I0810324

POSTCARD HISTORY SERIES

Waterville

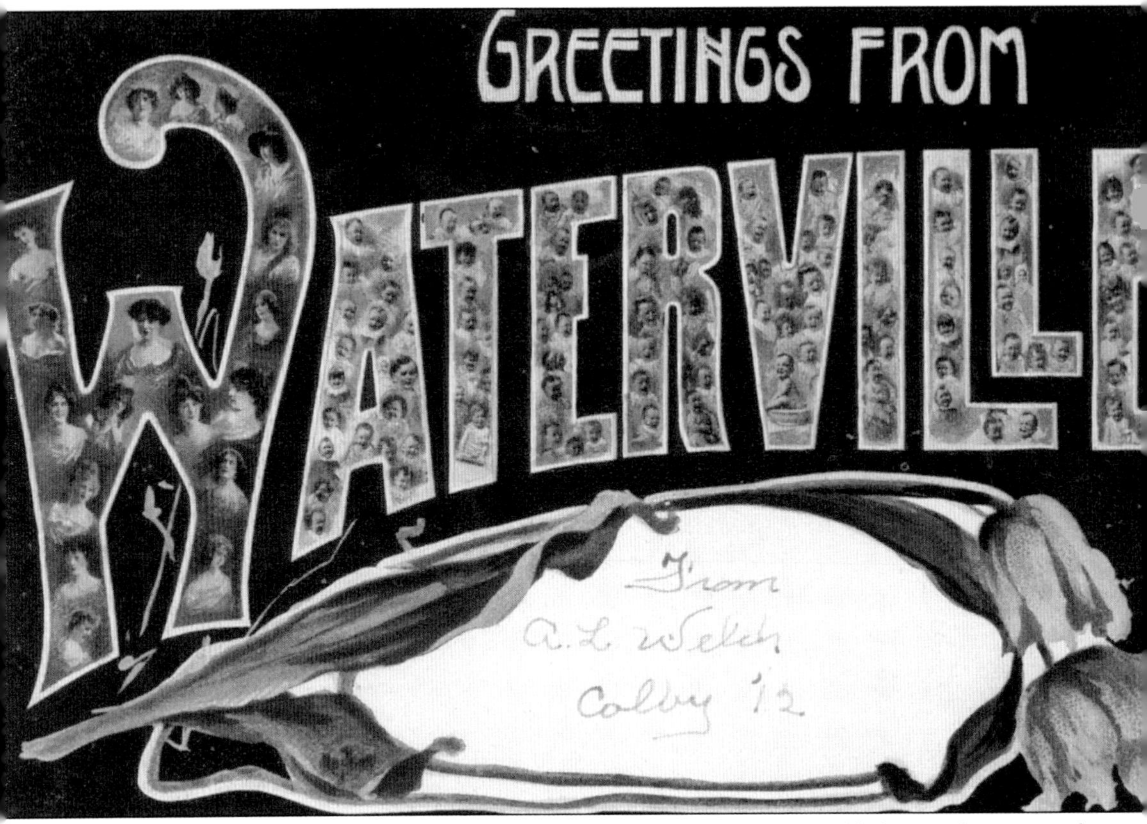

This postcard, mailed in 1908, declares "Greetings from Waterville" and left enough space on the front for the sender, A.L. Welch, to write his name and the fact that he belonged to the Colby College class of 1912. On the back, Welch, who was courting Janette Blanchard (the recipient of the card), included a message: "I told you I wouldn't forget you. Hope you won't forget to answer." (Courtesy of the Maine Historic Preservation Commission.)

On the Front Cover: This 1910 image shows Waterville firemen in front of Hose Company No. 1 and Hook and Ladder Company No. 1 on Main Street. Please see page 28 for more information. (Courtesy of the Maine Historic Preservation Commission.)

On the Back Cover: From 1899 to 1911, W.P. Putnam ran Putnam's Smoke Shop at Main and Common Streets. With the city hall in the background, this 1910 view captures the scene at the corner as a well-dressed gentleman walks by the store.

POSTCARD HISTORY SERIES

Waterville

Earle G. Shettleworth Jr.

ARCADIA
PUBLISHING

ISBN 978-0-7385-9848-2

Published by Arcadia Publishing
Charleston, South Carolina

Printed in the United States of America

Library of Congress Control Number: 2012950480

For all general information contact Arcadia Publishing at:
Telephone 843-853-2070
Fax 843-853-0044
E-mail sales@arcadiapublishing.com
For customer service and orders:
Toll-Free 1-888-313-2665

Visit us on the Internet at www.arcadiapublishing.com

This book is dedicated to Peter Warren Mackinlay (1948–1991), Colby College class of 1970, a gifted scholar and cherished friend.

Contents

ACKNOWLEDGMENTS

My connection to Waterville begins 90 years ago in the fall of 1923, when my mother, Esther Knudsen, entered Colby College as a freshman in the class of 1927. Her college friendships in Central Maine brought my family to spend summers in Skowhegan from 1955 to 1970. Each week in the 1950s and 1960s, my mother, my sister, and I would drive to Waterville to shop. During every trip, we would pass by the old Colby campus, and we would often meet my mother's professors on the street. Webster Chester, Ernest Marriner, Everett Strong, and Carl J. Weber became more than names in an old yearbook to me. In retrospect, it now seems incredible that I knew men who were teaching at Colby a century or more ago. Between 1966 and 1970, I attended college on the new Colby campus, witnessing the construction of the "new dorms" that made the first break from Georgian Revival architecture to modernism. When I return to the campus today, I marvel at how much it has grown in the last four decades while still retaining the essential character of Jens Frederick Larson's original vision of 1931.

I wish to thank several individuals for their valuable assistance in preparing this volume. Bryan Finnemore at the Waterville Historical Society provided scans of postcards from the society's extensive collection. Kevin Johnson of the Penobscot Marine Museum in Searsport furnished scans from the Eastern Illustrating and Publishing Company collection. Bill Taylor shared with me his Waterville postcard collection, as well as the two publications based on his collection—*Old Waterville Postcards* and *Vintage Pictures of Colby & Waterville*. Patricia Burdick, the assistant director for special collections at Colby College Libraries, gave me access to alumni magazines and past issues of the *Colby Echo* in an effort to aid my quest to research campus architecture.

In learning about Waterville, there are two essential reference books: *The Centennial History of Waterville*, edited by Edwin Carey Whittemore (1902), and *A Chronology of Municipal History and Election Statistics*, compiled and edited by Clement M. Giveen (1908). Colby is fortunate to have three excellent histories: *Colby College 1820–1925: An Account of Its Beginnings, Progress and Service* by Edwin Carey Whittemore (1927), *The History of Colby College* by Ernest Cummings Marriner (1963), and *Mayflower Hill: A History of Colby College* by Earl H. Smith (2006).

Unless otherwise noted, all images in this book appear courtesy of the Maine Historic Preservation Commission.

Introduction

The history of a place is punctuated by landmark events and significant people who are representative of the collective experience.

For example, any history of Waterville should include certain pertinent details, starting with the construction of Fort Halifax in 1754, followed by permanent settlers in the 1780s; the growth of the community and the partitioning of Waterville from Winslow in 1802; the development of the first industries (shipbuilding, sawmilling, and an iron foundry); and the founding of advanced schools of learning (Colby College in 1813, the Coburn Classical Institute in 1829, and Mount Merici Academy in 1911). The narrative continues with the arrival of the Androscoggin & Kennebec (A&K) Railroad in 1849 (later the Maine Central Railroad) and the sacrifices made by 525 native sons who fought in the Civil War, 71 of whom did not return home. After the Civil War, the fortunes of the town rose with the construction of the Lockwood Mill and the resulting increase in immigrants (French Canadians), economic prosperity, and incorporation as a city. This late-19th-century narrative includes a building boom, the development of community services provided by the board of trade (Waterville Opera House, an extensive sewer system, and a new cemetery), and a rapid increase in population. The 20th century saw Waterville weather the effects of two world wars, the Great Depression, and the relocation of Colby College. At mid-century, a second building boom signaled continued growth, even as the decline in textile manufacturing impacted the prosperity of Waterville's working citizens. Along the way, the names of influential statesmen (Gov. William T. Haines, Sen. George Mitchell), men of the cloth (Fr. Sebastian Rasle, Fr. Narcisse Charland), and industrialists (Amos Lockwood, Charles F. Hathaway) are interspersed with those of a leading inventor (Alvin O. Lombard), a respected doctor (Frederick C. Thayer, MD), a Civil War hero (Maj. Abner Small), and the successful merchants on Main Street.

But that narrative does not adequately convey the fullness of how the "place of fish"—Ticonic (or Taconnet) Falls—became Waterville, the "Elm City" in the 19th century, the "University City" at the beginning of the 20th century, and a place to "Converge and Create" in the 21st century. For a whole picture, readers need images—postcards, each perhaps worth a thousand words.

Take, for instance, the series of photographs depicting stylish homes "in Winter in Waterville, Me." Each shows a home with architectural merit sited on a tree-lined lawn and surrounded by a blanket of snow. Neither plow nor shovel has touched the snow at some houses, while the path to the street in one photograph indicates the level of work awaiting the residents. On each card, the name of the prominent property owner is written in gold ink at a jaunty angle. While these cards illustrate that even in cold, snowy Maine, the residents of Waterville have style, taste and prosperity, they also beg the question: for whom were they made?

Postcards also aptly illustrate why Waterville was known as "Elm City." The omnipresent trees line the roads, are glimpsed past the corners of buildings, populate the parks and squares, and lend their name to a street, a hotel, and other establishments, including a bowling alley and a bottling company. The corresponding lack of elms on the new Colby College campus in the mid-20th century is startling; the Colonial Revival buildings depicted on the stark, nascent landscape contrast with the maturity and warmth of the original brick buildings adjacent to the river. These images parallel the break with tradition and the fostering of expansion that characterized the college's move from the city to the suburbs.

The personal connections people felt with their schools is evident on the postcard of the Myrtle Street School with an arrow carefully drawn to point to a second-story classroom. Whether the sender, E.M. Sawyer, was a teacher or a student, the message seems to be, "here I am." At Mount Merici Academy, the carefully placed desks and chairs in the study hall and the lines of beds, dressing tables, and chairs in the "Minims' Dormitory" suggest the orderly decorum of the school run by Ursuline sisters. Even as their long white nightdresses blend into the bedding, the two little girls in the center of the dormitory photograph remind us that the school was originally a boarding school, and that even the youngest students left their families to attend.

Mount Merici Academy was one of several parochial schools that served the French Canadian population in Waterville. French immigrants settled in Waterville as early as 1827, but when the city's industrial base expanded after the Civil War, so did the French-speaking labor force. Currently, the French population in Waterville is about 15 percent of the whole, but it was three times that high in the 1900 census. The French Canadians were joined, in lesser numbers, by Irish, Scotch, Italian, and Polish immigrants, and in the early 1900s, Waterville also had Maine's largest population of Syrians/Lebanese, many of whom were weavers in the mills or worked for the railroad. St. Francis de Sales and Sacred Heart Churches, the Notre Dame School and Chapel, and Mount Merici Academy, as well as Poulin Furniture, Berube Bakery, L'Union Layfayette, and Joseph's Market, were not just institutions or commercial establishments, they were the loci of community.

Postcards are made so that someone can see a place without being there. They also record special events, promote businesses or interests, or simply capture moments of everyday life. These postcards illustrate that on an early morning, the wide streets of the business district could be quiet or full of firemen, military veterans, and spectators for a celebration. The same streets were equally welcoming to the rushing gentleman rounding the corner next to the peanut cart or his associate passing an idle moment sitting under the arch at Opera House Square. Winning teams, aspiring teams, a band of vaudeville performers, and the midway at the Central Maine Fairgrounds offered diversions at the end of a hard day cutting ice or working in the Hollingsworth & Whitney Company's paper mill across the river in Winslow.

The mighty Kennebec River was a constant presence in Waterville. Not only do the postcards illustrate the crucial industries fueled by its water power, they also show the infrastructure that connected Waterville to Winslow, including a pedestrian suspension bridge and a trolley that allowed residents easy access to jobs or homes on the other side of the river. On the west shore, the Waterville & Fairfield Electric Railway, the Androscoggin & Kennebec Railroad line, and the Oakland line connected Waterville with the communities of Fairfield and Oakland and beyond, each with their own business centers, residential neighborhoods, and industrial enterprises. Beyond the immediate vicinity, the railroad was Waterville's most important connection to greater Maine in the 19th and 20th centuries. The Maine Central Railroad roundhouse had no fewer than 35 locomotive stalls, and the nearby yard held the mechanical shops that serviced the entire fleet. Both freight and passenger service radiated from Waterville throughout the state, and the city's importance as a commercial transportation center was second only to Portland's.

To send a postcard from Waterville was to share a sense of the city, its inhabitants, its neighborhoods, its culture, and its enterprises. In the following pages, I welcome you to experience a city that, throughout its history, has always been a place to converge and create—Waterville, Maine.

One

Downtown

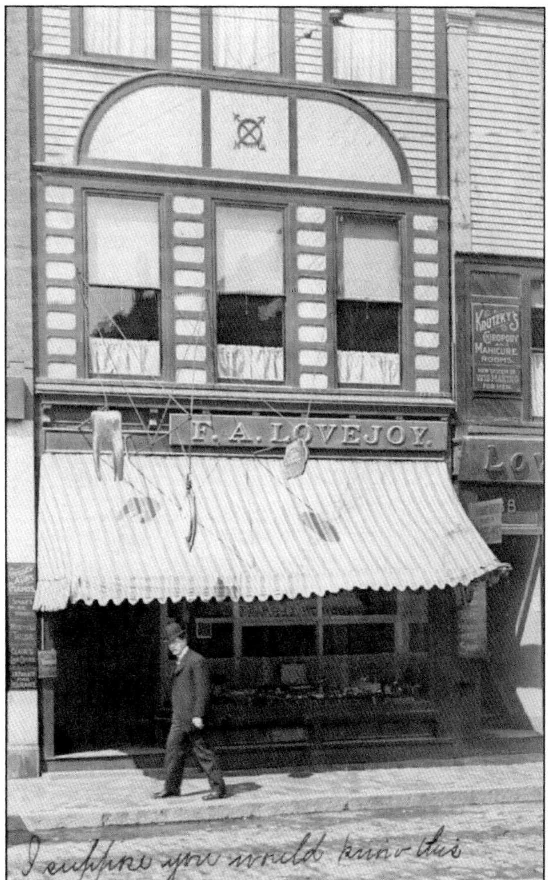

During the early 20th century, Waterville's Main Street was lined with many small frame commercial buildings that housed a myriad of goods, services, and professionals. Typical of these was the three-story block of F.A. Lovejoy, who dealt in watches, jewelry, silverware, and eyeglasses. A native of Bath, Maine, Lovejoy was a fixture of the Waterville business community from 1884 to 1920. (Waterville Historical Society.)

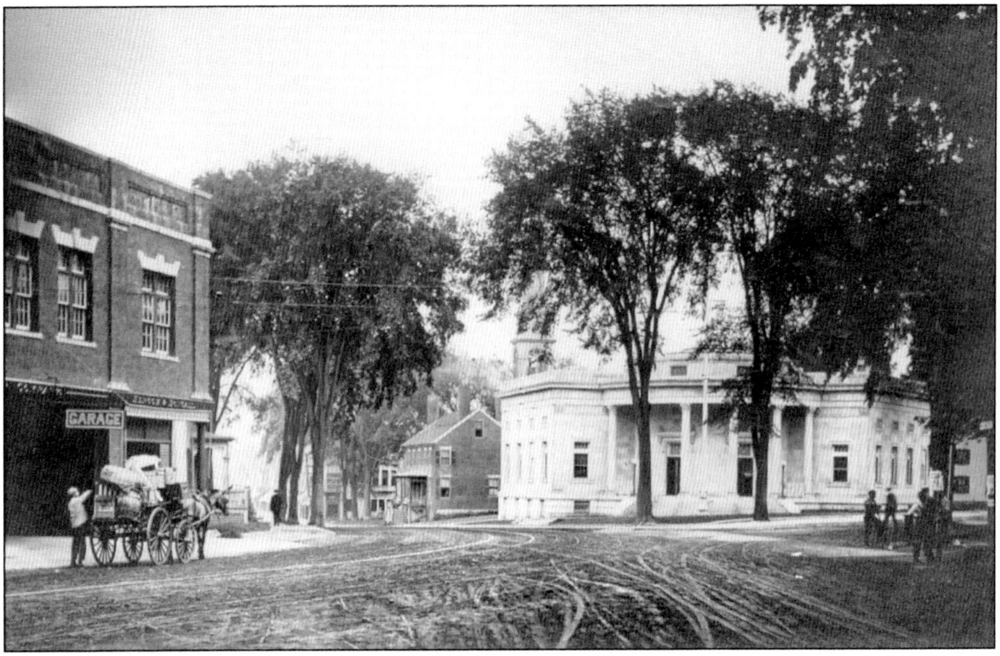

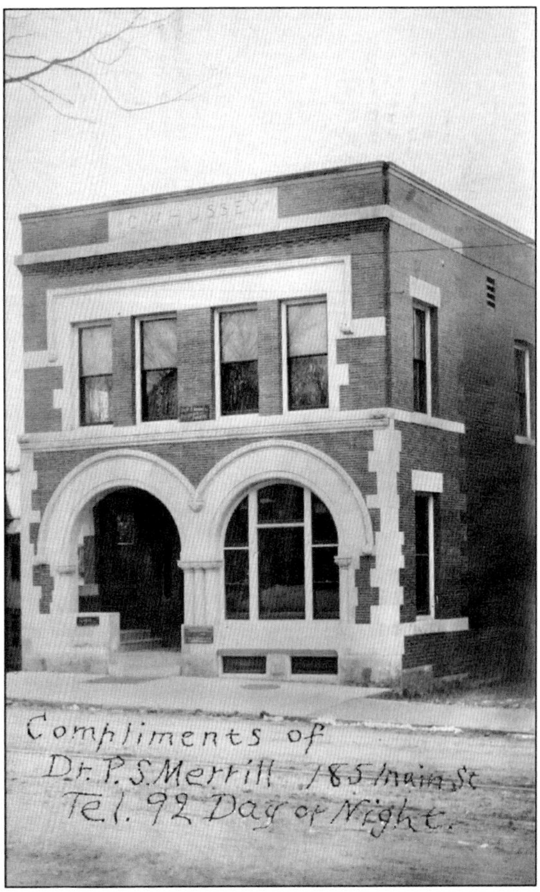

In the spring of 1913, two new buildings dominated the junction of Main and Elm Streets—the Waterville Motor Company at left and the post office at right. Built in 1911, the Waterville Motor Company was designed by Portland architect Frank M. Churchill to accommodate an automobile showroom and garage on the first floor and an amusement hall on the second. (Waterville Historical Society.)

One of Main Street's most distinctive commercial buildings is the C.W. Hussey Block, built in 1908 in the Romanesque Revival style from designs by William H. Butterfield. An attorney, Hussey occupied the first floor and leased the second floor to Dr. P.S. Merrill, an 1894 Colby College graduate who practiced medicine. Local contractor Horace Purinton constructed the building using brick with decorative stonework.

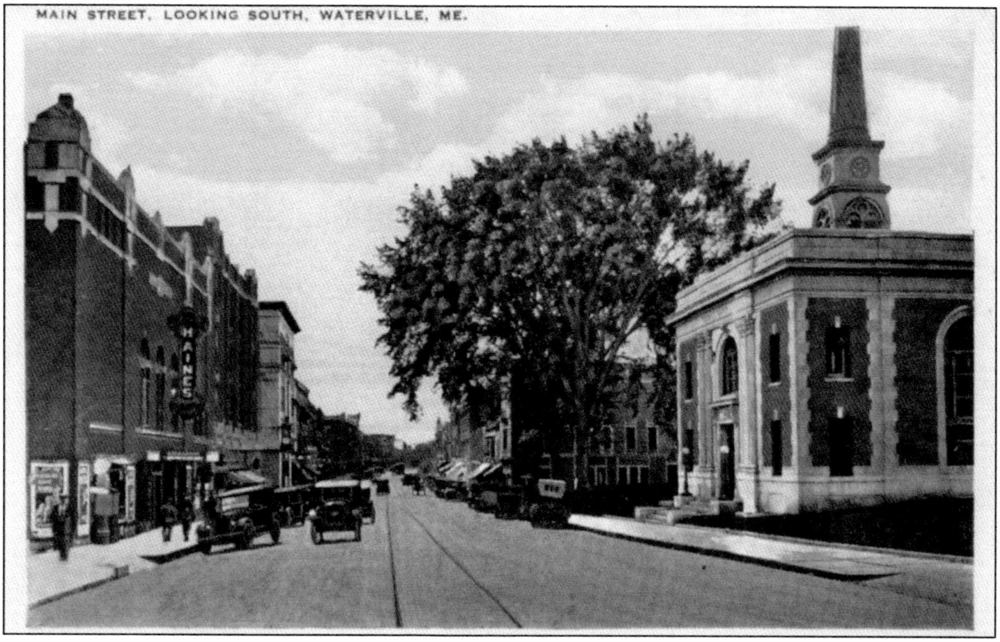

This postcard, entitled "Main Street, Looking South," shows the Haines Theater (built in 1917) at left and the Ticonic National Bank (built in 1919) at right with the tower of the Unitarian church behind it. Brick and stone were used to create the elegant Colonial Revival bank, which was designed by Thomas M. James, a Boston architect who specialized in planning bank buildings in New England.

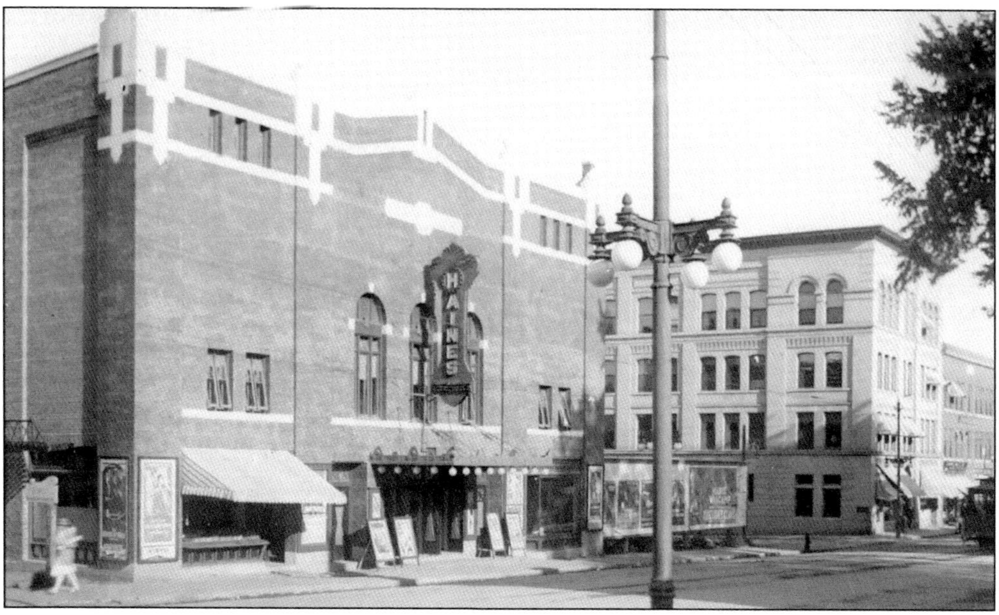

The Haines Theater was the largest of Waterville's three movie theaters when it was built on Main Street in 1917. Constructed by William T. Haines, a prominent local attorney and businessman, the theater was designed by the Boston architectural firm of Jackson and Salomonson in a distinctly modern style for its time. The Haines remained popular for nearly 60 years until it was destroyed by fire in 1967. (Waterville Historical Society.)

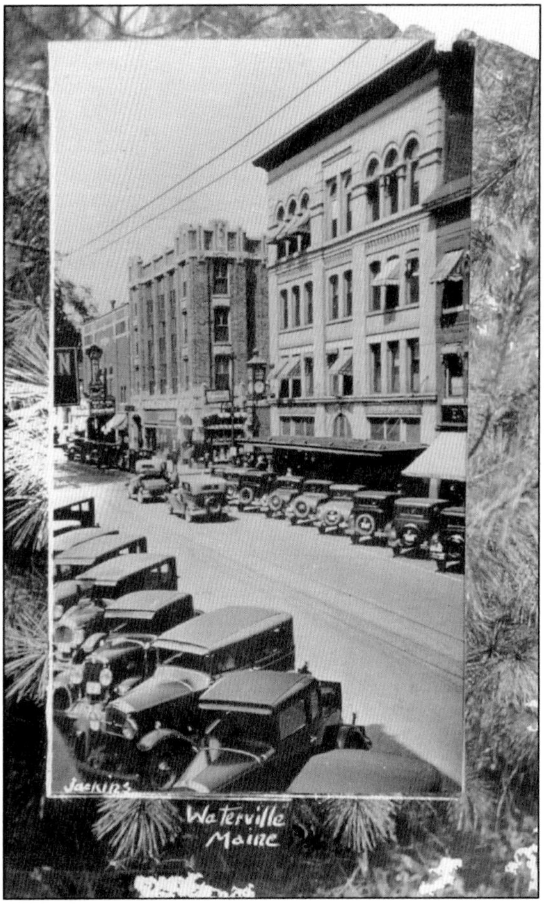

In this c. 1930 view of a car-lined Main Street, the Professional Building stands at the center with the Haines Theater at far left and the Savings Bank Block at right. Built in 1922–1923 by A.F. Cyr, the Professional Building contains street-level stores and three floors of offices. Its decorative exterior, the work of Portland architects William R. Miller and Raymond J. Mayo, exemplifies the Art Deco style. (Waterville Historical Society.)

One of Waterville's largest, most stylish early-20th-century buildings is the Savings Bank Block built in 1903 at Main and Appleton Streets. Constructed of gray brick, this block was planned by William M. Butterfield, who grew up in Waterville and practiced architecture in Manchester, New Hampshire, from 1881 until his death in 1932. Butterfield maintained close ties with his boyhood community, designing several buildings in town between 1900 and 1910. (Waterville Historical Society.)

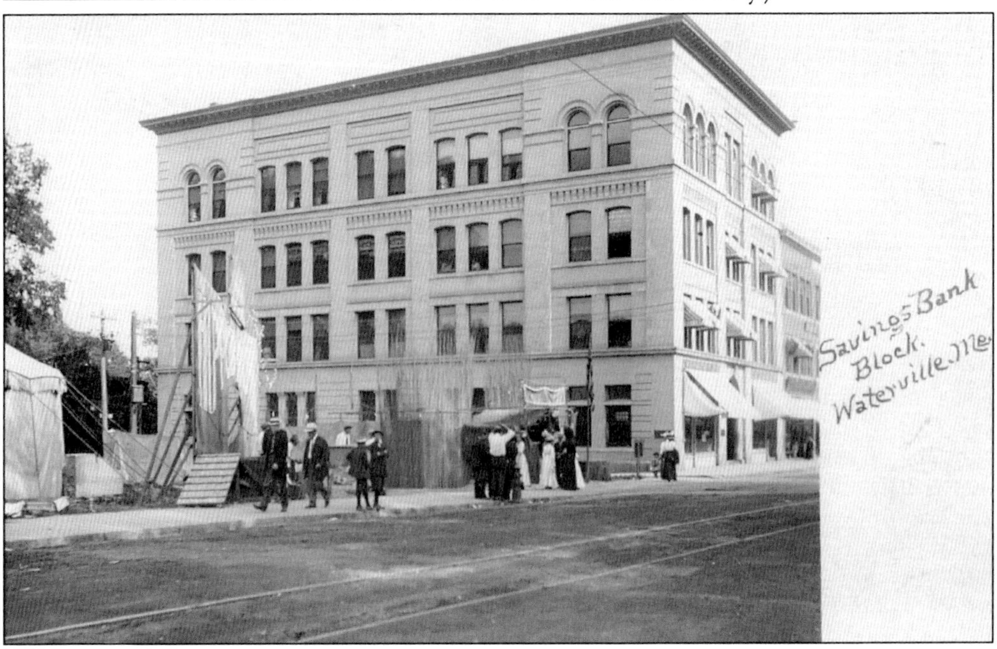

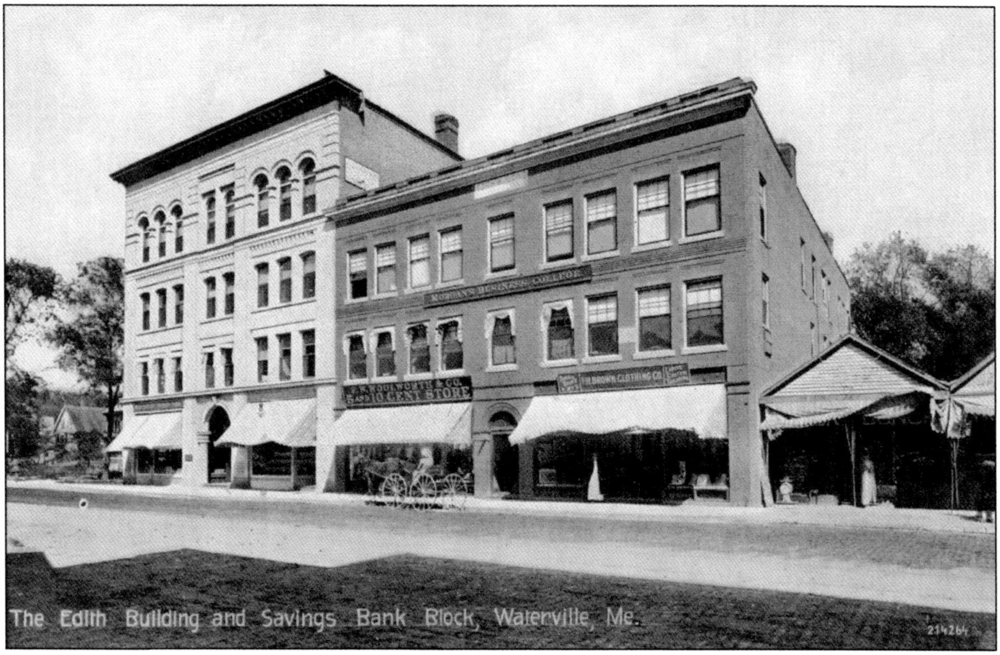

In 1910, William T. Haines constructed the three-story brick Edith Building—named for his wife, Edith—next to the Savings Bank Block on Main Street. The building contained an F.W. Woolworth's five-and-dime store and an F.H. Brown clothing store on the street level and Morgan's Business College on the second and third floors. Note the one-story lunchroom at right.

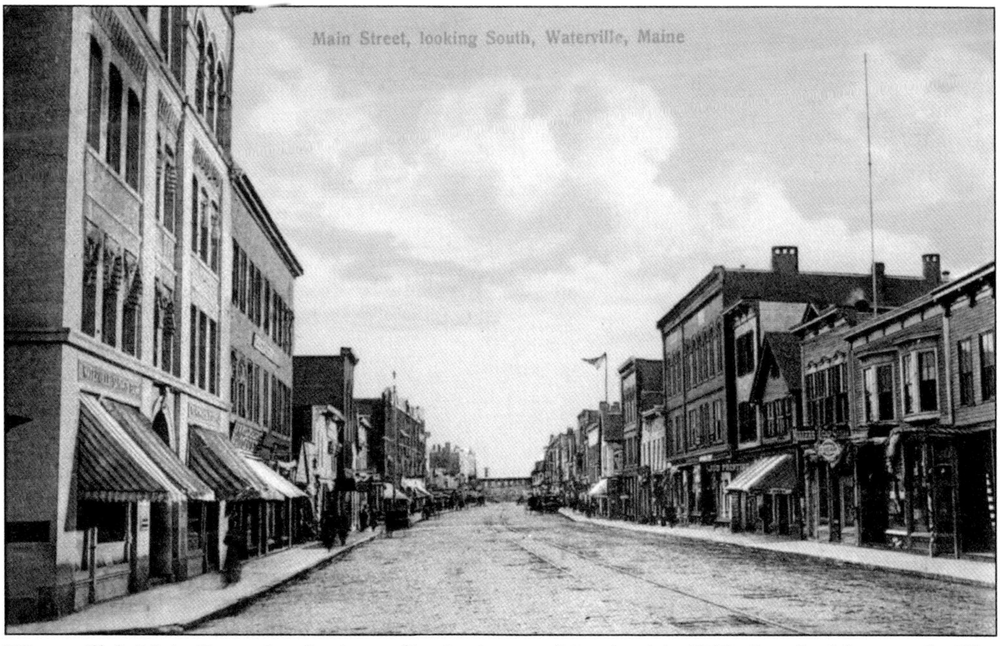

Waterville's Main Street is a business district in transition in this 1910 view looking south. The new Savings Bank Block and Edith Block are at left, while the brick Pulsifer and Flood Blocks of 1901 overshadow the row of small frame shops in the foreground at right.

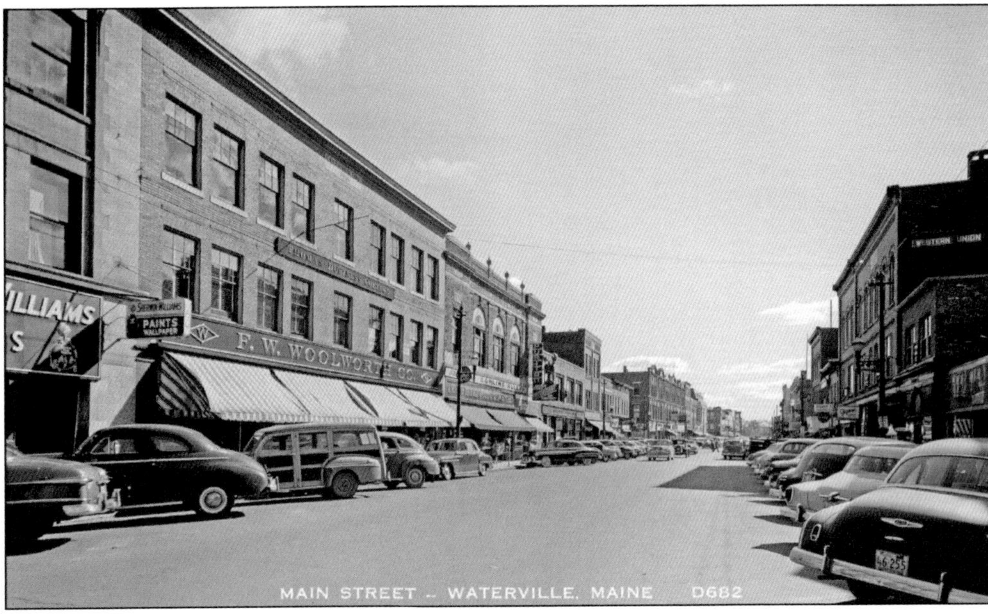

Main Street thrived as Waterville's commercial center in the post–World War II years, as reflected in this 1950s postcard. By 1931, Woolworth's occupied the entire first floor of the Edith Block (at left), and it remained there until the early 1970s. Next to the Edith Block is the Eaton Block, built by attorney Harvey Doane Eaton Sr. in 1923 from plans by the Augusta firm of Bunker and Savage. (Penobscot Marine Museum.)

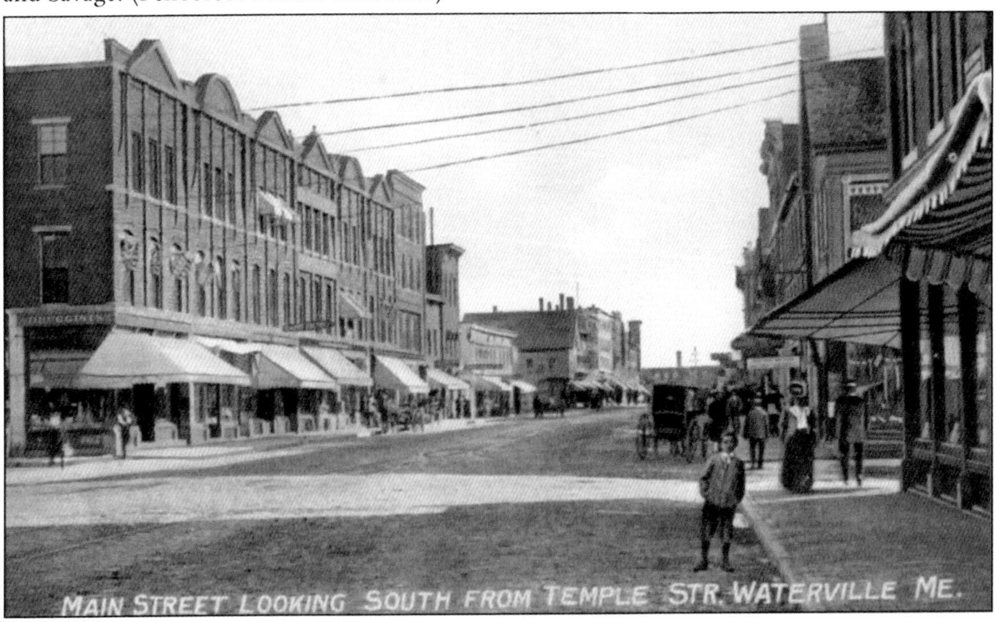

At left are the Arnold-Boutelle-Elden Blocks at Main and Temple Streets, a three-story brick Queen Anne–style row consisting of three sections. W.B. Arnold, a hardware merchant, built the store on the corner between 1886 and 1887; Dr. George Boutelle constructed the middle store in 1887 and leased it to a newsstand; and J.F. Elden built the final part of the block for his furniture store in 1893. By the time this postcard was printed around 1910, some of these businesses had changed.

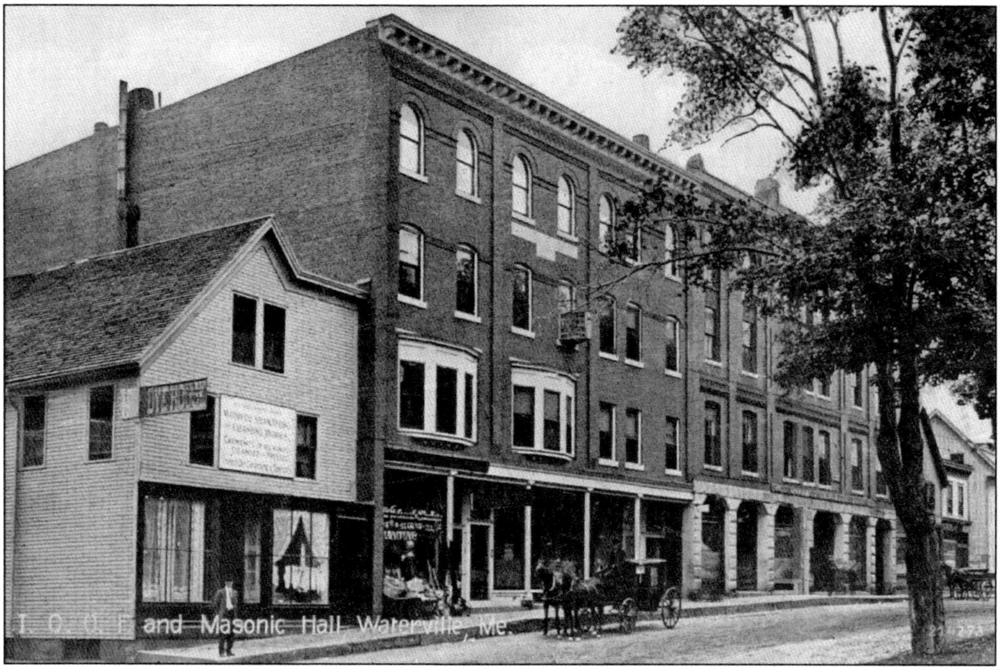

Today, only the first two stories remain of the four-story brick building built by William T. Haines on Common Street in 1897. The first story contained the post office and various stores, the second contained offices, and the third and fourth held the Odd Fellows' room and hall. The small wooden building at left housed a laundry, and the Masonic Building is at right.

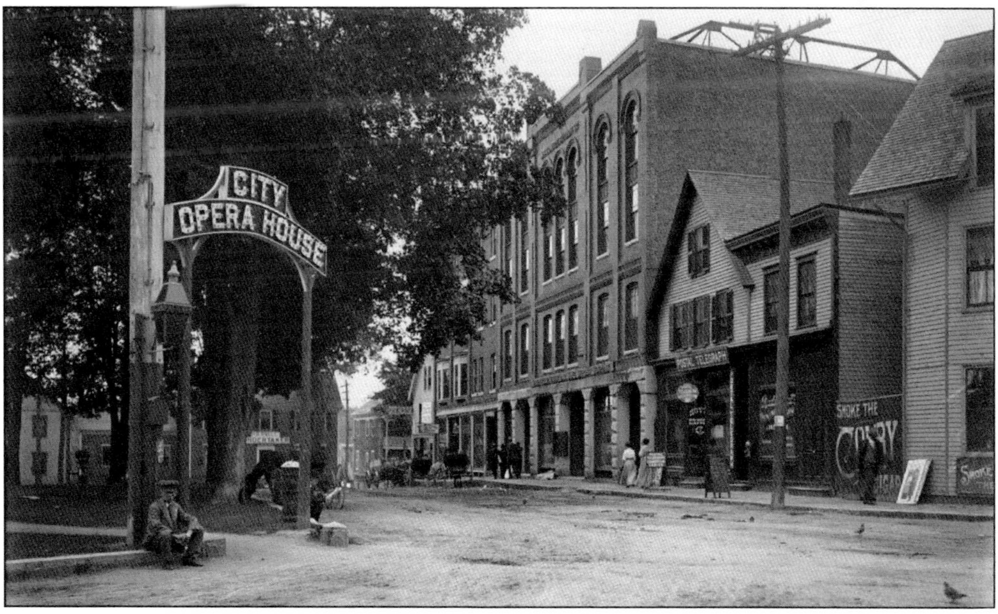

The Masonic Building, constructed in 1890 and designed by Edwin E. Lewis of Gardiner, is the focal point of this view of Common Street from Main Street. At left is City Hall Park (now Castonguay Park), and at right, next to the Masonic Building, are three wooden commercial buildings that were destroyed by fire in 1911. An electrified sign invites patrons to the City Opera House, located in Waterville's city hall. (Waterville Historical Society.)

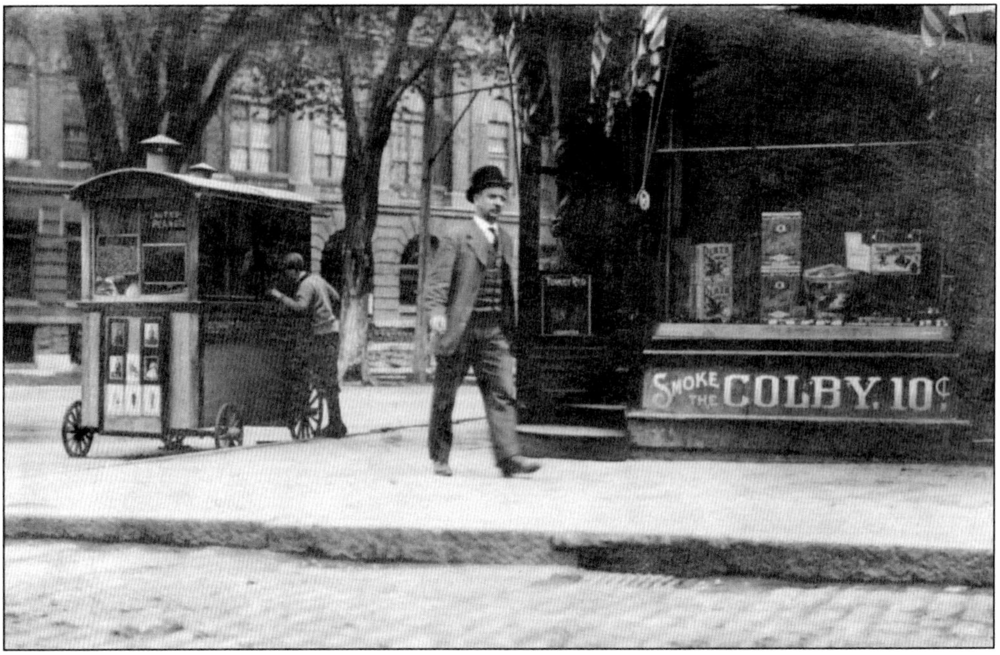

W.P. Putnam ran Putnam's Smoke Shop at Main and Common Streets from 1899 to 1911. The city hall is in the background in this 1910 view that captures the scene at the corner. On display in the window are boxes of Plaza pipe tobacco and Bull Durham chewing tobacco. A cart at left is selling roasted salted peanuts.

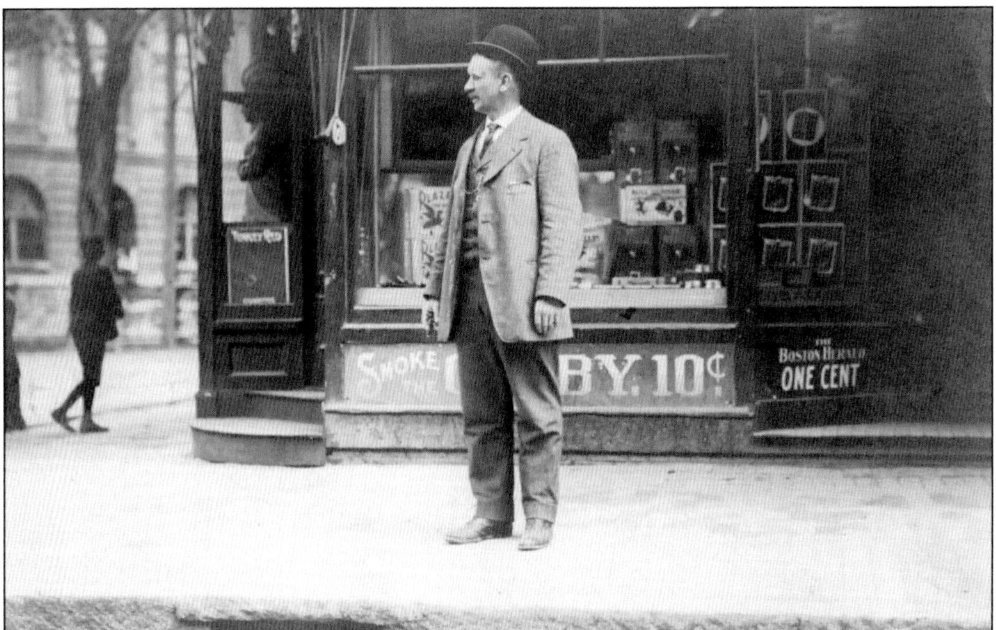

Another view of Putnam's Smoke Shop at Main and Common Streets shows a cigar store Indian in the window at left and signs for a Colby cigar for 10¢ and the *Boston Herald* for a penny. Like many tobacconists, Putnam manufactured cigars with names aimed at capturing a specific market—in this case, Colby College. (Waterville Historical Society.)

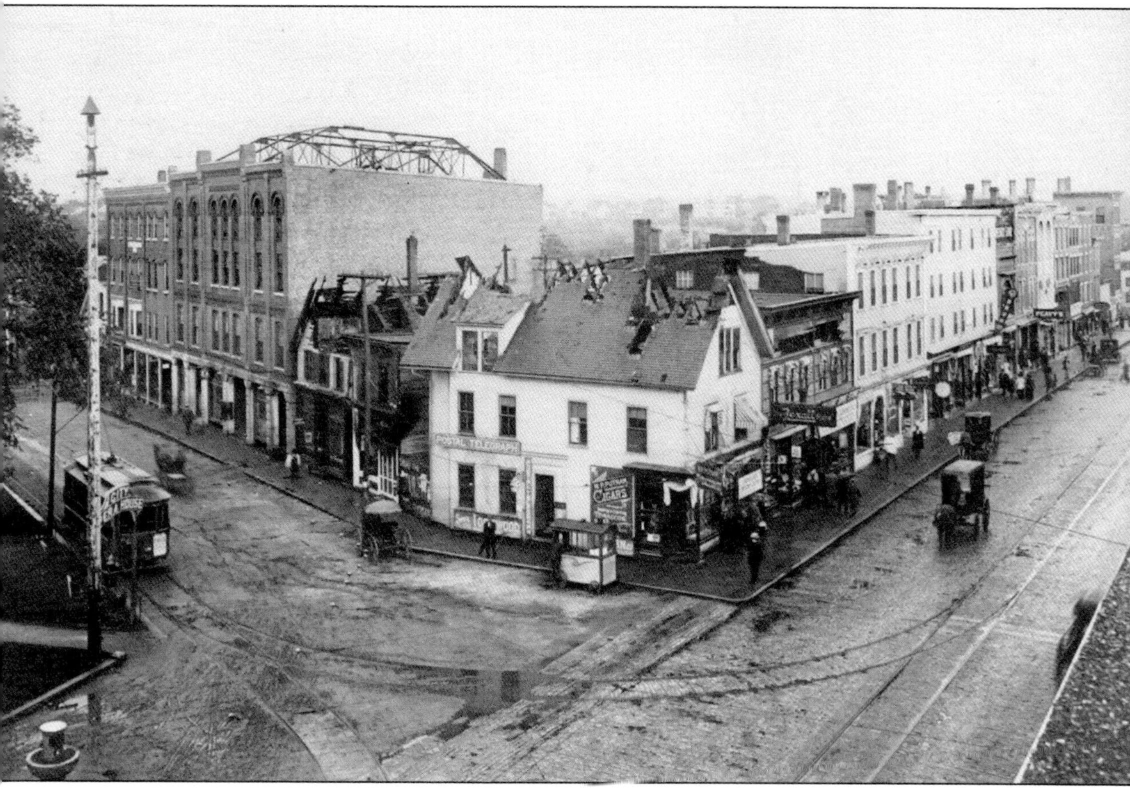

In 1911, fire severely damaged Putnam's Smoke Shop at Main and Common Streets, along with adjacent shops. Putnam's and the two buildings to its left were replaced the next year by brick blocks, while the Rexall drugstore to the right was renovated and reopened. The Putnam building was a local landmark starting in the 1850s, when it served as the studio of photographer Simon Wing.

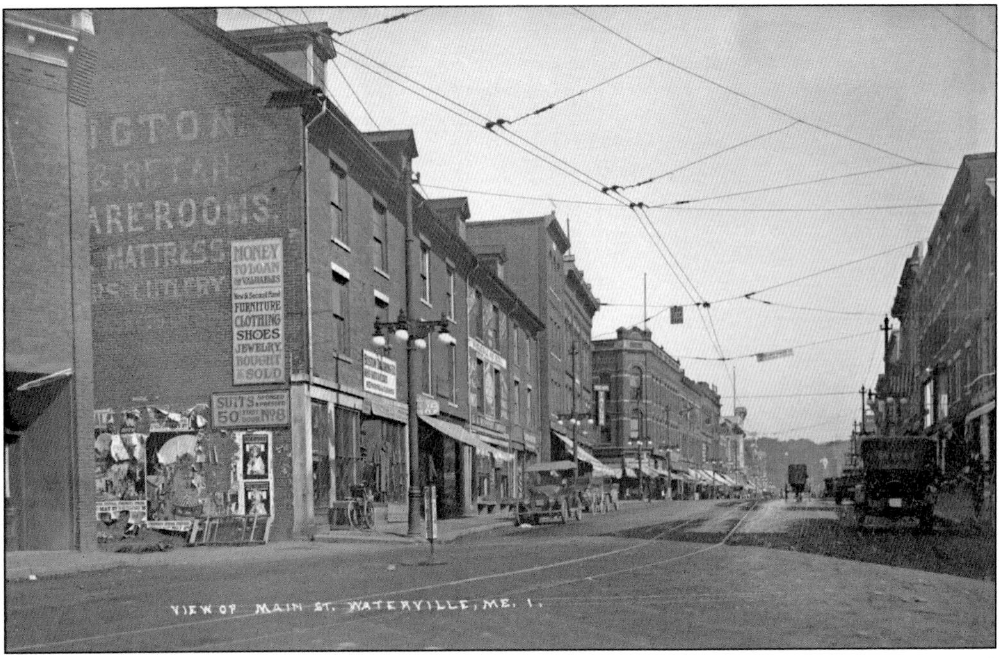

This view of the west side of Main Street looking north shows the Ticonic Row in the foreground as it appeared from 1836 until 1924, when a fourth story was added. Ticonic Row is one of Waterville's first brick commercial buildings. The two blocks beyond it are the Parent Block (1909) and the Milliken Block (1877). (Penobscot Marine Museum.)

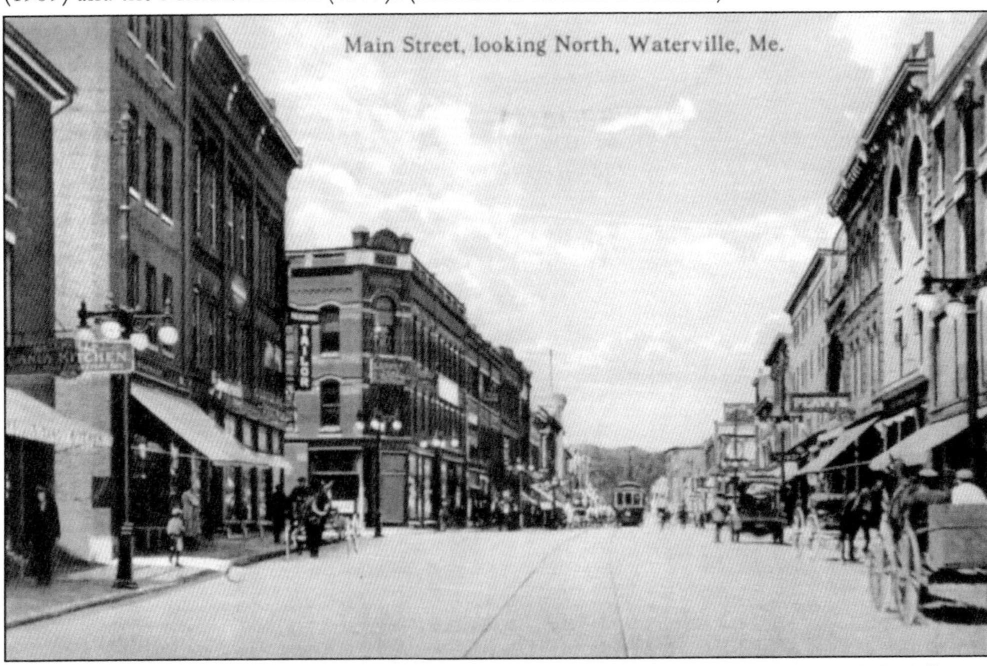

This view of Main Street looking north includes the Parent and Milliken Blocks at left, followed at Main and Silver Streets by the brick corner block occupied from 1901 to 1908 by Clukey and Libby's department store. That business was succeeded by the Corner Store Dry Goods, which inhabited the space from 1908 to 1911.

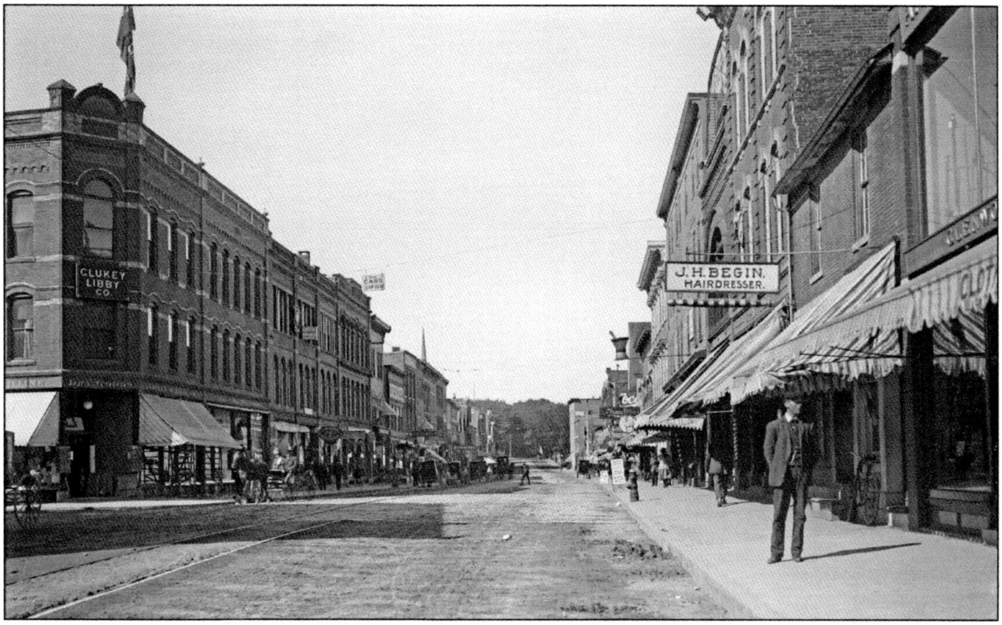

In the late 19th century, many of Main Street's wooden shops were replaced by substantial brick commercial buildings. The trend is evident in this view showing the west (left) side of the street looking north. Beginning in the left foreground, at the corner of Silver Street, are the Clukey Block (1890); the Plaisted Block (1883, 1890), designed by Fassett and Stevens; and the Sopher Block (1890), designed by Fassett and Tompson. (Penobscot Marine Museum.)

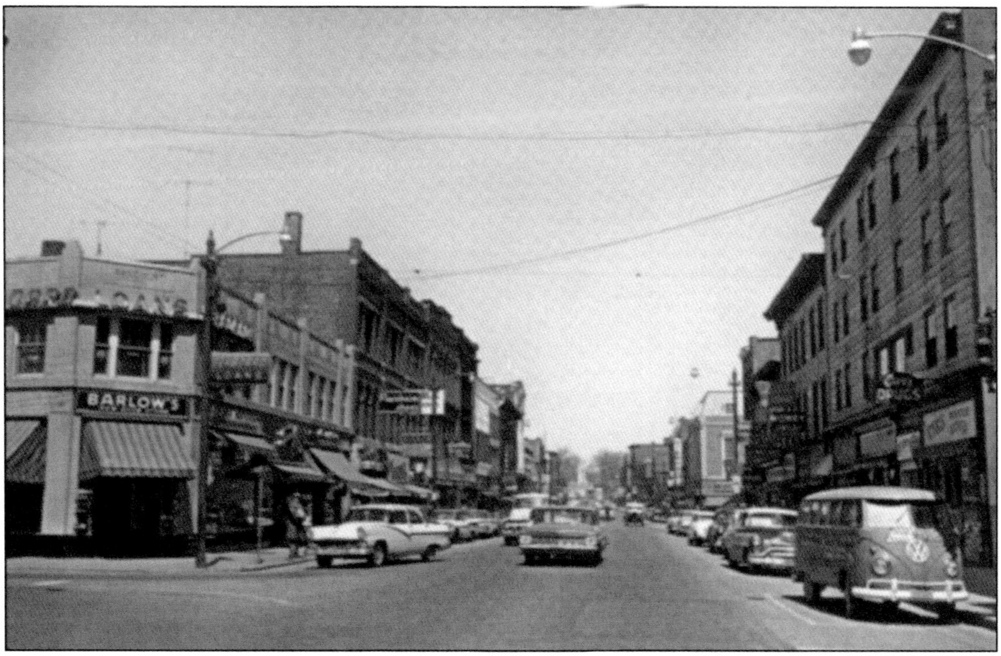

In 1936, the Clukey Block at Main and Silver Streets was replaced by the Rancourt Block, shown at left in this c. 1960 photograph. Built by Charles G. Rancourt, this distinctive Art Deco building was designed by Bunker and Savage of Augusta to accommodate a jewelry store and a shoe store on the first floor and offices and small shops on the second.

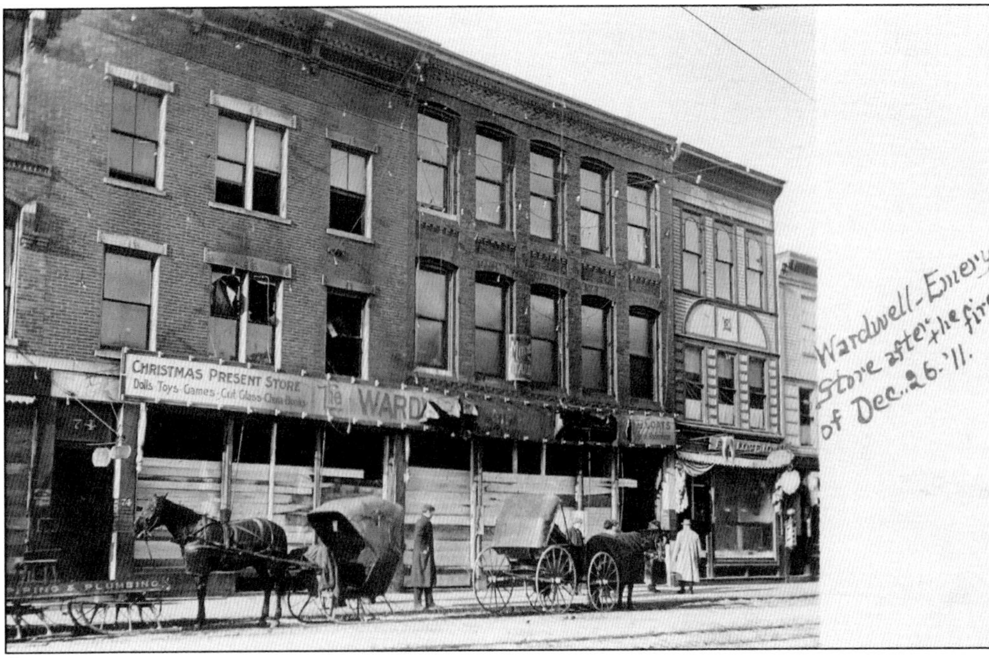

In 1911, the Wardwell-Emery Department Store occupied the first floor of two blocks on Main Street. On December 26 of that year, a furnace explosion destroyed the store and other businesses in the blocks, including William R. Pattangall's law office and Samuel A. Mitchell's tailor shop. The fire also resulted in water damage to the building at right, which housed F.A. Lovejoy's jewelry store and Dr. S.A. Cobb's dental office.

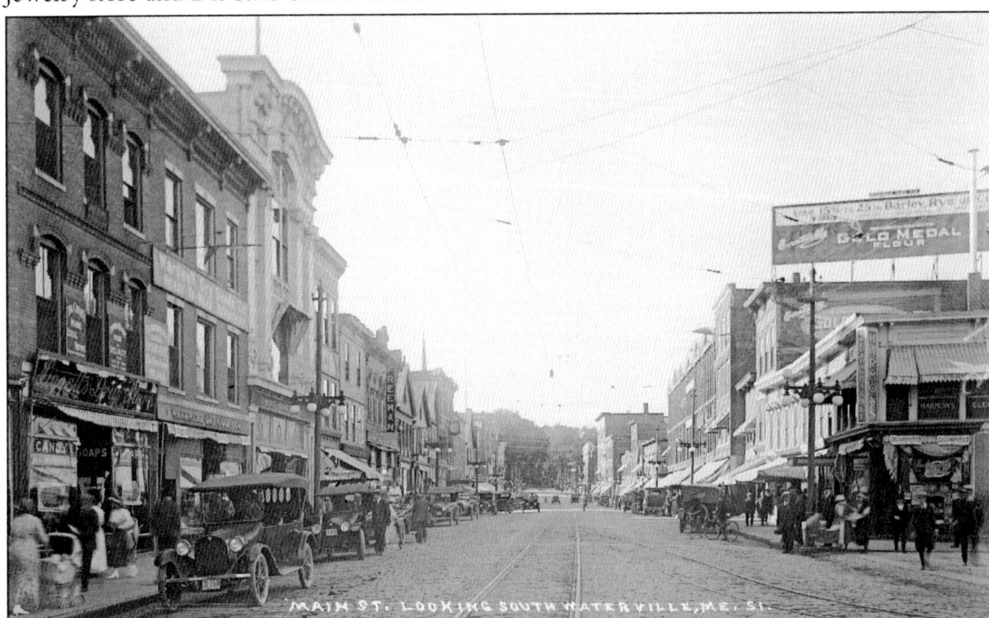

Following the fire of December 26, 1911, the Wardwell Dry Goods Company rebuilt its Main Street store, which appears second from the left in this view looking north. Next to Wardwell, the Emery Department Store was built in 1912, the elaborate Beaux-Arts facade of which was designed by William R. Miller and Raymond J. Mayo of Portland. (Penobscot Marine Museum.)

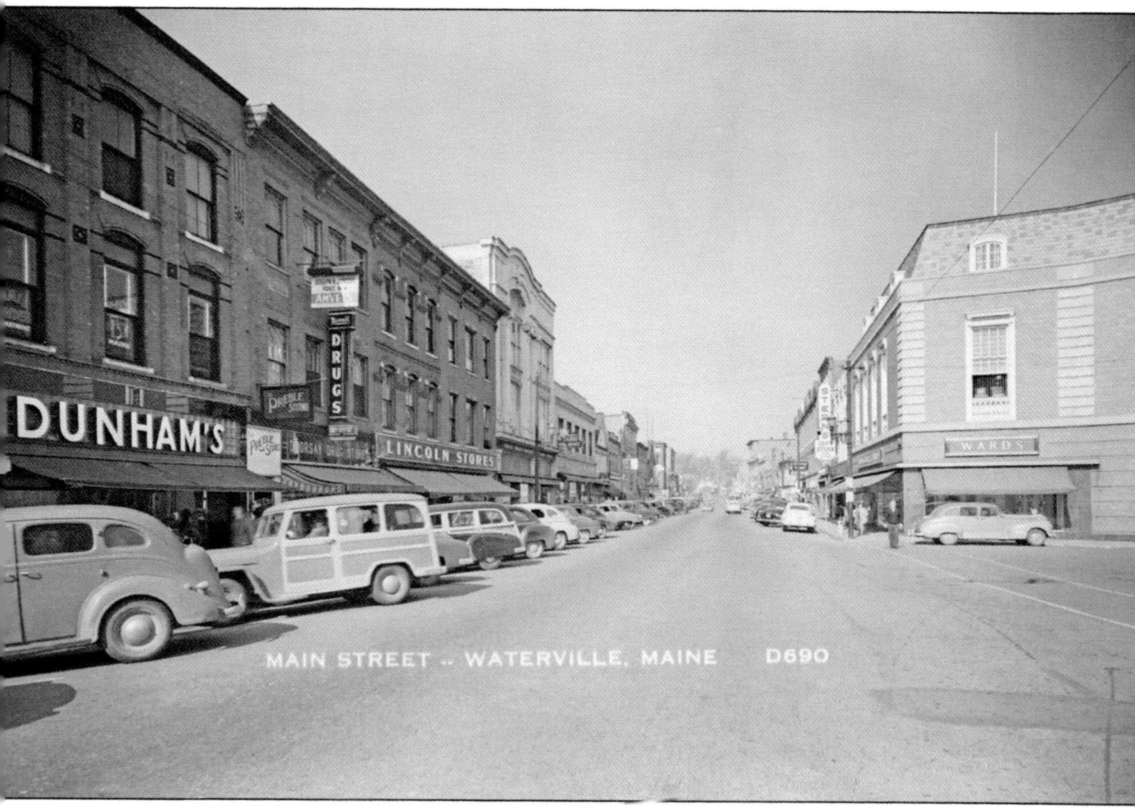

This c. 1950 view of Main Street looking north shows the Montgomery Ward department store (built in 1938) at right. This large brick commercial building replaced the two-story wooden block that had occupied the corner for decades. Montgomery Ward's mansard roof was added to the building sometime before 1948. At left is the widely known Dunham's clothing store, founded by Horatio R. Dunham, an 1886 Colby College graduate (Penobscot Marine Museum.)

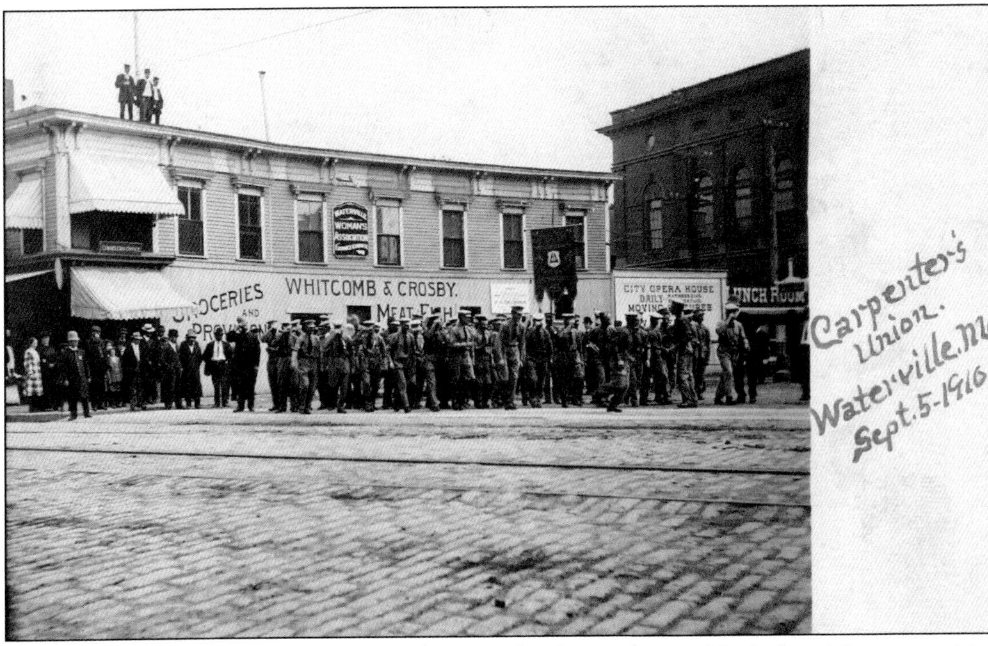

Since its national inception in 1894, Labor Day has been observed in industrial communities like Waterville with parades that include policemen, firemen, barbers, masons, plasterers, textile workers, paper makers, and printers. Here, about 40 members of the carpenters' union march down Main Street on September 5, 1910, with the city hall shown at right. Many of these carpenters participated in Augusta's parade on the same day.

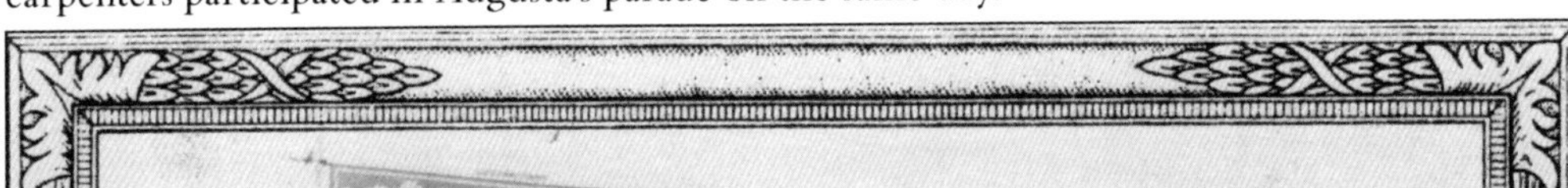

Nearly 50 years after the Battle of Gettysburg in 1863, Civil War veterans marched down Main Street on May 30, 1913, in Waterville's annual Memorial Day parade. The decades since the war had thinned the ranks of these proud members of the Grand Army of the Republic (GAR) who fought to preserve the Union.

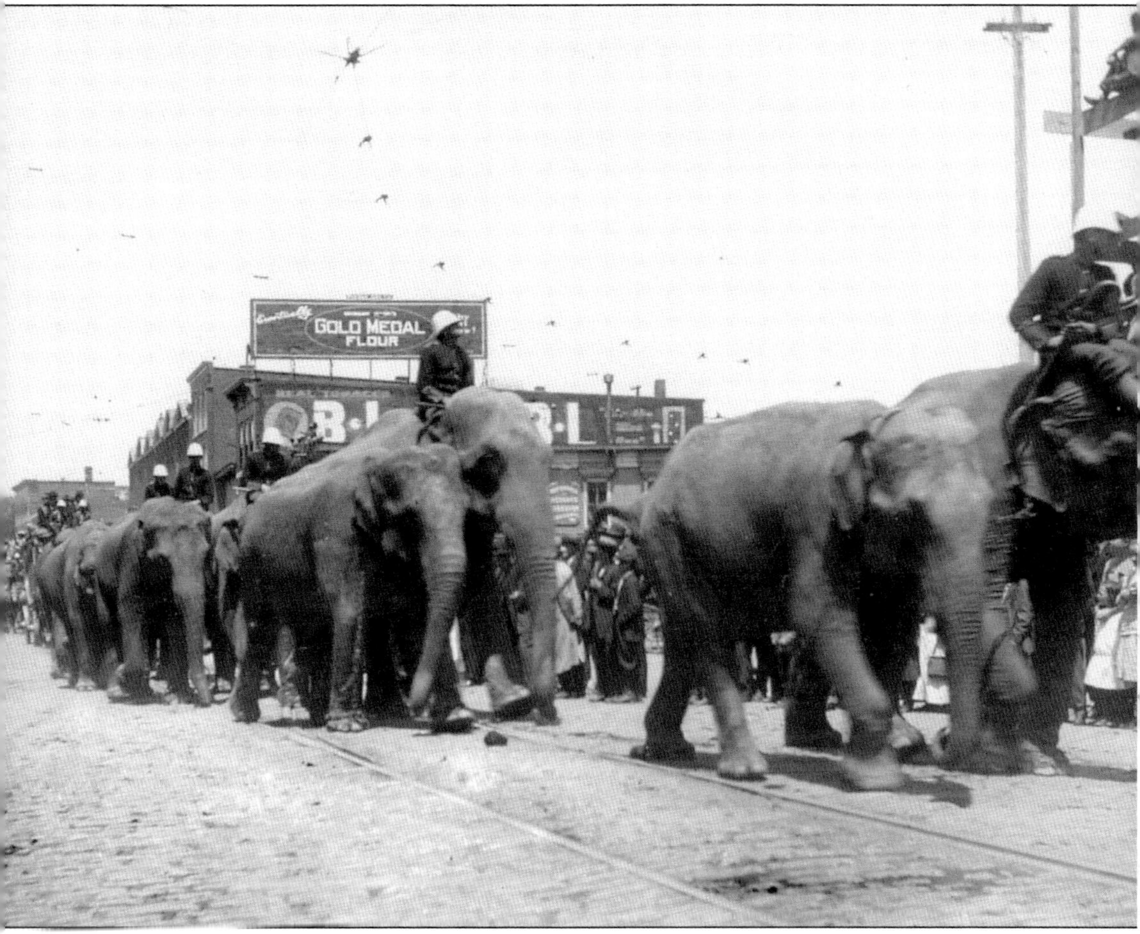

Four pairs of elephants march down Main Street as part of a colorful circus parade on Circus Day—June 5, 1913. In the early 1900s, traveling circuses were popular forms of entertainment, and the circus owners used parades to advertise their arrival and provide a preview of the attractions offered to those who could attend the actual show. (Waterville Historical Society.)

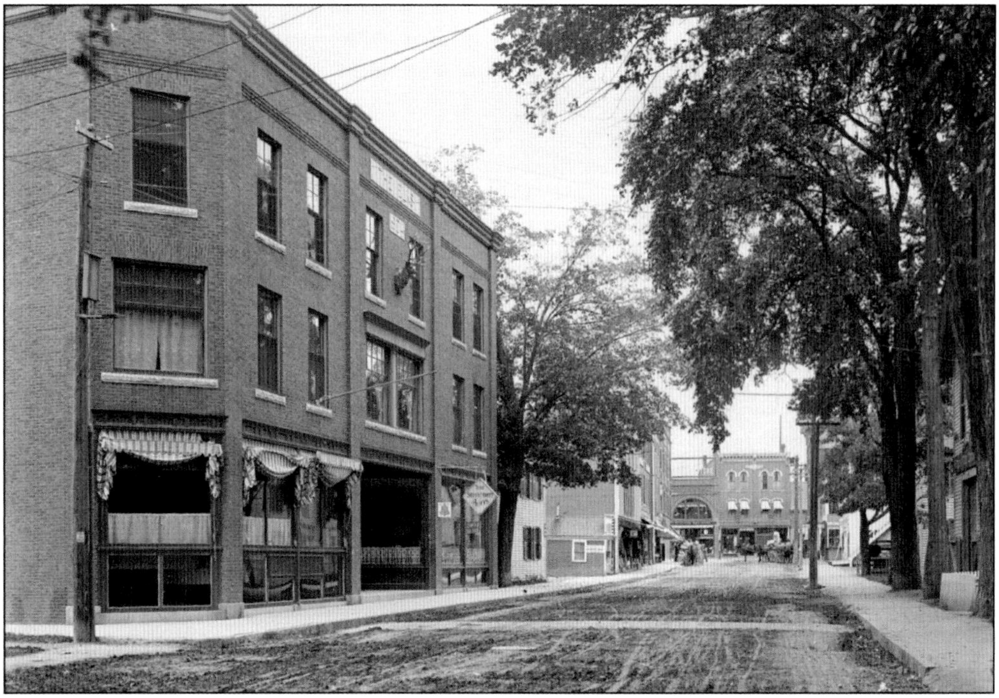

In 1904 and 1905, local businessman and politician Cyrus Davis built the Elks Block on Silver Street to provide office space for his recently established newspaper, the *Waterville Morning Sentinel*, as well as to provide a meeting space for the Elks club. At that time, the paper sold for 2¢ and had a daily circulation of 3,500. Waterville architect A.G. Bowie designed this building. (Penobscot Marine Museum.)

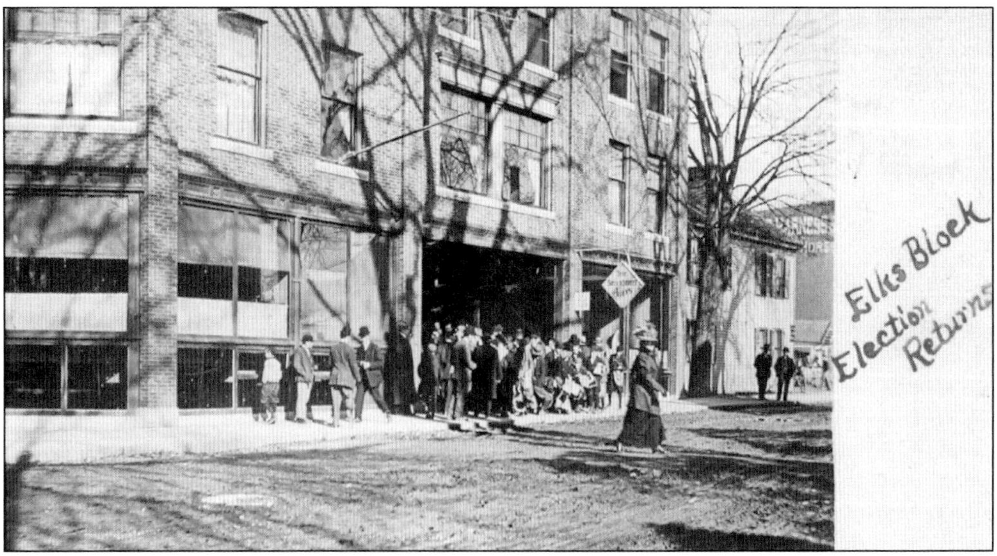

In the days before radio and television, the public relied on newspapers to provide election results. In this c. 1910 image, a crowd is gathered in front of the Elks Block on Silver Street to catch the latest news about voting returns from the *Waterville Morning Sentinel*. While the *Sentinel* printed election coverage in its daily issues, the paper also provided a public service by posting results outside of its offices. (Waterville Historical Society.)

Two

Public Buildings and Spaces

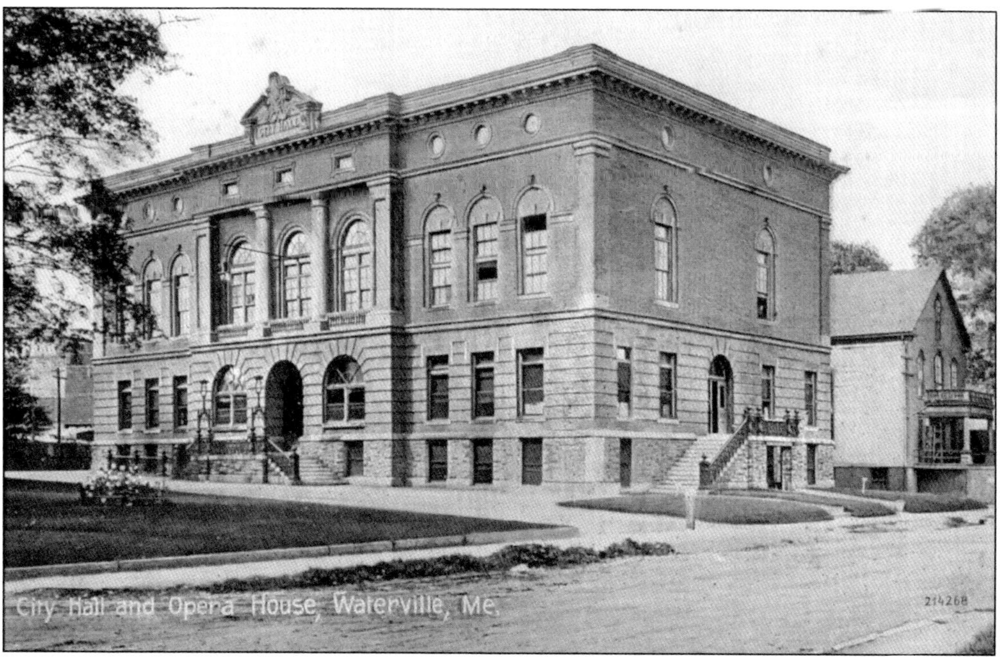

The Waterville City Hall and Opera House (built in 1902) reflect an 1890s trend in Maine cities and towns to construct municipal buildings that combined government offices with a public auditorium. Efforts to replace Waterville's wooden city hall, seen at right (behind the new structure), with this more permanent brick one began in 1896 and culminated in 1901 with the decision to go forward with architect George D. Adams's plans for a new facility.

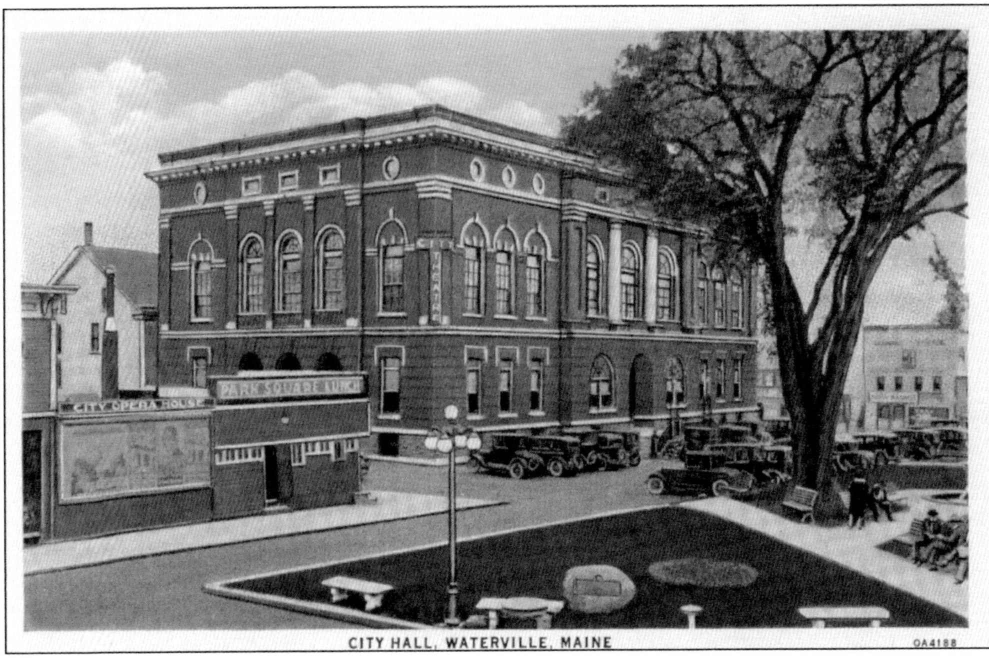

The Waterville Opera House is a grand early-20th-century theater that has hosted celebrities for more than a century, including Pres. Herbert Hoover, Rudy Vallée, and Marian Anderson. A successful 2012 campaign to restore the opera house resulted in a distinguished historic interior combined with state-of-the-art performance hall standards.

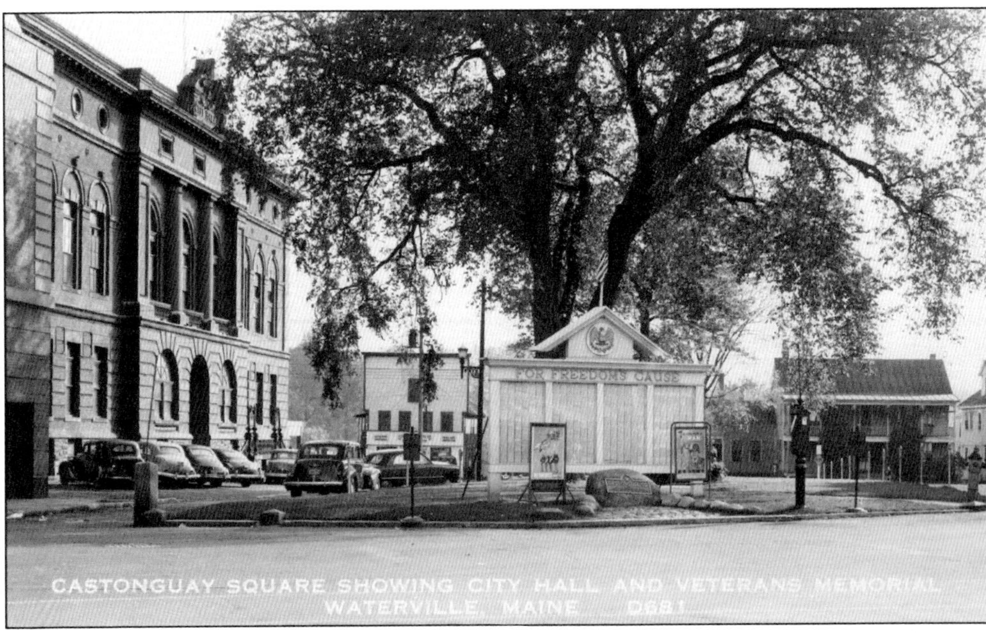

The park in front of Waterville City Hall was originally known as "The Common." The space was renamed Castonguay Square in 1921 after Sgt. Arthur L. Castonguay, a Waterville native who died in 1918 while fighting in France during World War I. This post–World War II view shows the veterans' memorial listing the names of Waterville citizens who served in that conflict.

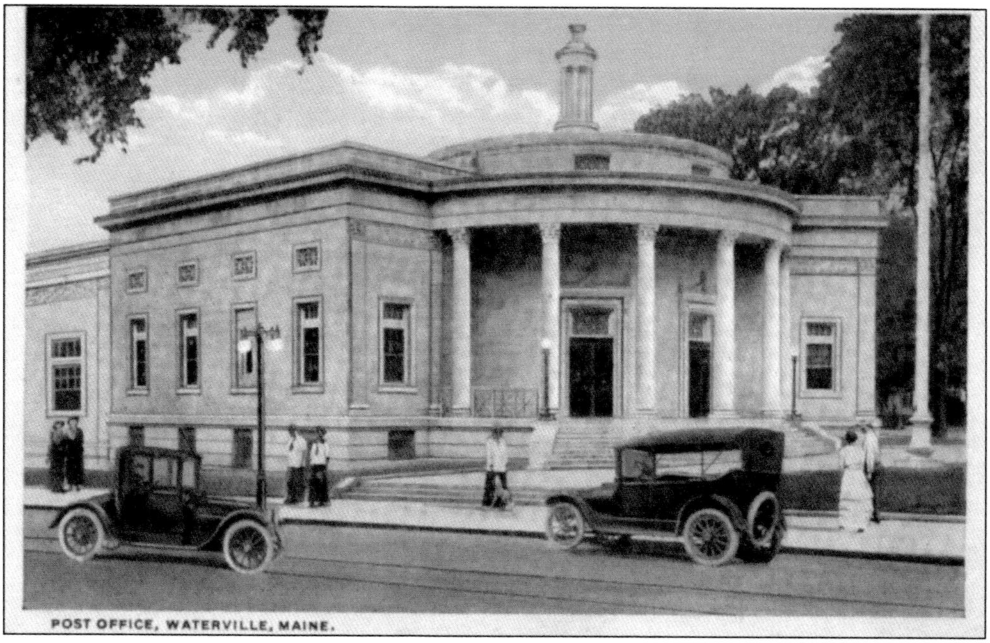

The Waterville Post Office, which was built between 1911 and 1913, is located at the juncture of Main and Elm Streets. US Department of the Treasury architect James Knox Taylor designed this elegant neoclassical stone building based on William Strickland's Philadelphia Exchange. The post office's Indiana limestone walls stand on a Maine granite foundation.

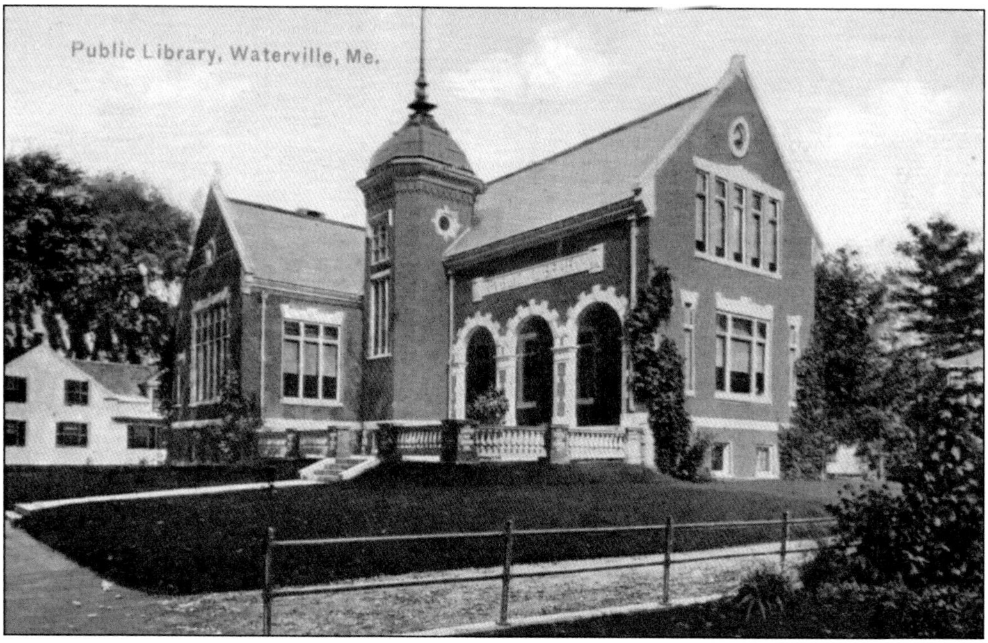

Philanthropist Andrew Carnegie made a $20,000 gift to Waterville in 1902 to construct a public library, contingent on the building being constructed in a suitable location and the city making an annual appropriation for its operation. Between August 1903 and December 1904, the Waterville Public Library was built on Elm Street from an eclectic design by William R. Miller, architect of similar libraries in Fairfield and Auburn.

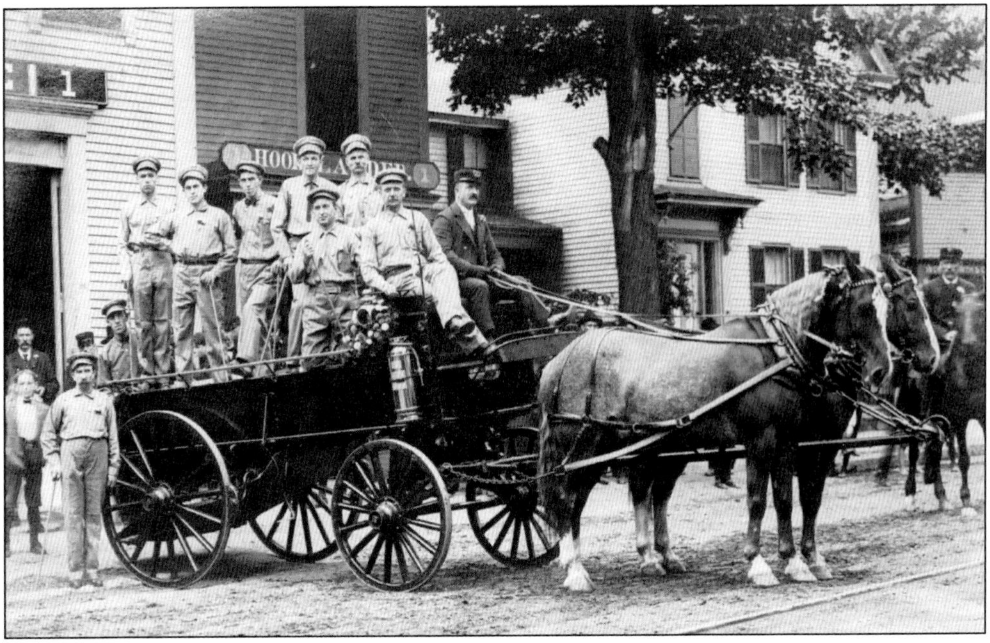

In this 1910 image, Waterville firemen pose aboard a horse-drawn wagon in front of the Main Street buildings housing Hose Company No. 1 and Hook and Ladder Company No 1. In 1911, these two companies were relocated to the new Central Fire Station, and the old wooden firehouses were demolished.

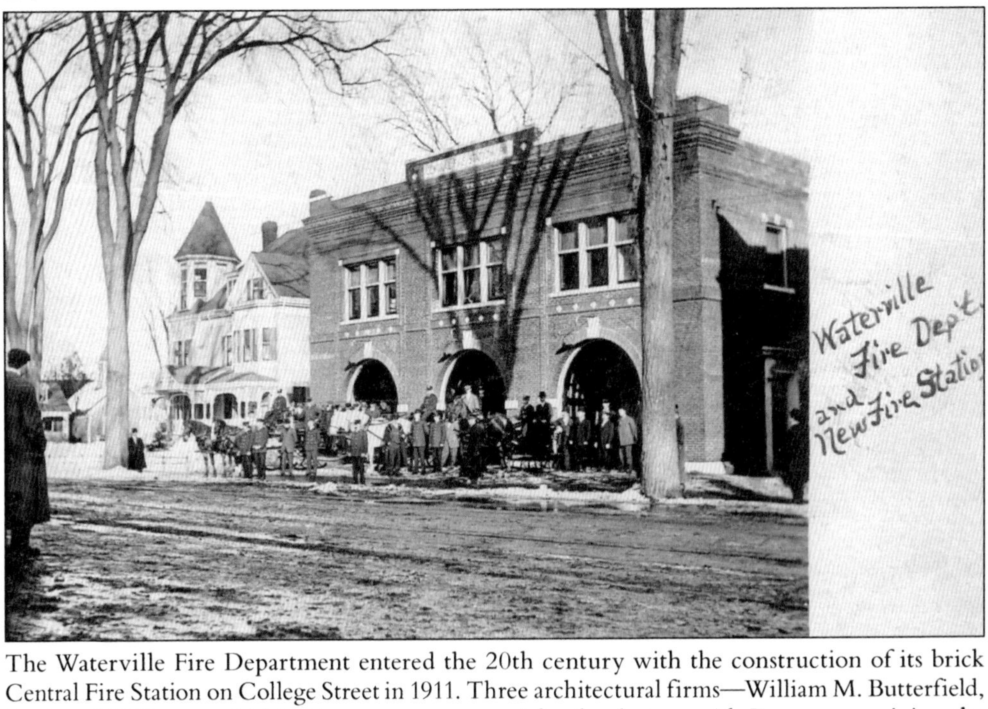

The Waterville Fire Department entered the 20th century with the construction of its brick Central Fire Station on College Street in 1911. Three architectural firms—William M. Butterfield, Funk and Wilcox, and H.L. Freeman—competed for the design, with Freeman receiving the commission. The fire station consolidated two hose companies and a hook and ladder company into one location, all of which were still horse-drawn as of opening day in January 1912.

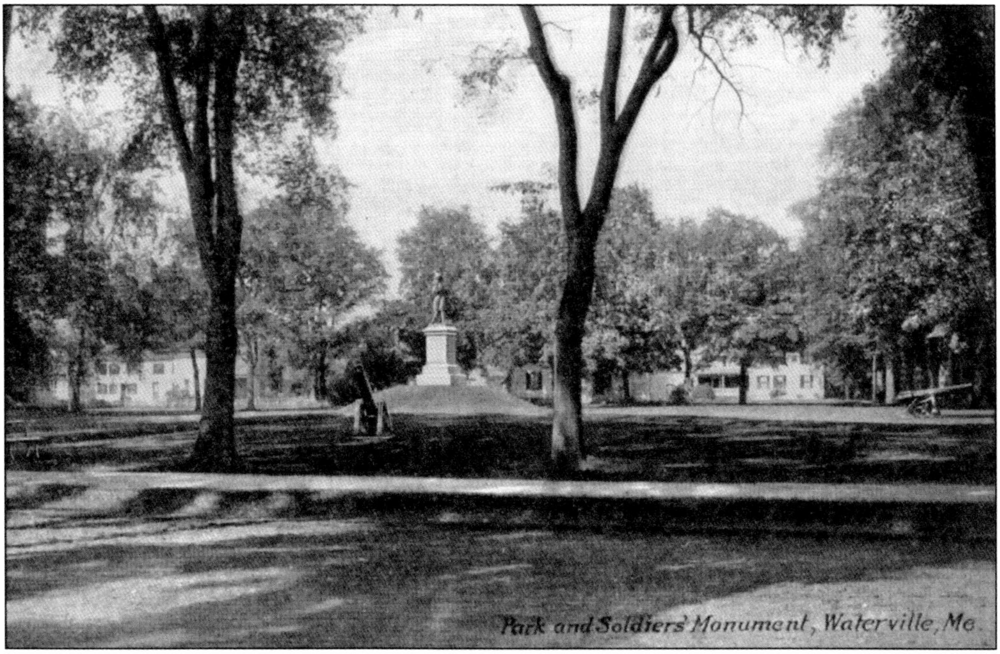

Like many communities across Maine after the Civil War, Waterville was quick to memorialize local citizens who had served in the conflict. Even before the war ended in 1865, townspeople were raising funds to erect a suitable monument, and that year, the town granted the use of the park at Elm and Park Streets as the site for a statue.

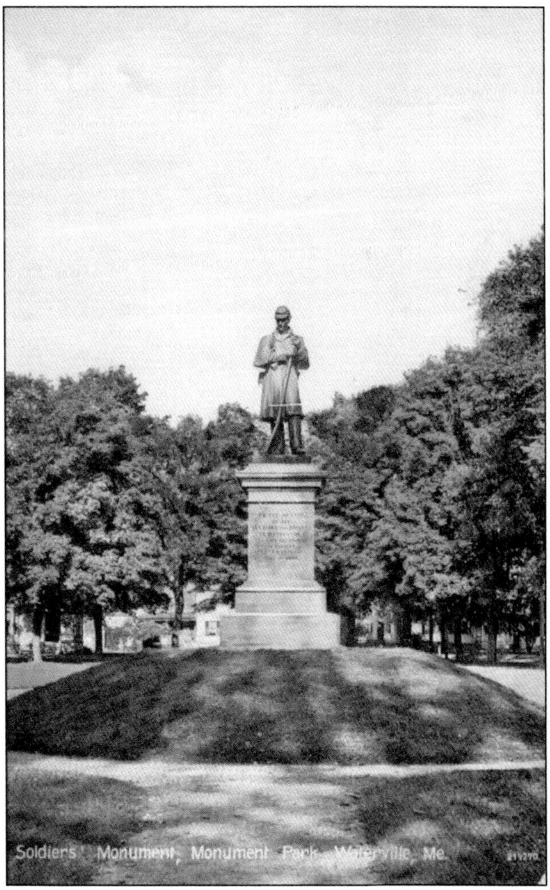

By 1875, $1,000 was raised for a Civil War monument. That year, the town voted for another $1,000 to enable the Waterville Soldiers' Monument Association to acquire a bronze casting of *The Citizen Soldier* by Boston sculptor Martin Milmore. Additional funds were contributed for the statue's granite pedestal, and the monument was dedicated on Memorial Day, May 30, 1876.

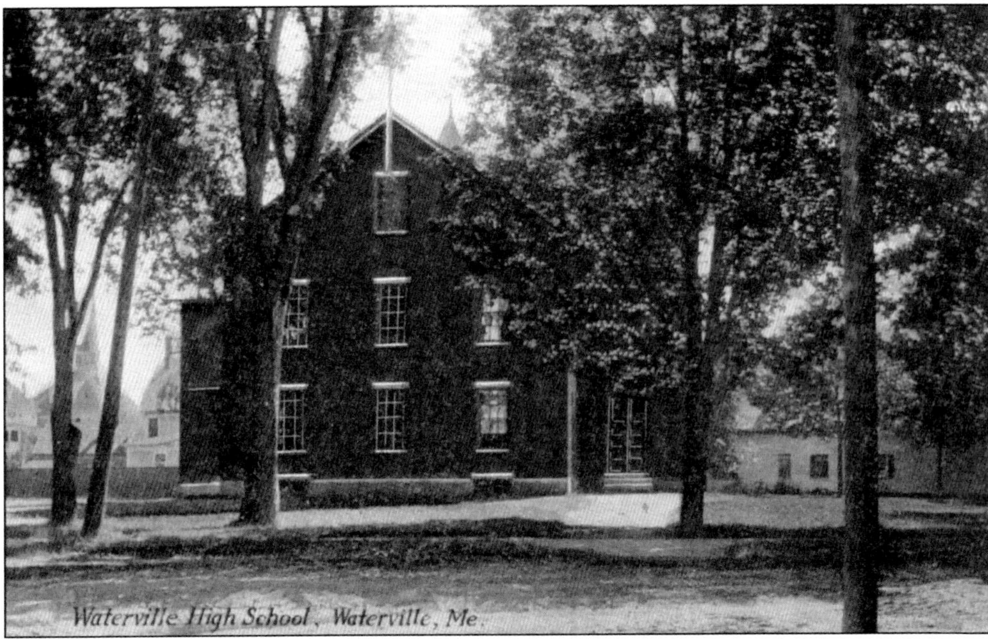

This modest brick building, which was constructed on Pleasant Street in 1853 as a grammar school, represents a long record of public service. Waterville High School used the building from its establishment in 1876 until its removal to new facilities on Gilman Street in 1913. This building was demolished in 1922 to make way for the new junior high school.

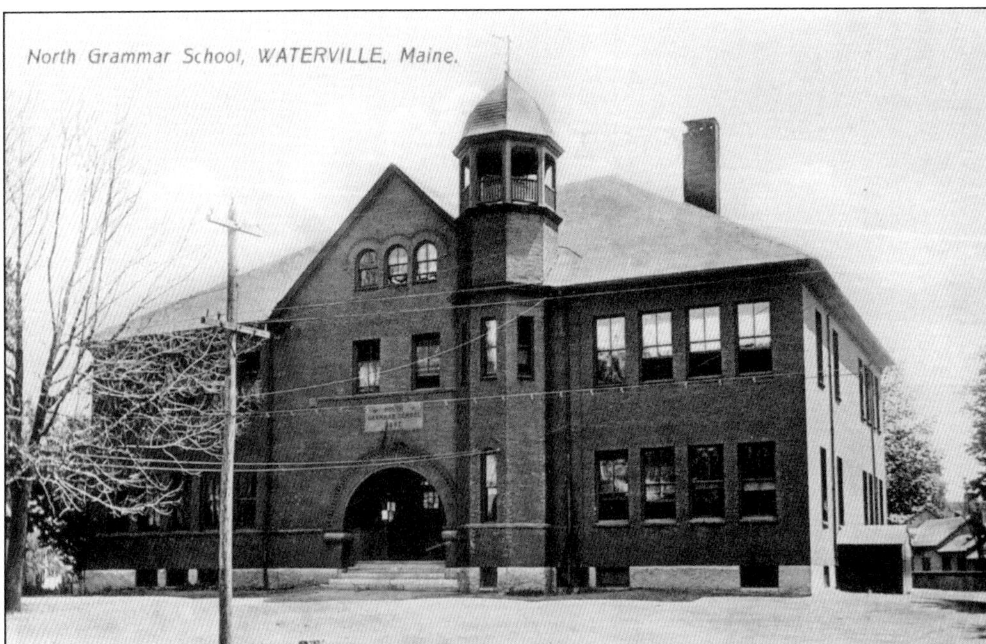

In 1887, John Calvin Stevens of Portland designed North Grammar School on Pleasant Street as an eight-room brick school to be built for $19,000. Its broad, arched entrance and picturesque tower are features of the Romanesque Revival style. Construction began in the spring of 1887, and the building opened on February 28, 1888, with a capacity of 400 students.

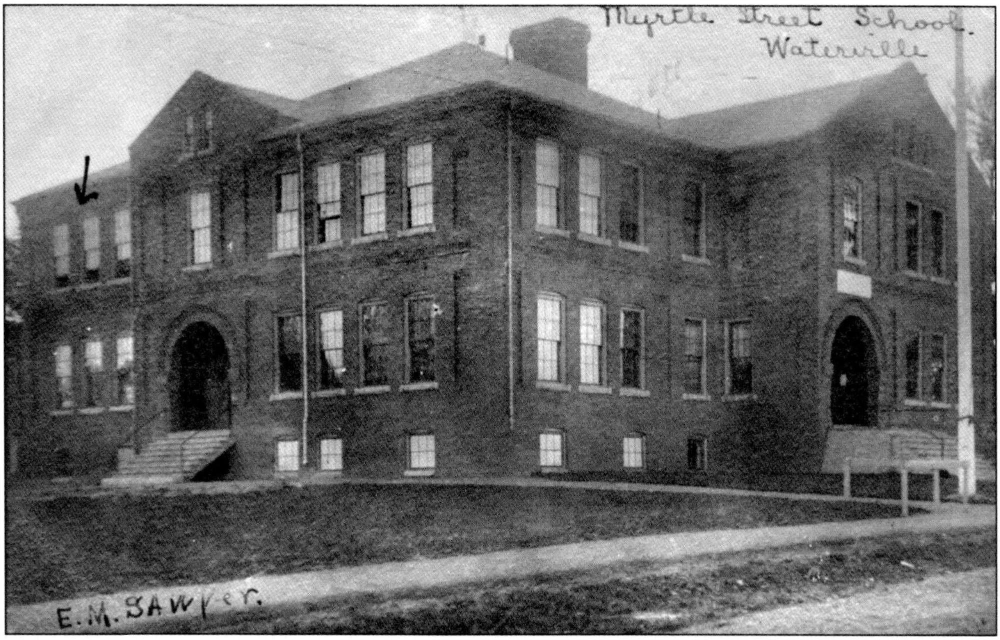

When the Myrtle Street School was constructed in 1897, ***Industrial Journal*** described this $15,000 brick building as the "best school which the city has, there being eight large school rooms and two small rooms for the use of the assistants and for recitation rooms." The Myrtle Street School was designed in the Romanesque Revival style by Edwin E. Lewis of Gardiner and erected by local contractor Stephen F. Brann.

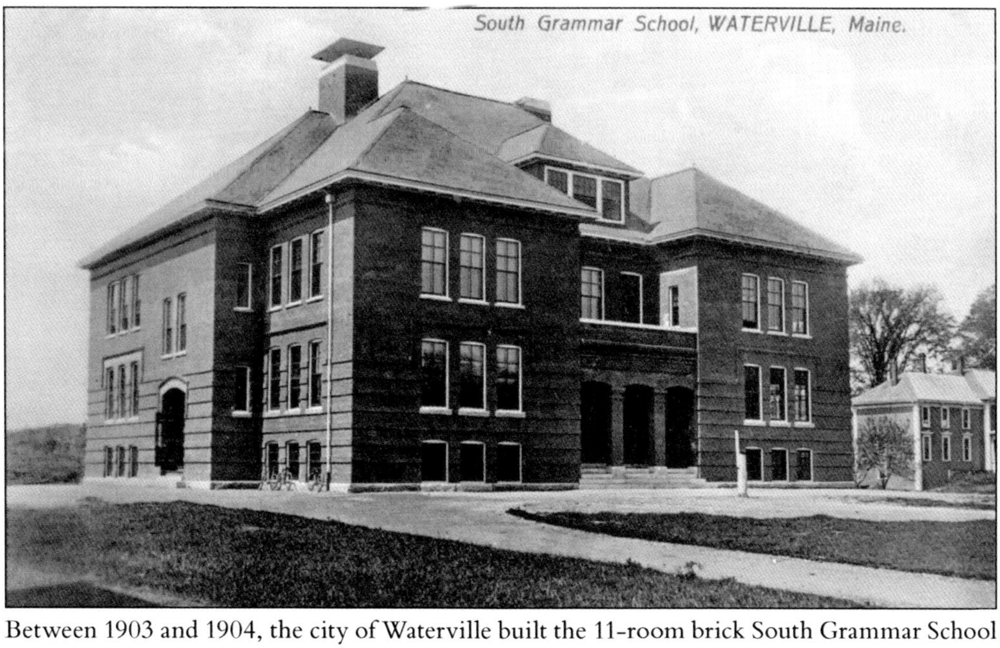

Between 1903 and 1904, the city of Waterville built the 11-room brick South Grammar School on Silver Street for $36,000. Architect William M. Butterfield drew the plans. After opening in January 1905, the school burned down in March 1906. The city immediately hired Butterfield to furnish designs based on the previous building, and in 1906, a new South Grammar School rose from the ashes of the old one at a cost of $34,500.

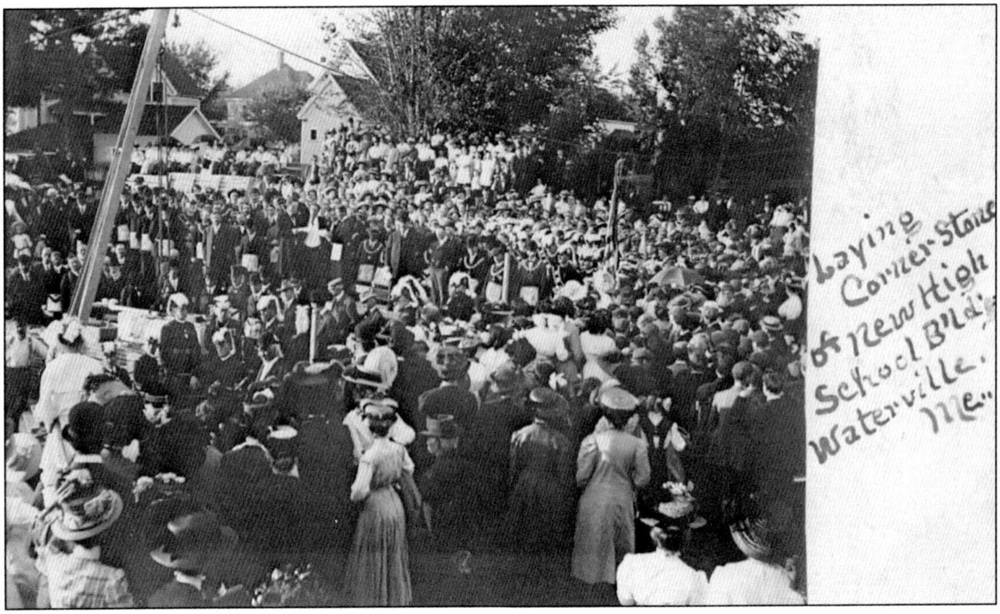

On October 5, 1909, builders laid the cornerstone for Waterville High School on Gilman Street. The next day, the *Waterville Morning Sentinel* reported that, "The cornerstone of the new high school was set in place yesterday afternoon in the presence of a large concourse of citizens, men and women, and hundreds of children from the high and common schools. The exercises were carried out without a hitch." (Waterville Historical Society.)

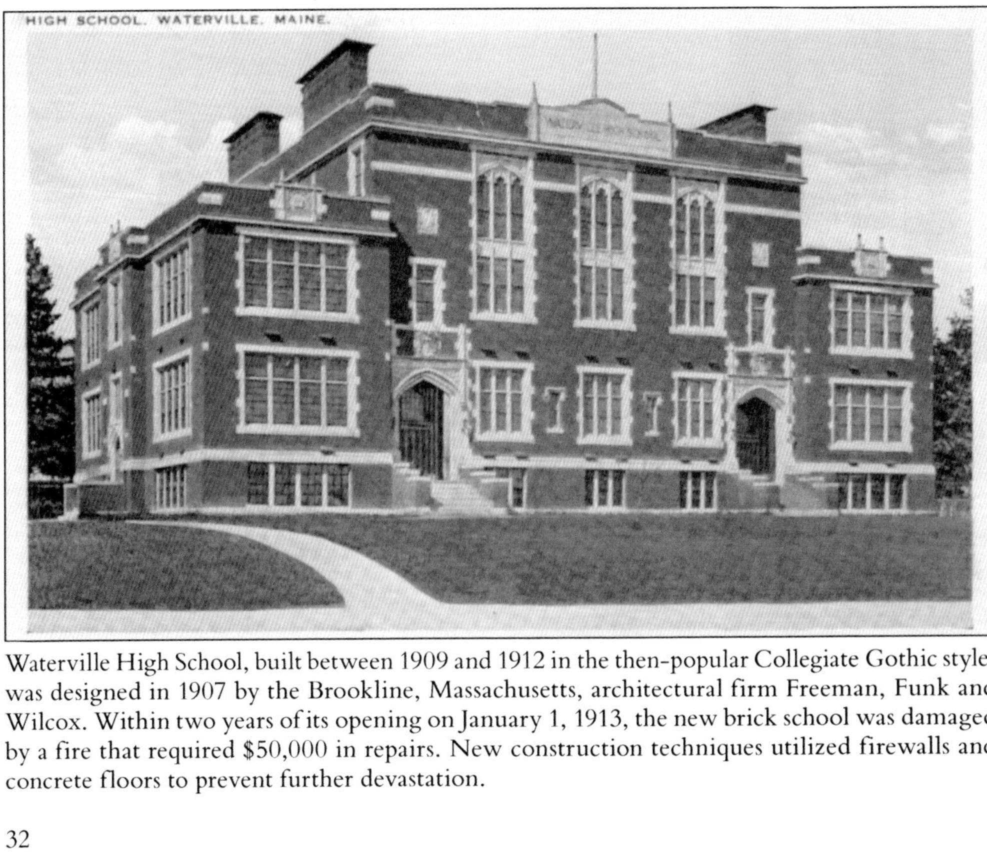

Waterville High School, built between 1909 and 1912 in the then-popular Collegiate Gothic style, was designed in 1907 by the Brookline, Massachusetts, architectural firm Freeman, Funk and Wilcox. Within two years of its opening on January 1, 1913, the new brick school was damaged by a fire that required $50,000 in repairs. New construction techniques utilized firewalls and concrete floors to prevent further devastation.

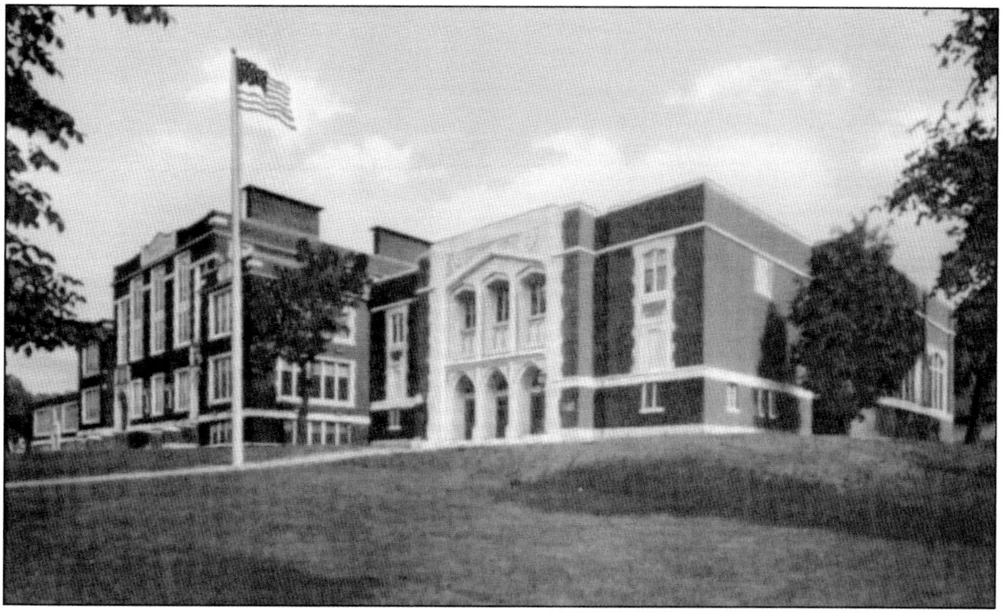

By the 1930s, Waterville High School had become overcrowded. The problem was addressed by constructing two additions—the manual arts training wing (left, built in 1936) and the auditorium and gymnasium (right, built in 1938–1940). These additions were designed by the Augusta architectural firm Bunker and Savage in a style compatible with the original building. The federal Works Progress Administration helped pay construction costs for both wings.

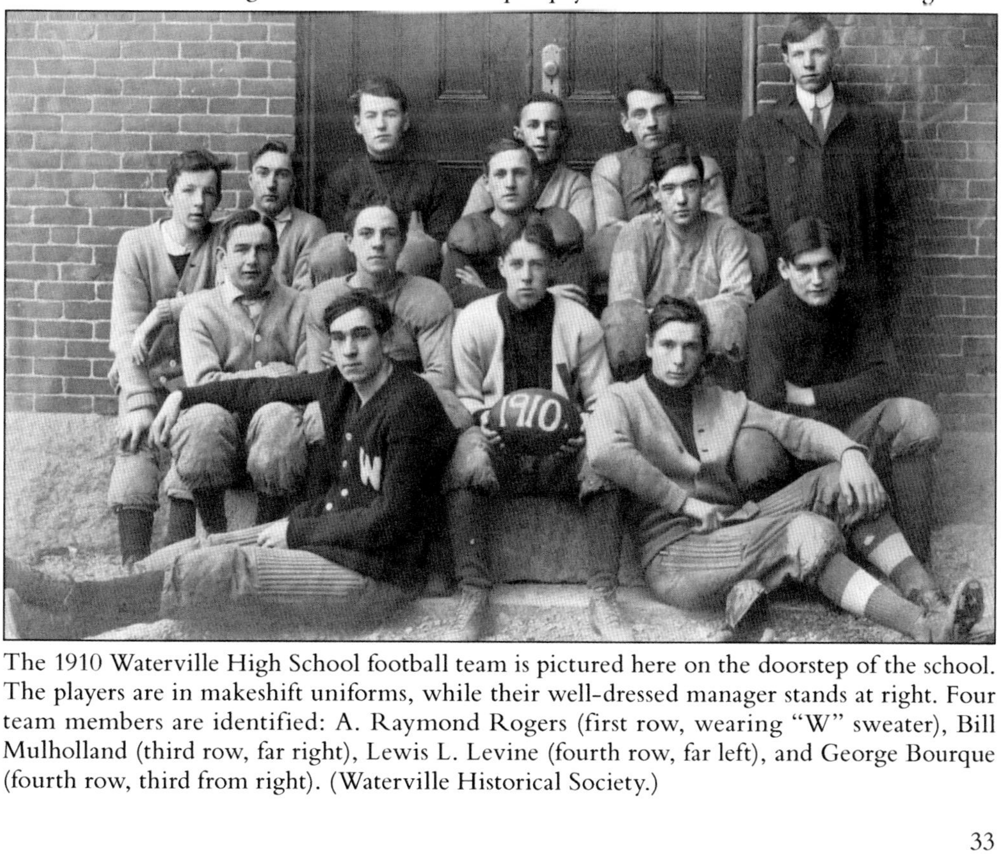

The 1910 Waterville High School football team is pictured here on the doorstep of the school. The players are in makeshift uniforms, while their well-dressed manager stands at right. Four team members are identified: A. Raymond Rogers (first row, wearing "W" sweater), Bill Mulholland (third row, far right), Lewis L. Levine (fourth row, far left), and George Bourque (fourth row, third from right). (Waterville Historical Society.)

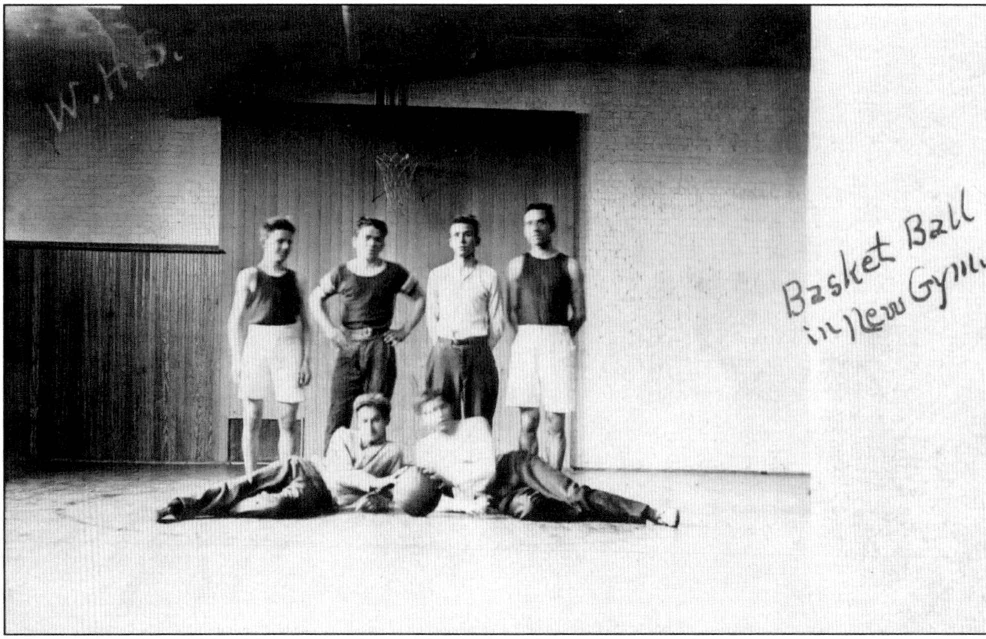

After James Naismith invented the game of basketball at a YMCA training school in Springfield, Massachusetts, in 1891, its popularity quickly spread throughout the country. By the time Waterville's new high school opened in 1913, basketball was an established sport in most American high schools and colleges. Here, Waterville High School players pose in their new gymnasium.

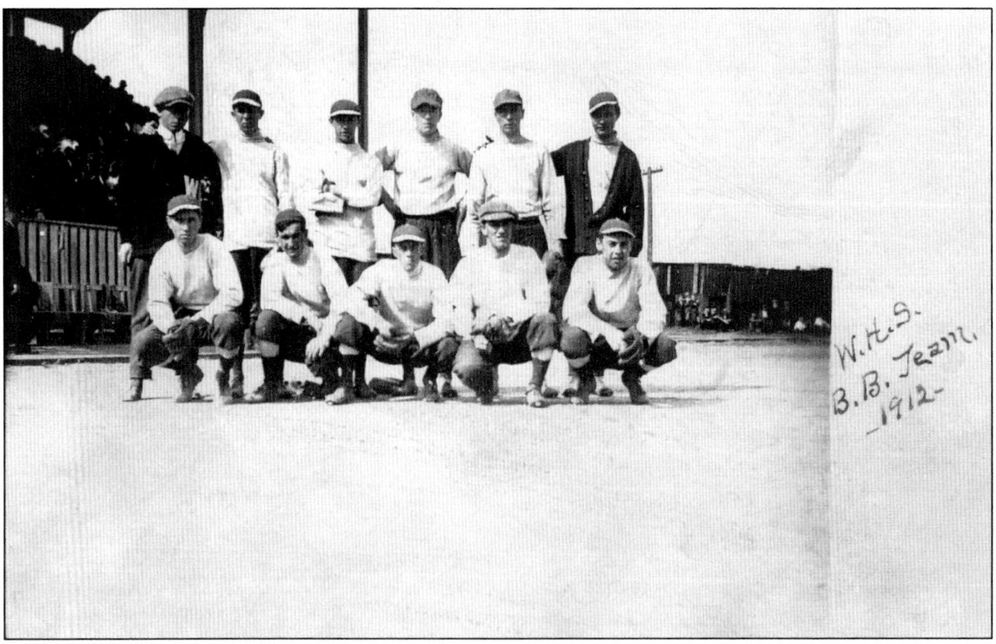

The Waterville High School baseball team won the first of three highly touted contests against Coburn Classical Institute in 1912, but, as the *Waterville Morning Sentinel* reported, if they "went into the [second] game with the idea of coming out victor, it certainly was not evident to the spectators." During the third game (another Waterville loss), the western end of the grandstand at Colby's Alumni Field briefly caught fire, causing a near-panic.

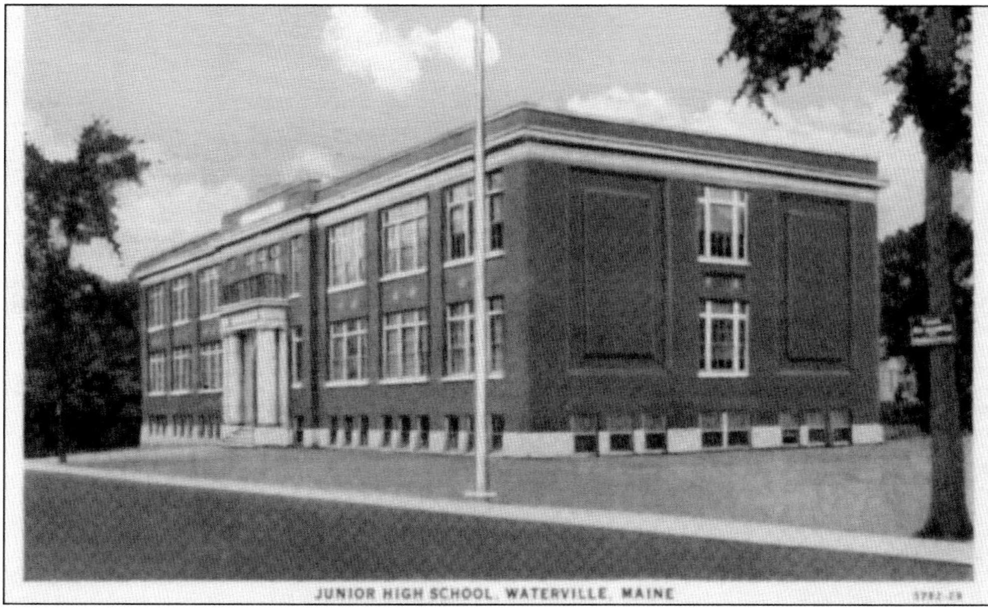

In 1922, the old Waterville High School building on Pleasant Street was demolished, and a new junior high school was erected on the site. Designed by local architect Horace True Muzzy in the Colonial Revival style, this building was constructed for $195,000 and could accommodate 570 students. The curriculum included domestic science, textile design, automotive repair, and manual training, and the school contained an auditorium and a gymnasium.

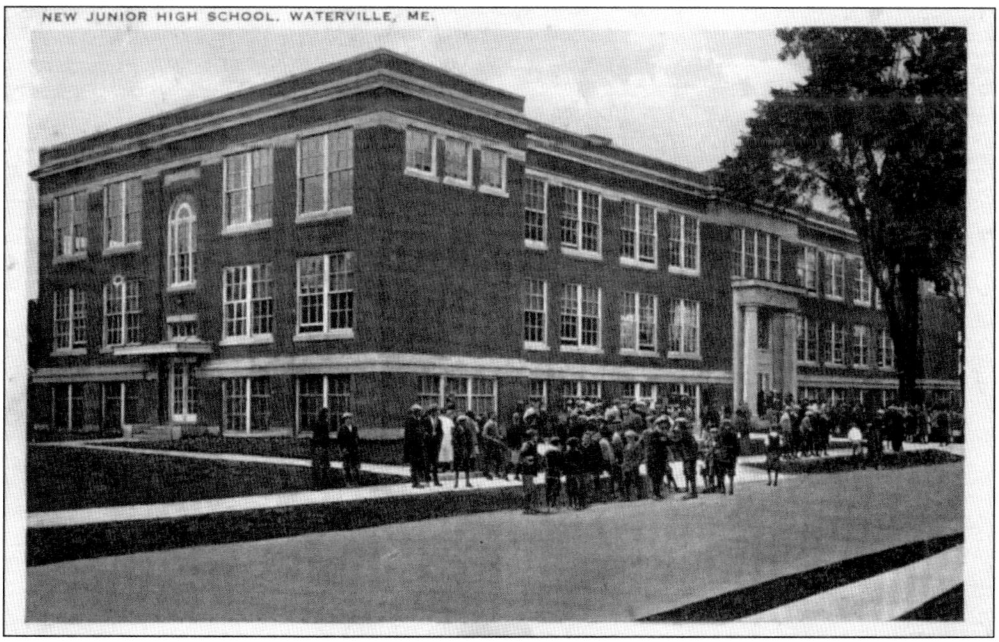

Waterville Junior High School opened in the fall of 1923 and was soon expanded by the additions of wings on both sides. In 1936, the junior high school moved into the old high school on Gilman Street, and the old junior high building became the Pleasant Street School, which served students in kindergarten through sixth grade. In 1994, the Pleasant Street School was renamed for Albert S. Hall, a longtime Waterville teacher and school administrator.

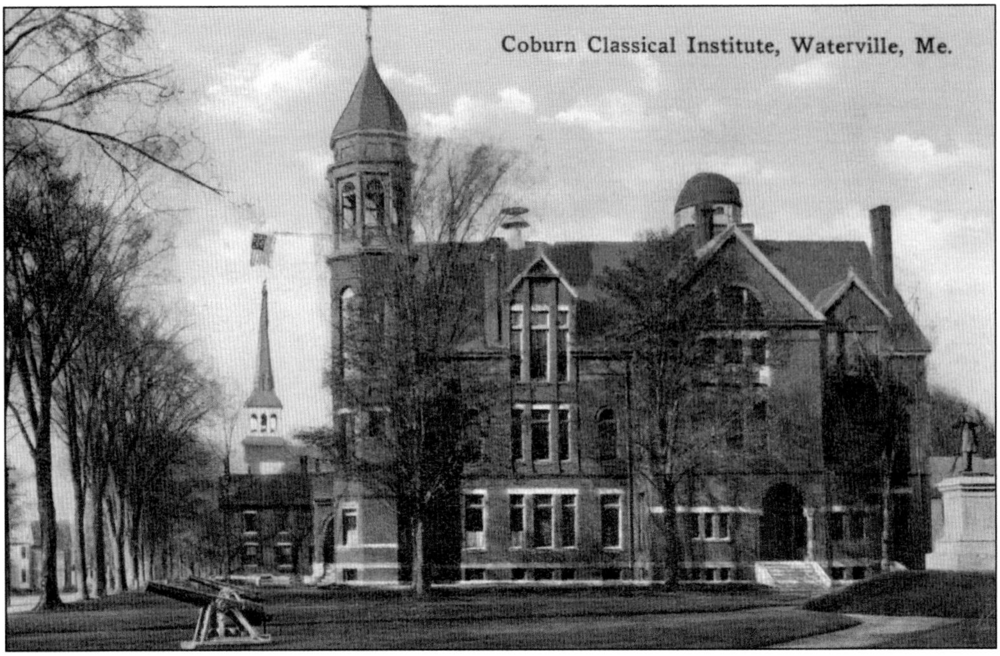

Coburn Classical Institute, founded as Waterville Academy in 1829 and renamed Waterville Classical Institute in 1865, was located on Elm Street adjacent to Monument Park. The institute, initially meant to be a preparatory school for Colby College, was renamed in 1883 for Gov. Abner Coburn of Skowhegan after he donated funds to construct this building in memory of his brother Stephen Coburn and his nephew Charles Coburn.

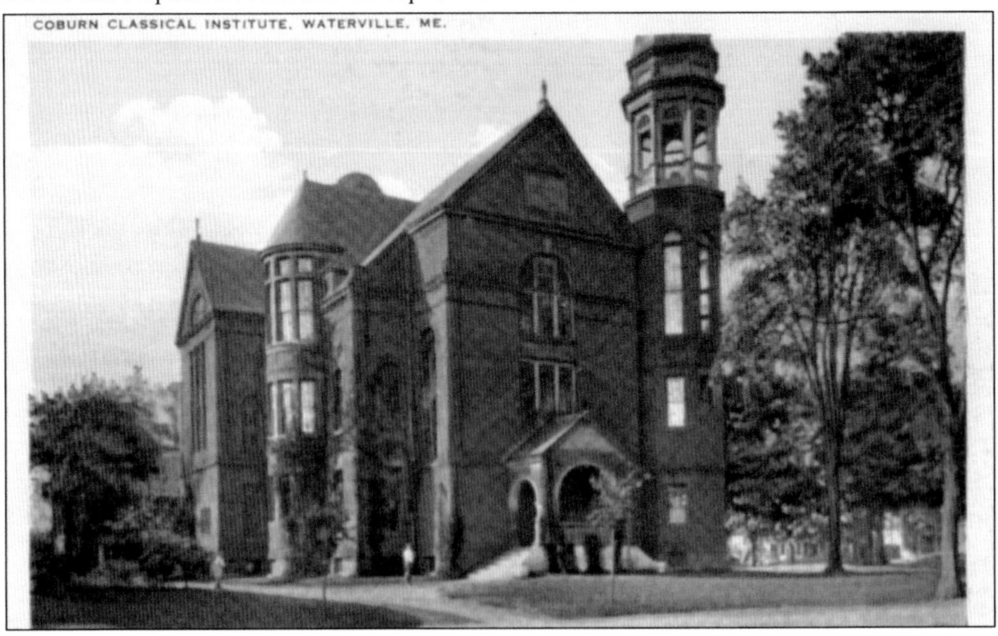

When the Coburn Classical Institute was dedicated in 1884, this $50,000 building was considered one of the finest educational facilities in Maine. Designed in the Queen Anne style by Francis H. Fassett and John Calvin Stevens of Portland, this three-story brick structure included classrooms, lecture halls, a library, a chapel, and an astronomical observatory.

The domed belfry on the picturesque corner tower was the symbol of Coburn Classical Institute until the building was destroyed by fire in 1955.

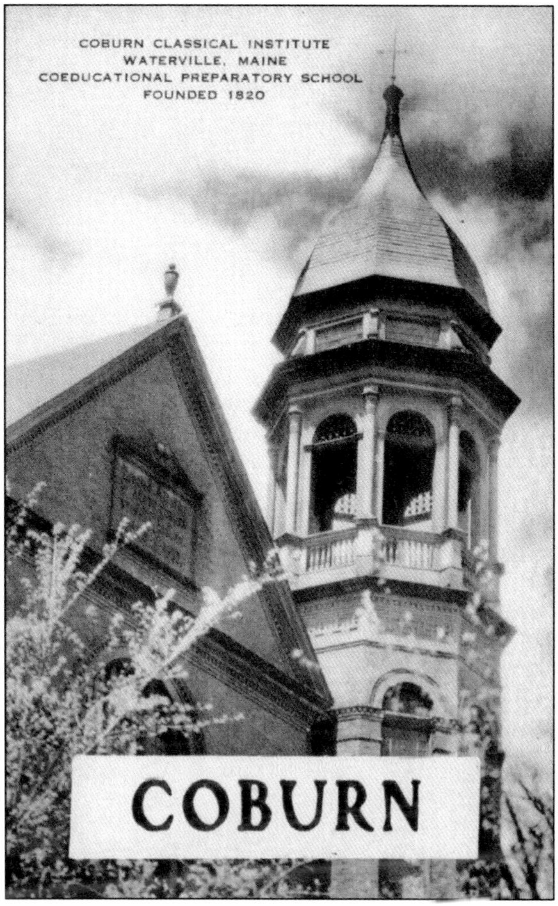

In this c. 1910 postcard image, Coburn Classical Institute students watch a fall football game from seats in the grandstand at the school's athletic field. The institute's 1900 catalogue described the school's athletic program as follows: "Football, baseball, tennis, track, and field sports all receive attention. Athletic sports have their rightful place in the school. Their purpose is to give the students needed exercise and healthful recreation."

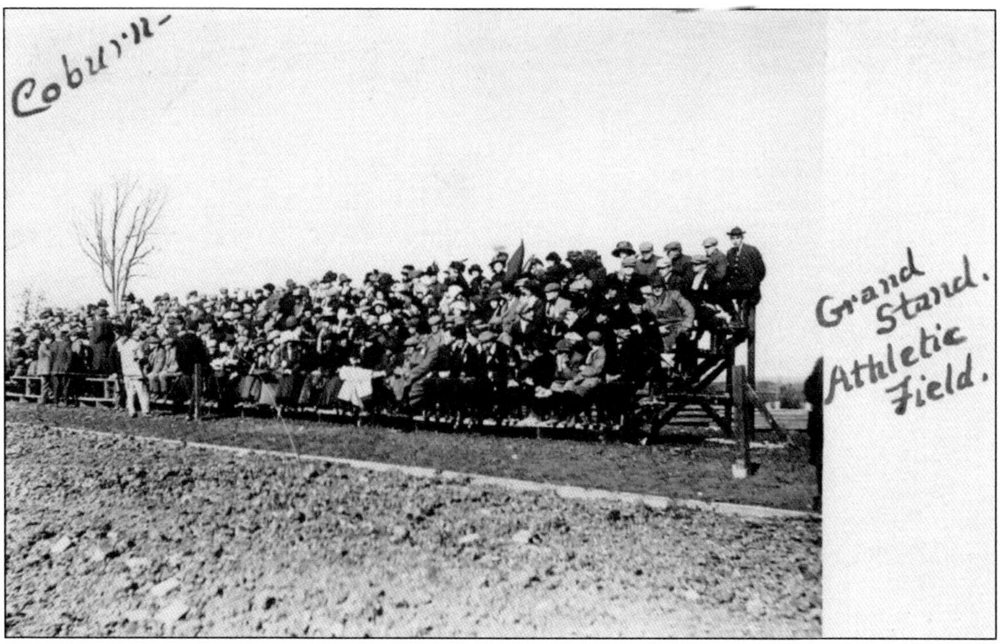

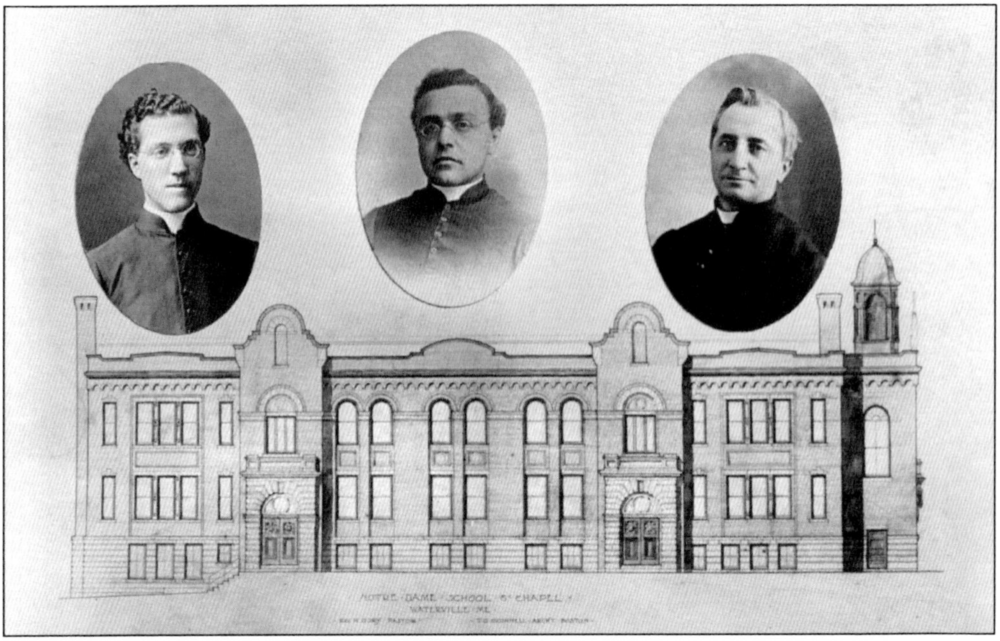

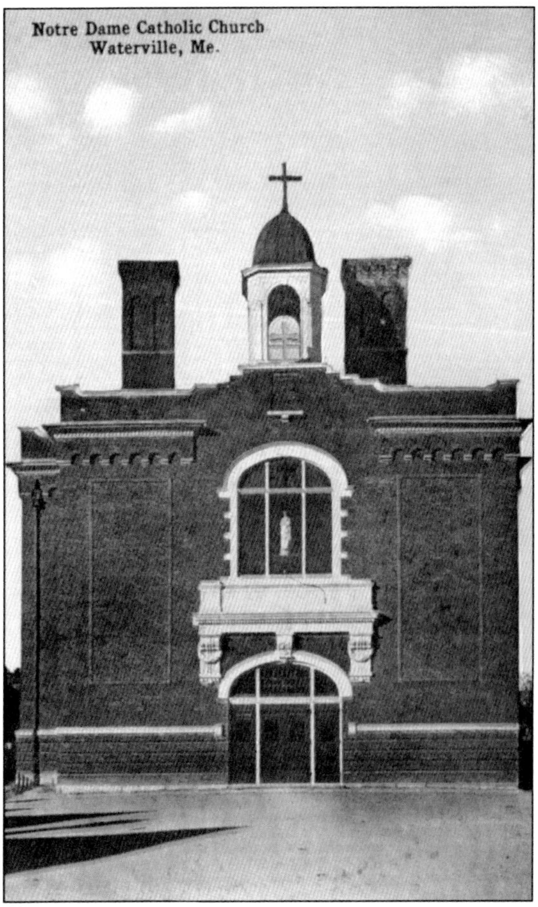

Notre Dame Parish was founded in 1910 by Fr. Henri Gory. In contrast to prior Catholic parishes in Waterville, Notre Dame was planned at the outset to provide both religious services and parochial schooling, and its first building reflected this dual mission. In March 1913, the school and chapel burned down and were quickly replaced by the large brick structure shown in this architect's drawing by Timothy G. O'Connell of Boston.

Notre Dame Catholic Church on Silver Street is located at one end of the large brick structure built in 1913 to house the parish chapel and school. From 1910 to 1920, Ursuline nuns from France taught classes at the school. They were replaced in 1920 by Ursulines from Mount Merici Academy in Waterville.

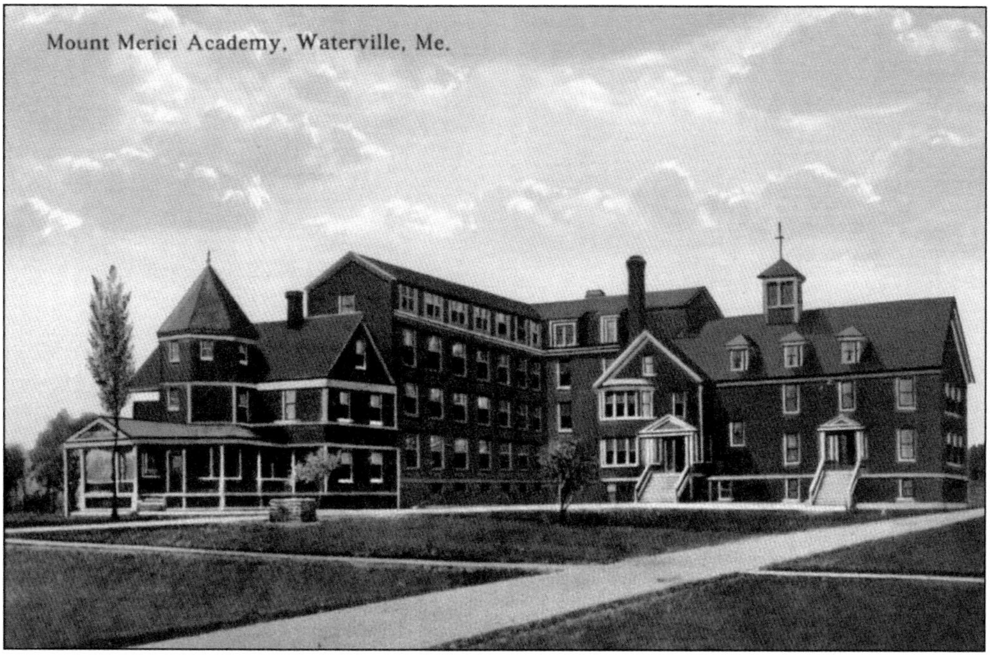

Six Ursuline sisters came to Waterville from Canada in 1888 at the request of St. Francis de Sales Catholic Church. Their teaching mission grew to the extent that Mount Merici Academy was founded in 1911 on Western Avenue. In February 1912, the academy opened its classroom, dormitory, and convent complex to accommodate 125 students. After more than a century of service, the academy remains a vital educational institution.

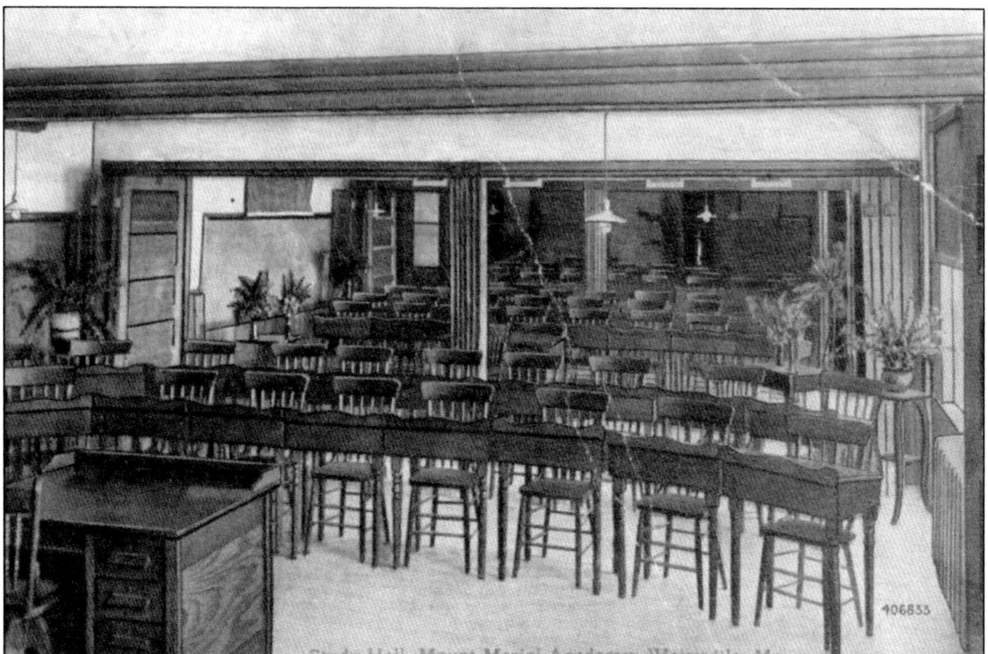

Shortly after Mount Merici Academy opened in 1912, Fairfield photographer W.H. Langley published a series of postcards of the school's interior. This view shows the study hall.

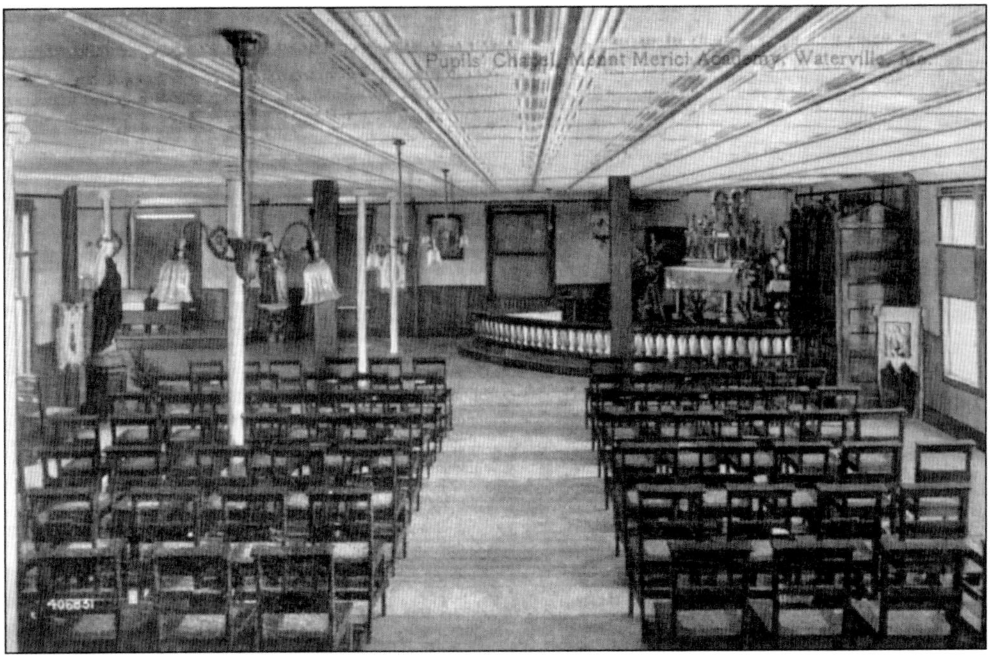

W.H. Langley created this c. 1912 view of the pupils' chapel at Mount Merici Academy.

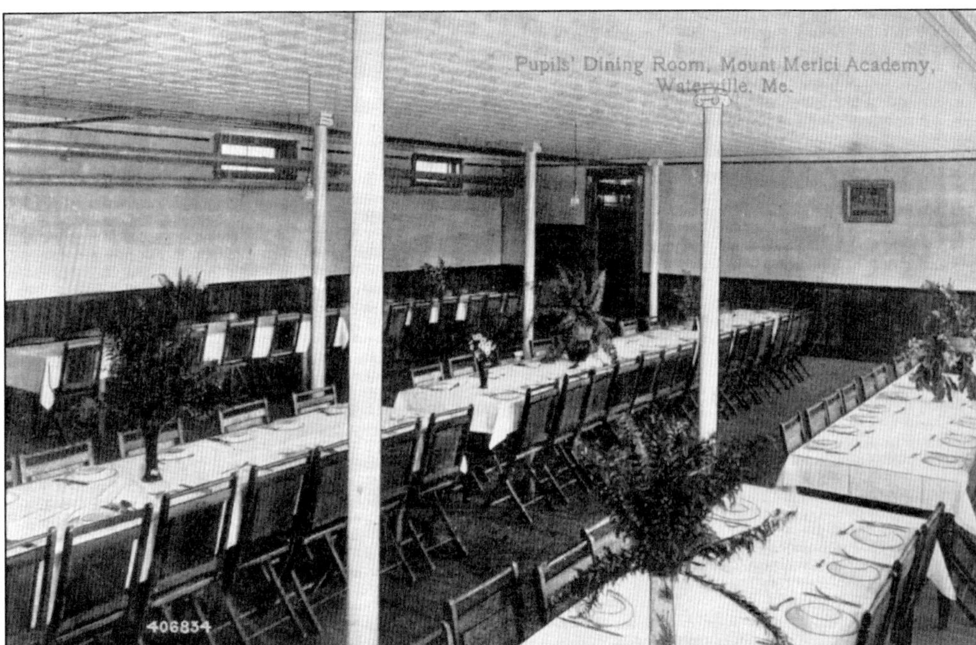

W.H. Langley created this c. 1912 view of the pupils' dining room at Mount Merici Academy.

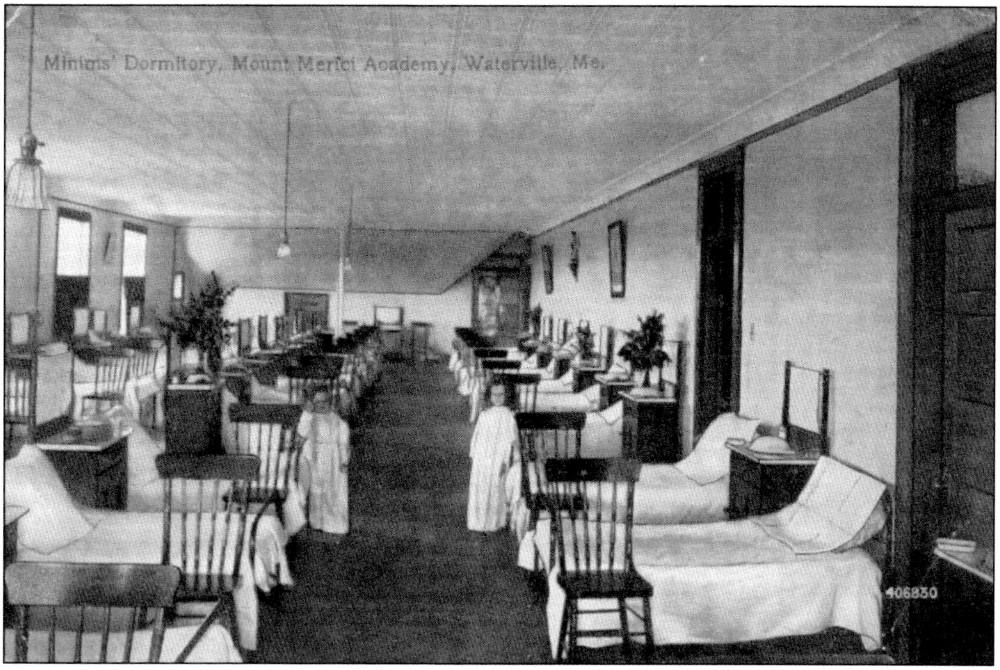

W.H. Langley created this c. 1912 view of the minims' dormitory for young girls at Mount Merici Academy.

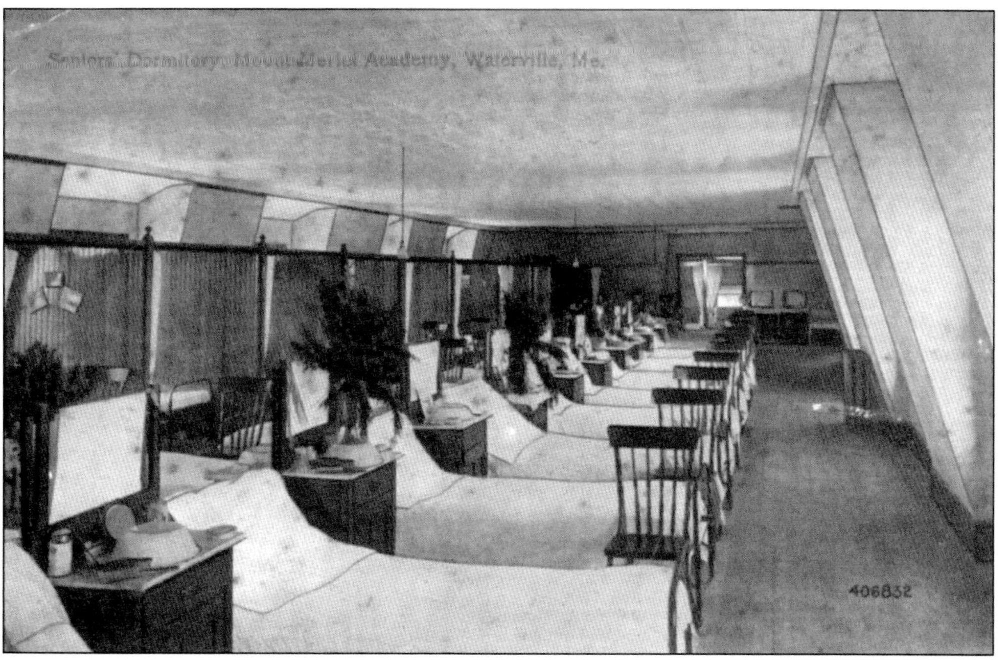

W.H. Langley created this c. 1912 view of the seniors' dormitory at Mount Merici Academy.

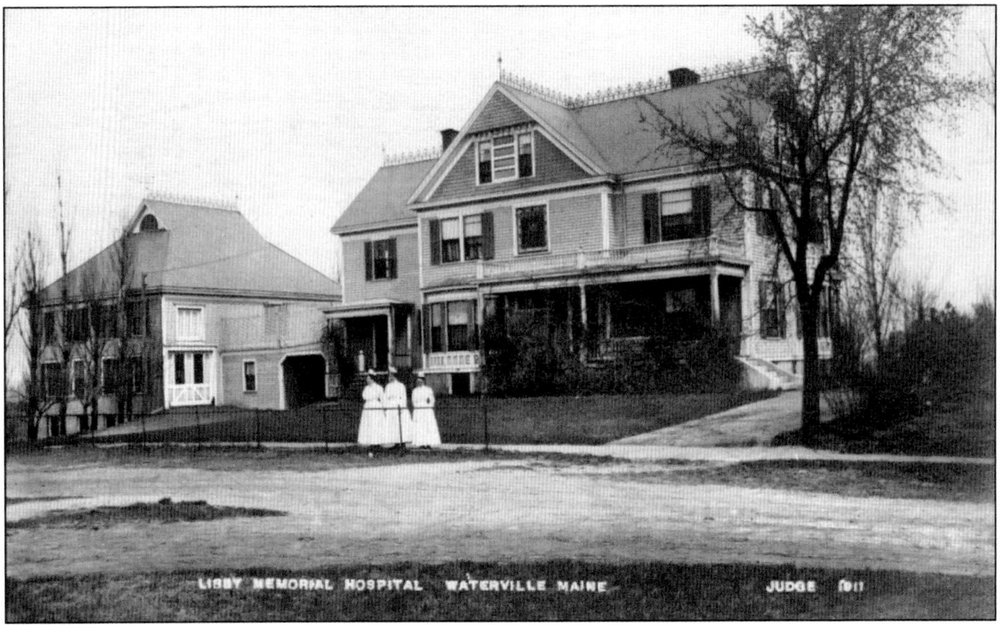

The Libby Memorial Hospital opened in 1911 in the former home of I.C. Libby on College Street. According to the March 1911 *Board of Trade Journal*, its purpose was to "furnish hospital accommodations and facilities for sufferers who would otherwise have to go to Augusta, Lewiston, or Portland." Up to 56 patients could be cared for at a time. The founding physicians, Drs. E.W. Boyce and D.B. Craigin, were supported by the community's leading citizens and businesses.

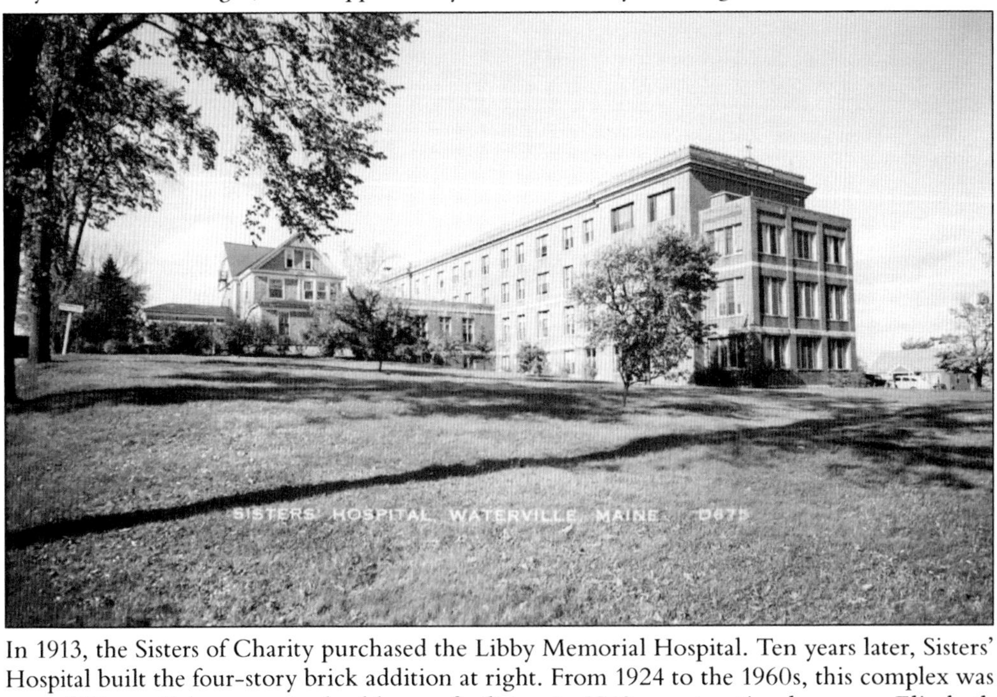

In 1913, the Sisters of Charity purchased the Libby Memorial Hospital. Ten years later, Sisters' Hospital built the four-story brick addition at right. From 1924 to the 1960s, this complex was one of Waterville's two major health care facilities. In 1963, construction began on Elizabeth Ann Seton Hospital, a new Catholic hospital near Mount Merici Academy. Seton merged with Thayer Hospital in 1975 to form Mid-Maine Medical Center. (Penobscot Marine Museum.)

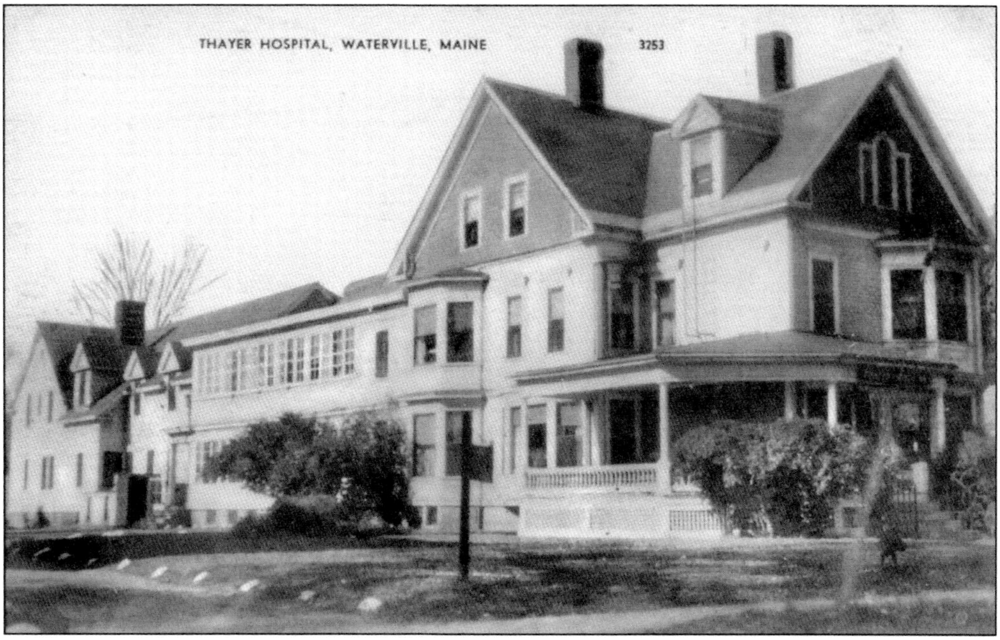

Dr. Frederick C. Thayer, a graduate of Colby College and Bowdoin's Medical School of Maine, practiced medicine in Waterville from 1867 until his death in 1926. Dr. Thayer's spacious home on Main Street was described in the 1898 *Souvenir of Waterville* as being "in one of the prettiest locations in the city, in the cool shade of majestic elms." After Thayer died, this house was converted into Thayer Hospital, which opened in 1931. (Waterville Historical Society.)

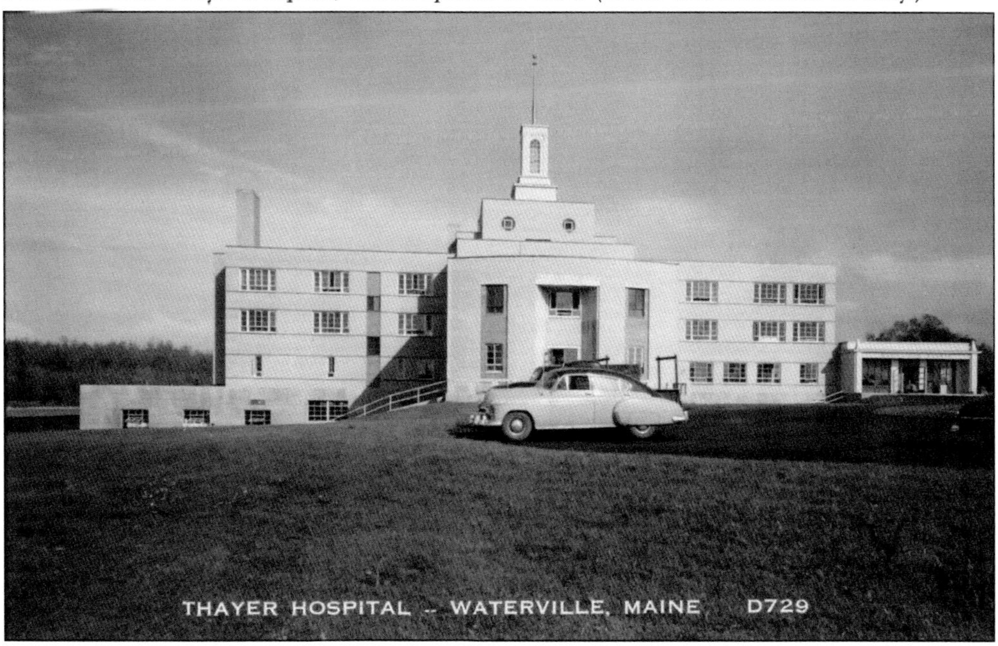

Thayer Hospital operated in Dr. Thayer's Main Street house for two decades. In 1951, the facility was replaced with this modern 63-bed hospital on North Main Street. Today, this building forms the core of the Thayer Campus of MaineGeneral Medical Center, which serves the health care needs of the Waterville/Fairfield region.

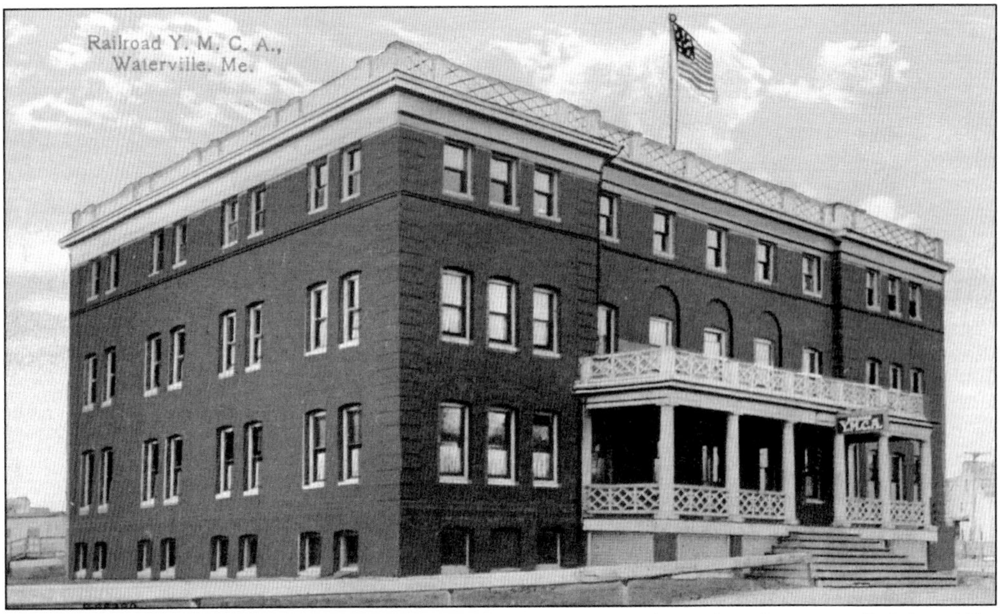

In the early 1900s, Waterville was second only to Portland as the railroad center of Maine. The large number of railroad employees passing through the city resulted in the construction, in 1910, of the Railroad YMCA adjacent to the rail yard. Built for $25,000, this facility offered a restaurant, recreation, and 57 rooms for guests (often workers) to stay in. The Railroad YMCA ended its days as the Hotel Emma, which burned down in January 1977.

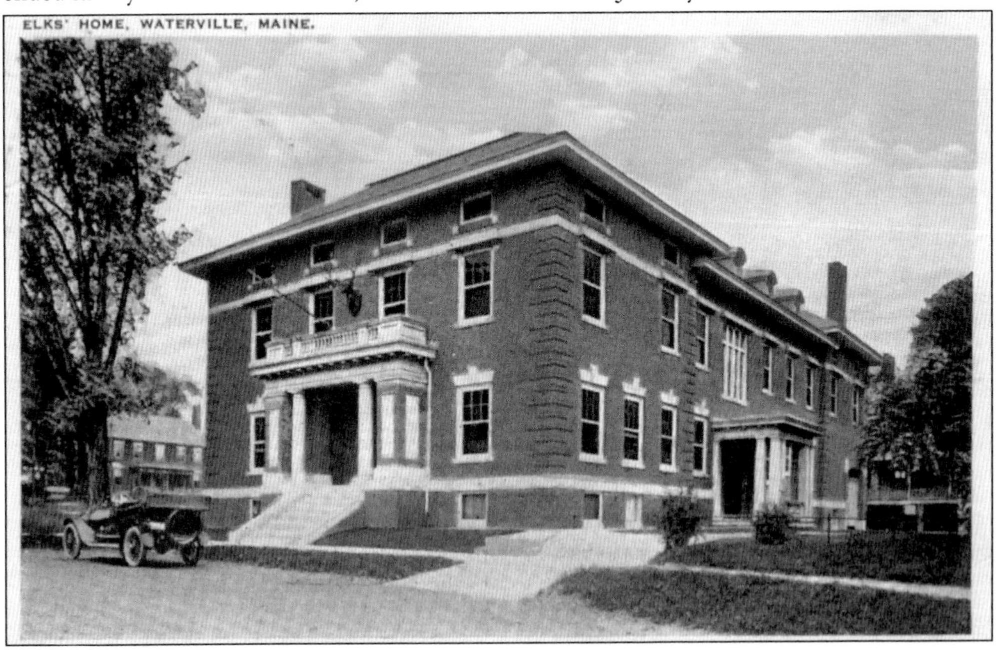

This stately brick Colonial Revival building on Appleton Street was built between October 1913 and June 1914 as the headquarters of the Waterville Elks Club. Constructed at a cost of $27,000 from plans by William R. Miller and Raymond J. Mayo of Portland, the Elks Home was equipped with rooms for dining, banqueting, dancing, reading, smoking, playing billiards, and bowling, as well as lodge rooms for club meetings.

Three

CHURCHES

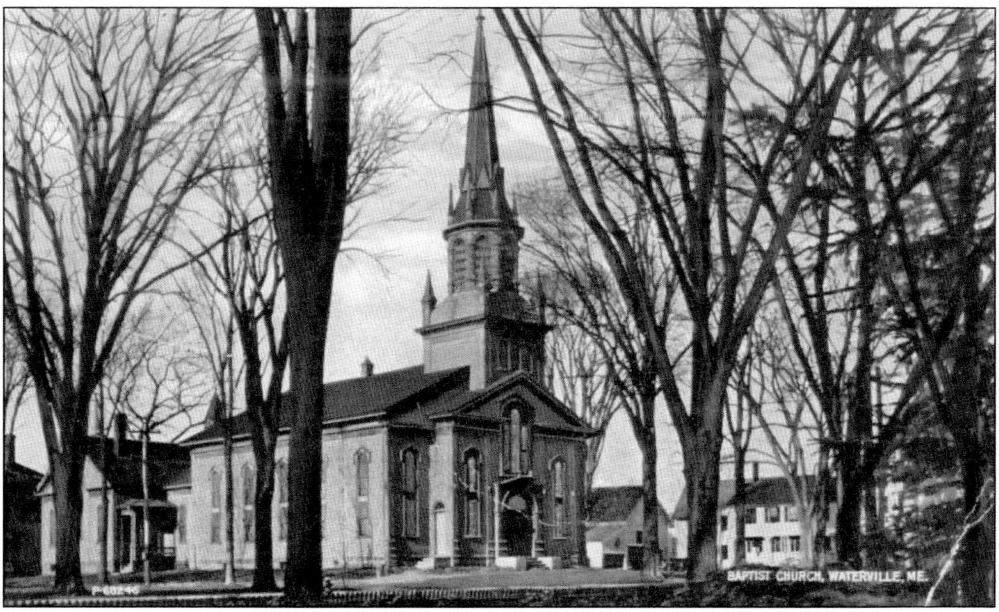

The First Baptist Church at Elm and Park Streets is Waterville's oldest denominational building. The church was founded in 1818 by Rev. Jeremiah Chaplin. In 1826, the Baptists paid Joseph Packard of Readfield $3,856 to construct a Federal-style meetinghouse, which was dedicated on December 6 that year. In 1875, the church underwent an extensive Victorian remodeling based on designs by Francis H. Fassett of Portland; the church is pictured here after the remodeling.

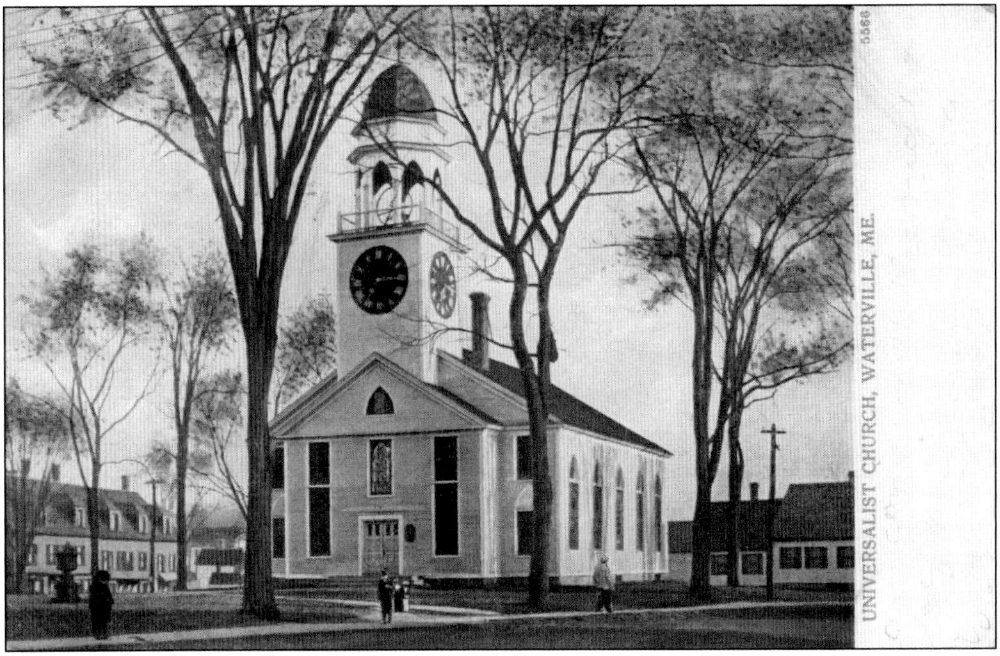

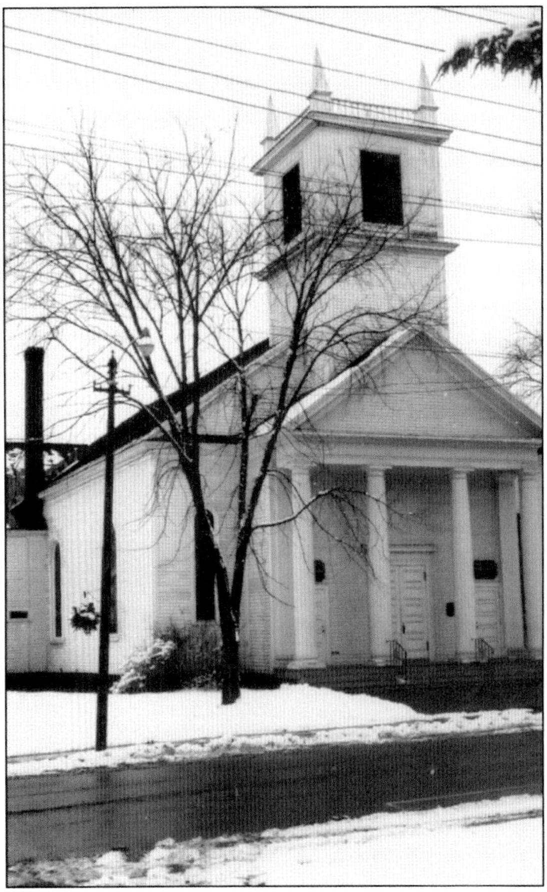

Located on a highly visible site at Elm and Silver Streets, the Universalist Unitarian Church of Waterville is the town's second-oldest religious building, having been constructed by the Universalists in 1832 for $4,100. Federal in style with Gothic Revival features, the church was dedicated on January 1, 1833. In 1952, local Unitarians united with the Universalists to form the current church.

After its construction in 1836, the First Congregational Church on Temple Street spent most of its first century as an unadorned Federal-style meetinghouse (with the exception of the Gothic pinnacles on the tower). In 1923, local architect Horace T. Muzzy added the columned portico on the front. In 1965, the Congregationalists sold their church to the Urban Renewal Authority, which demolished the building in 1966 to make way for downtown commercial development. (Waterville Historical Society.)

The First Unitarian Society of Waterville was organized in 1863. Between 1865 and 1866, the society erected this Italianate church on Main Street. James P. Blunt designed and constructed the building. The church closed its doors in 1936 and was demolished in 1939; the society has been part of the Universalist Unitarian Church of Waterville since 1952. (Waterville Historical Society.)

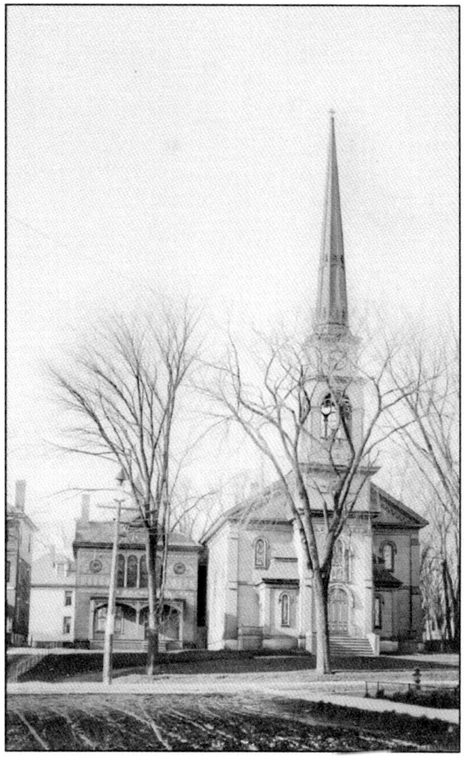

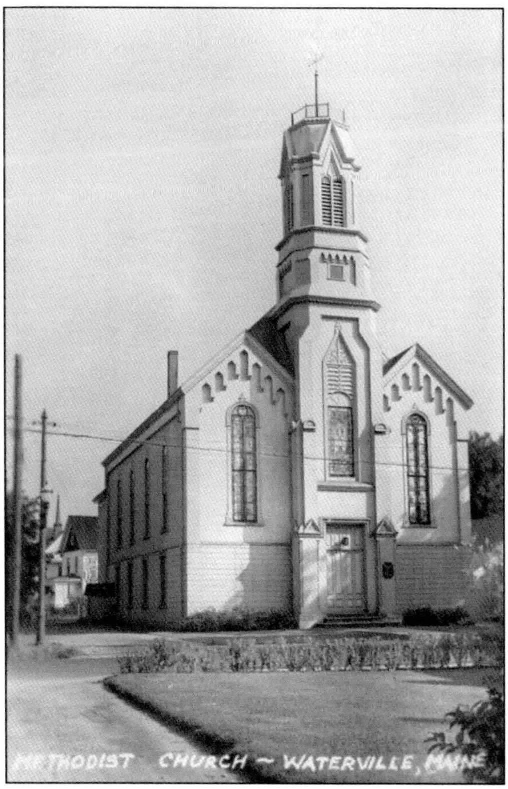

The earliest known Methodist service in Waterville took place in 1827, but more than four decades passed before the first Methodist church was built in the area. In 1869, local businessman Reuben B. Dunn financed most of the $18,000 cost of an elaborate, Romanesque church on Pleasant Street designed by architect Charles F. Douglas. By the time this early-20th-century postcard was created, the spire of the Pleasant Street United Methodist Church had been removed from the steeple. (Waterville Historical Society.)

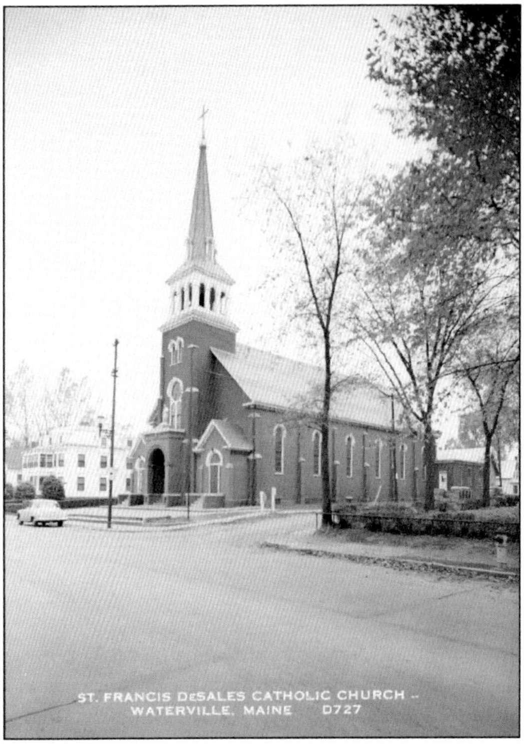

The Lockwood Textile Mills attracted French American workers to Waterville after the Civil War, expanding the city's Catholic population. In 1870, Fr. David J. Halde arrived for the purpose of building St. Francis de Sales Catholic Church to serve this population. In 1872, construction began on a 600-seat structure at Elm and Winter Streets. Two years later, in 1874, the parish completed this substantial brick church with a distinctive blend of Romanesque and Gothic features. (Penobscot Marine Museum.)

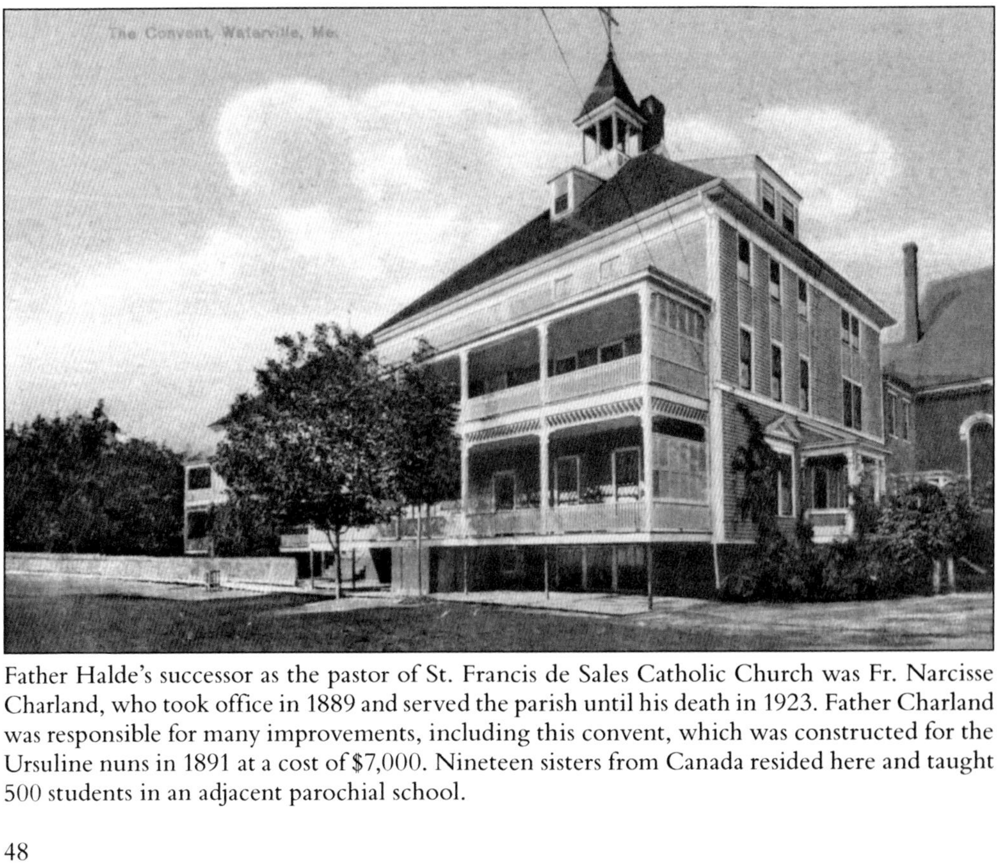

Father Halde's successor as the pastor of St. Francis de Sales Catholic Church was Fr. Narcisse Charland, who took office in 1889 and served the parish until his death in 1923. Father Charland was responsible for many improvements, including this convent, which was constructed for the Ursuline nuns in 1891 at a cost of $7,000. Nineteen sisters from Canada resided here and taught 500 students in an adjacent parochial school.

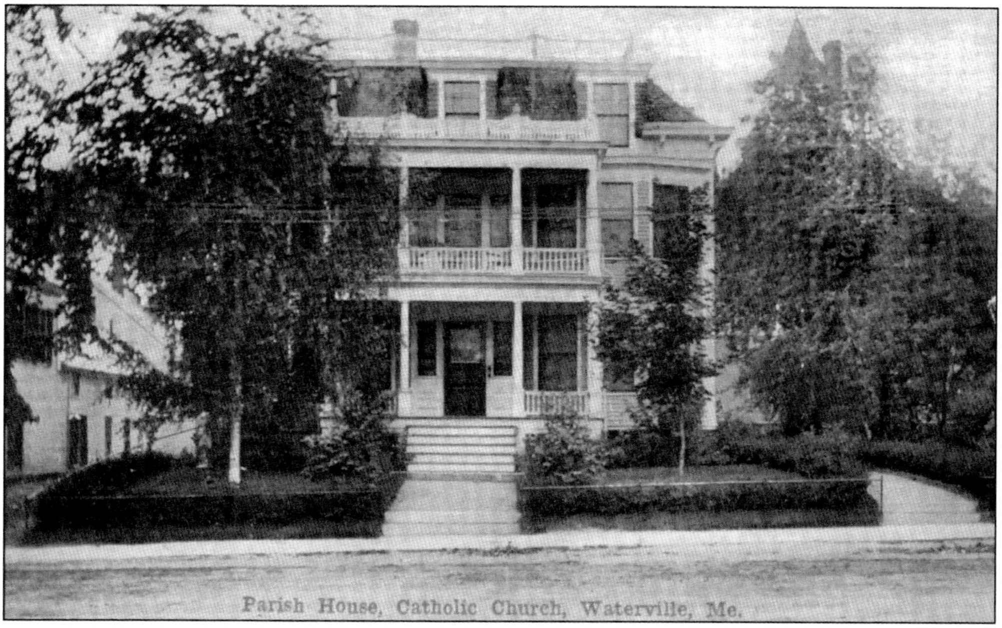

In 1895, Fr. Narcisse Charland built a three-story wooden rectory and parish house on Elm Street immediately south of St. Francis de Sales Catholic Church; he resided there until his death in 1923. Period accounts such as the *Souvenir of Waterville* (published in 1898) describe the structure as "a very fine addition to the present buildings belonging to the church" and a "very excellent rectory which adorns the southerly end of the parochial property."

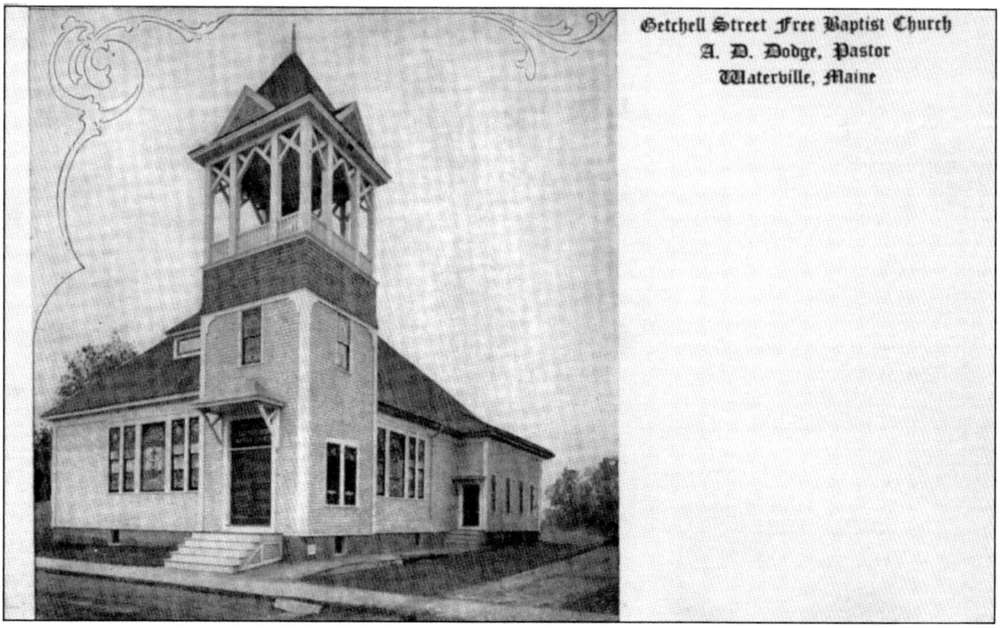

The Getchell Street Free Baptist Church was organized in 1901 with Rev. A.D. Dodge as its first pastor. Designed by Waterville architect H.L. Gilman, the building was constructed in 1904 for $10,000 and continues to serve the current congregation after the more than a century of use. In 1928, the church adopted a new constitution and changed its name to the Getchell Street United Baptist Church.

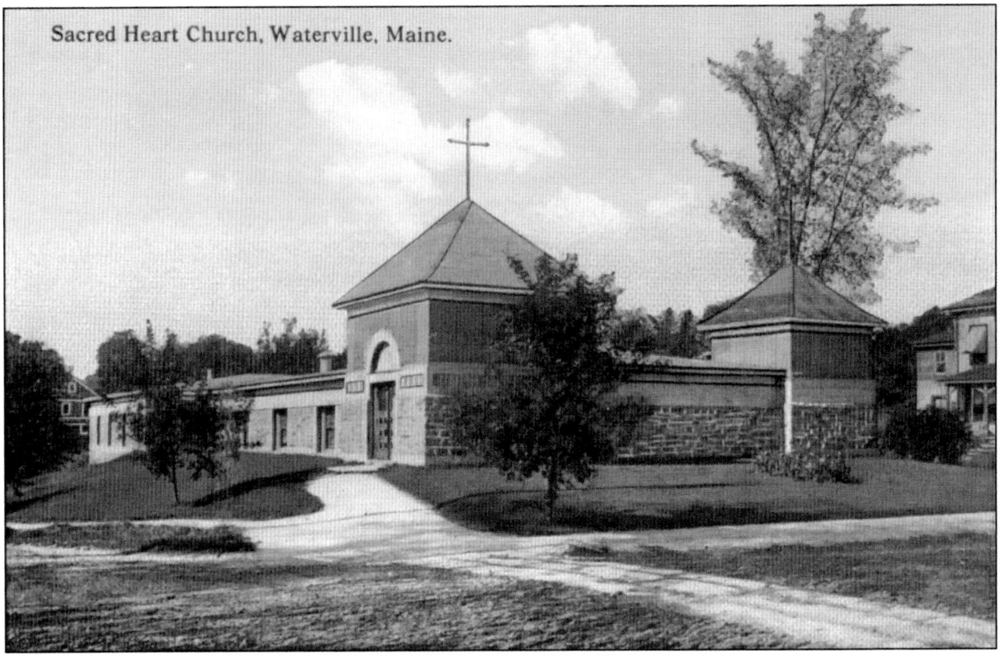

In 1905, Sacred Heart Parish was created to address the spiritual needs of Waterville's Irish, Lebanese, and Syrian Catholics. The next year, the parish purchased a lot at Pleasant and Gilman Streets and began construction on the basement of a new church. This basement structure served as the church's place of worship from 1908 to 1929.

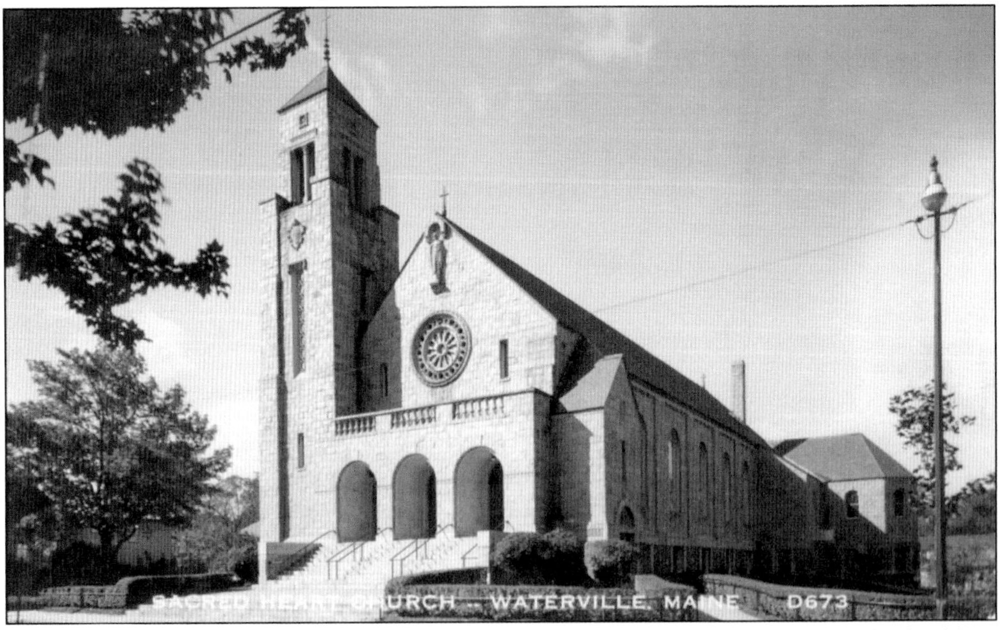

In 1929, Sacred Heart Parish decided to complete the construction of its church by building on its basement foundation. Boston architects Timothy G. O'Connell and Richard J. Shaw, who planned Catholic buildings throughout New England, then designed this impressive stone Romanesque church, and Sacred Heart Church was consecrated on Easter Sunday, April 20, 1930. (Waterville Historical Society.)

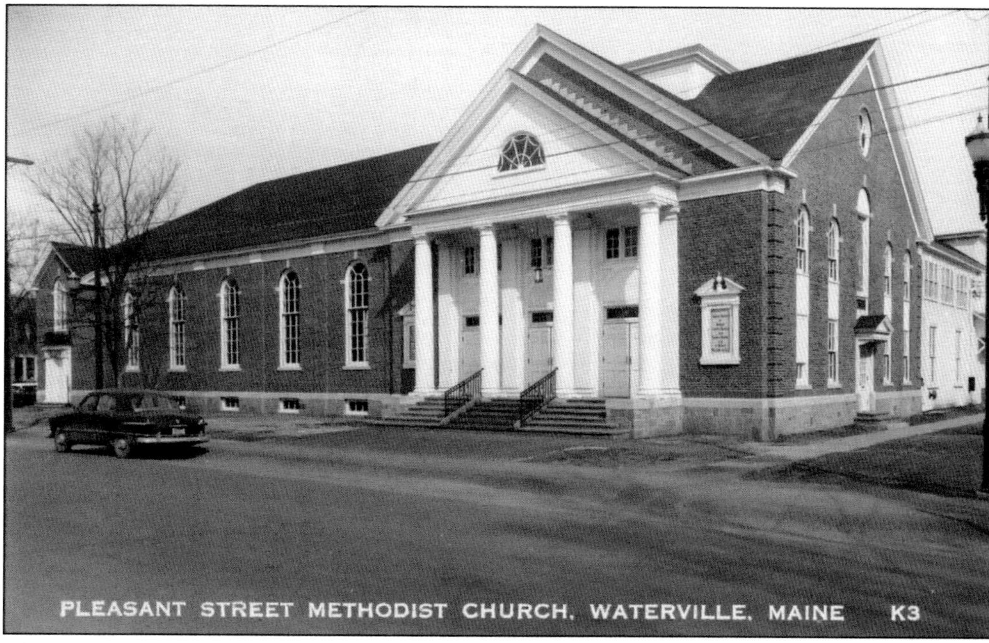

The new sanctuary of the Pleasant Street United Methodist Church was built in 1953 and 1954 from designs by the Augusta architectural firm of Bunker and Savage. The congregation dedicated this brick Georgian Revival building on June 13, 1954. Trustee Henry T. Winters donated $100,000 toward the $187,000 construction cost. The old sanctuary was remodeled into function rooms for the church.

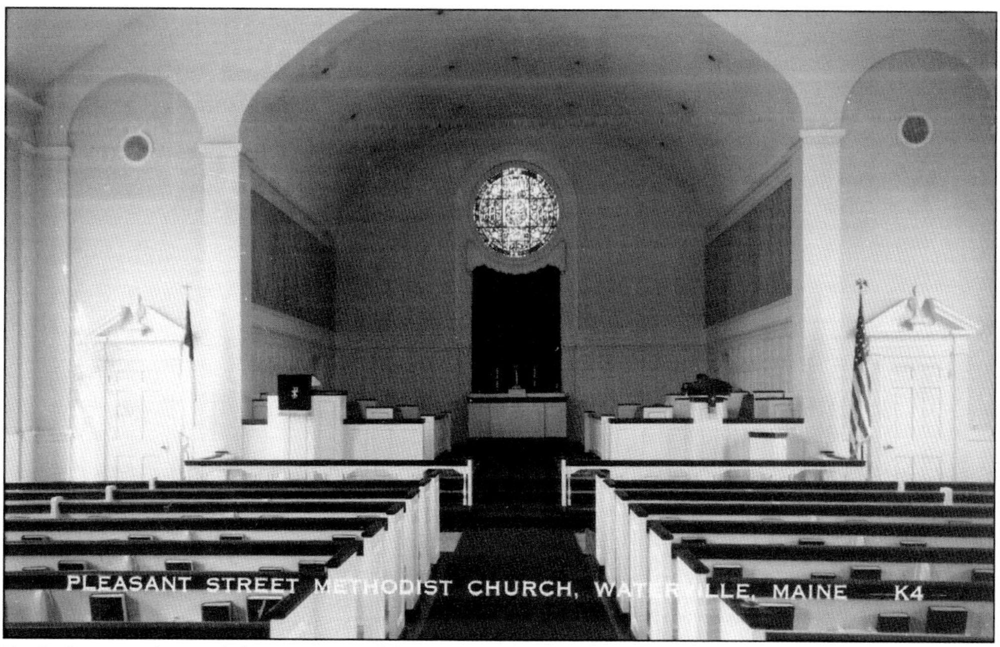

Both the exterior and the interior of the new sanctuary of the Pleasant Street United Methodist Church reflect a mid-20th-century enthusiasm for 18th-century Georgian architecture. This beautiful building is stylistically related to two other Waterville religious landmarks—Colby's Lorimer Chapel (built in 1938) and the First Congregational Church (built in 1967).

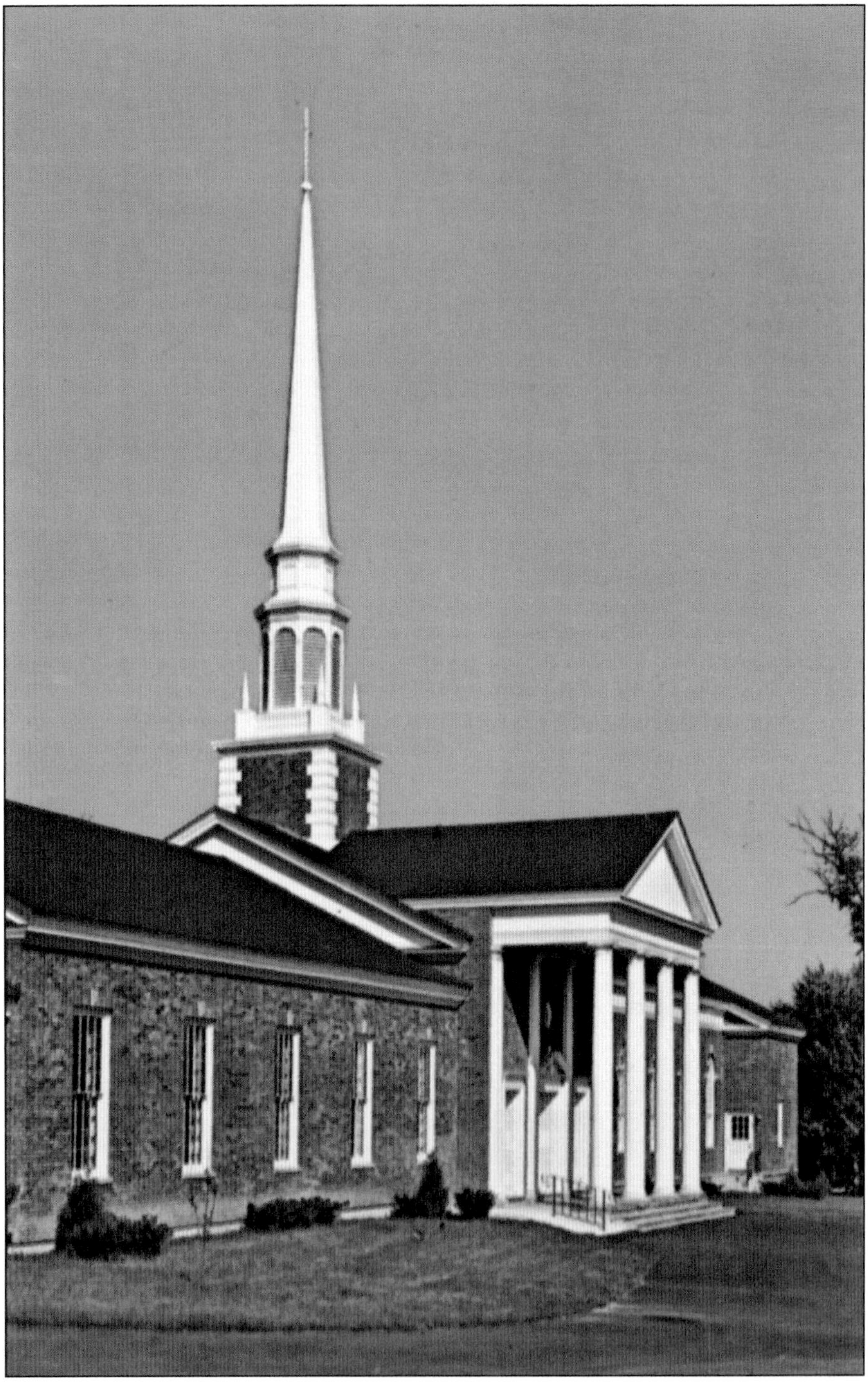

To replace its historic meetinghouse (see page 46), the First Congregational Church purchased a site at Upper Main Street and Eustis Parkway in 1965 and commissioned architect Arland A. Dirlam of Boston to design a new building. Construction on Dirlam's handsome brick Colonial Revival church began in 1966 and was completed the next year at a cost of $412,000. This portico captures the spirit of the one on the previous church.

Four

Homes

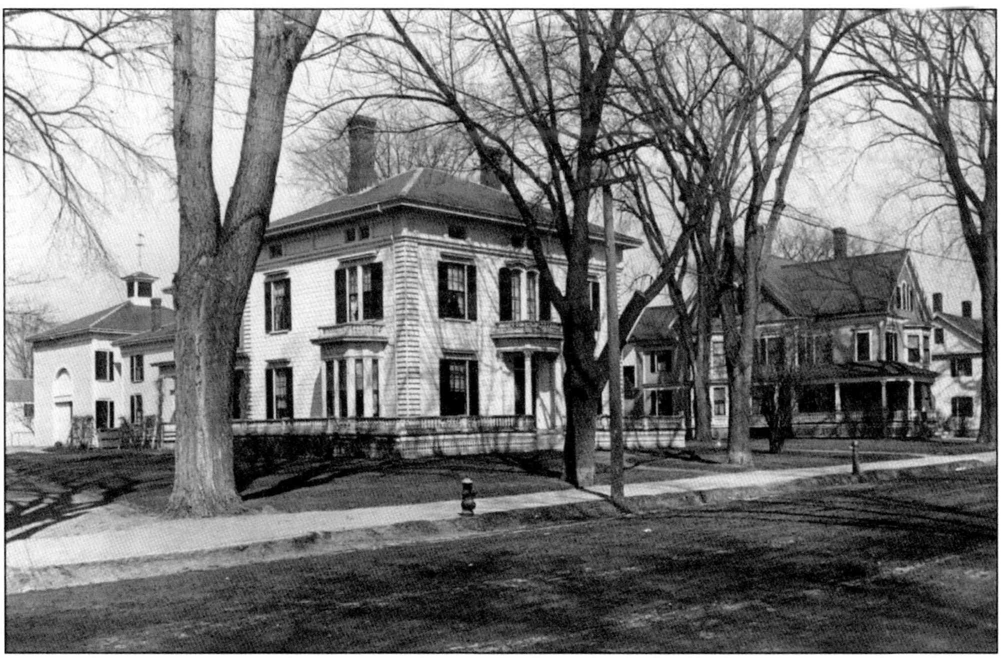

Successful lumberman Franklin Smith lived in this stately white Italianate home on Main Street from 1859, when it was constructed, until his death in 1888. A Waterville native born in 1802, Smith was in the lumber business for 60 years and represented Kennebec County in the Maine state senate. His residence was designed by local architect-builder J.P. Blunt. Dr. Frederick C. Thayer's house is visible immediately to the right of the Smith residence.

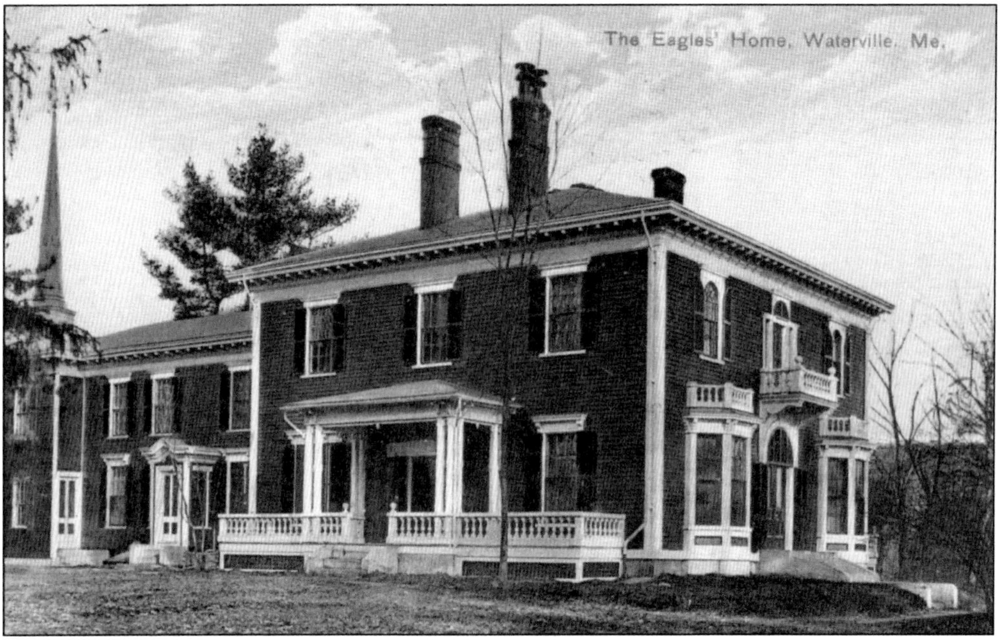

Edwin Noyes's Italianate residence on Temple Street dated from before the Civil War. Noyes came to Waterville in 1837 to teach at Waterville (Colby) College. Two years later, he began studying law with his future father-in-law, Timothy Boutelle, whose practice Noyes joined in 1842. Noyes was active in the development and management of Central Maine railroads and served in the state senate. His house later served as the Eagles' Home and the YMCA.

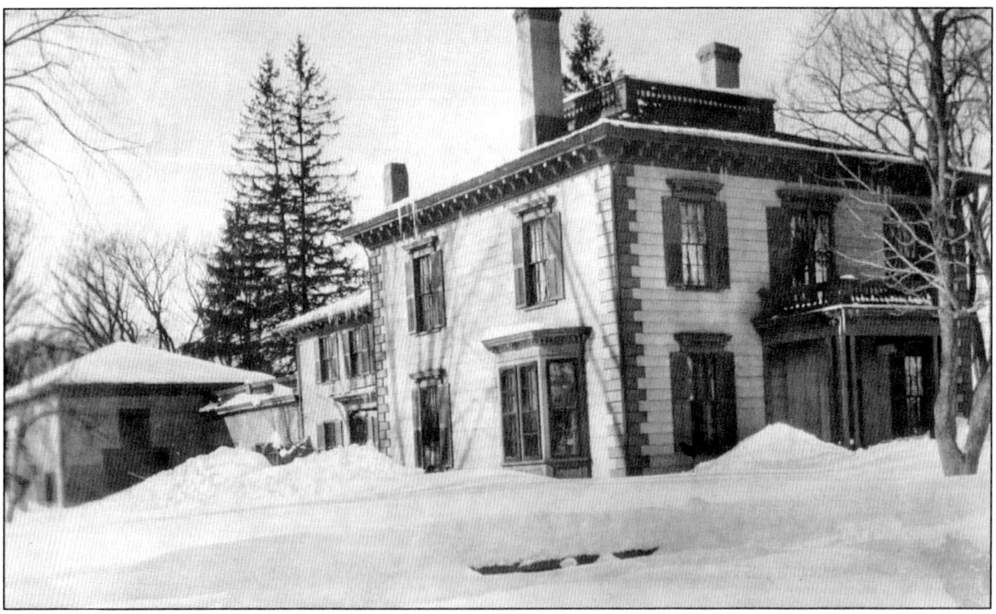

Dr. Samuel Plaisted built this fine Italianate house at Main and Center Streets in 1857–1858 from plans by J.P. Blunt. Born in Gardiner in 1801, Dr. Plaisted practiced medicine in Waterville from 1828 until his death in 1860. The doctor was also involved in banking and papermaking. His wife, Mary Appleton Plaisted, received a substantial inheritance in 1853 from her uncle Samuel Appleton of Boston. (Waterville Historical Society.)

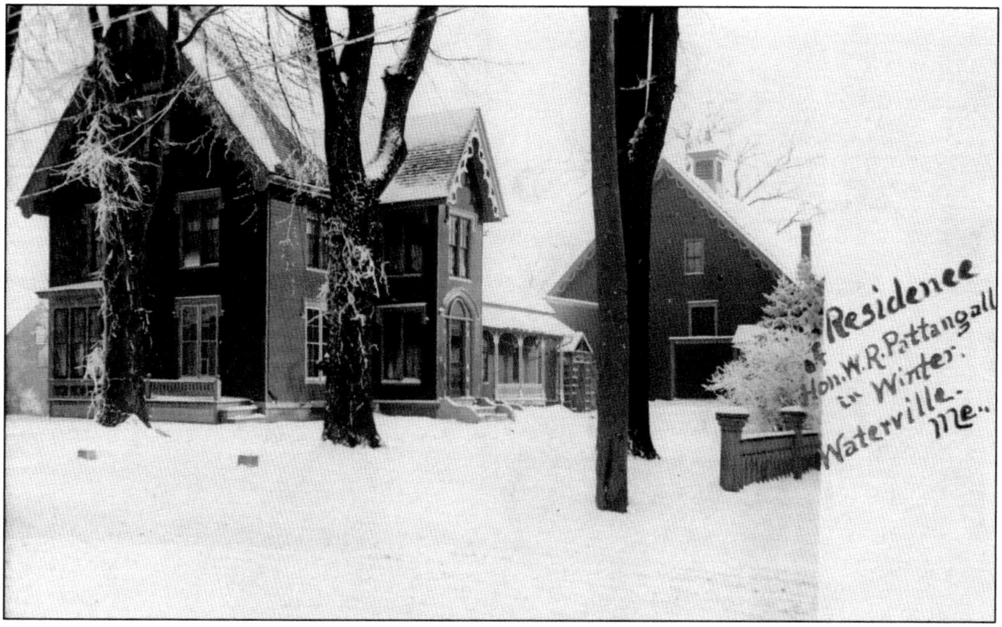

In the early 20th century, this Gothic Revival house on Silver Street was home to William R. Pattengall. A newspaper editor, attorney, political satirist, and prominent Democrat, Pattengall served as a state representative from 1897 to 1911 and as Waterville's mayor in 1911 and 1912. After unsuccessfully running for governor in 1922 and 1924, he spent eleven years on the state supreme court, including five as chief justice.

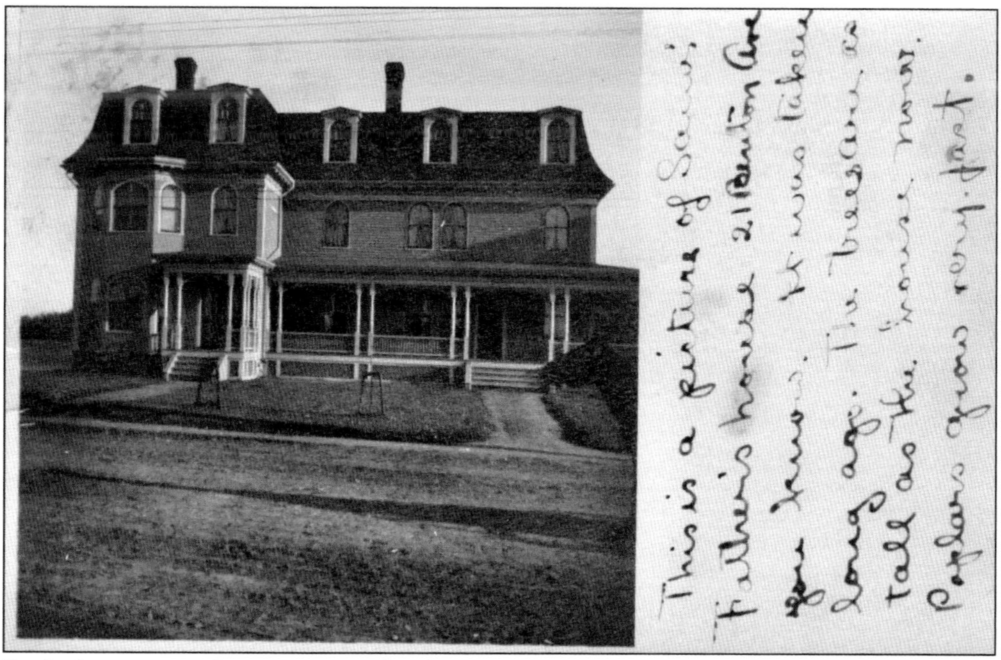

Real-photo postcards are a source of early-20th-century images of local homes. A homeowner would order a small number of cards bearing a picture of their house, then send them to family members and friends. This 1918 card shows a large Victorian mansard-roofed residence in Winslow. The message reads, "This is a picture of Sam's father's house 21 Benton Ave. you know."

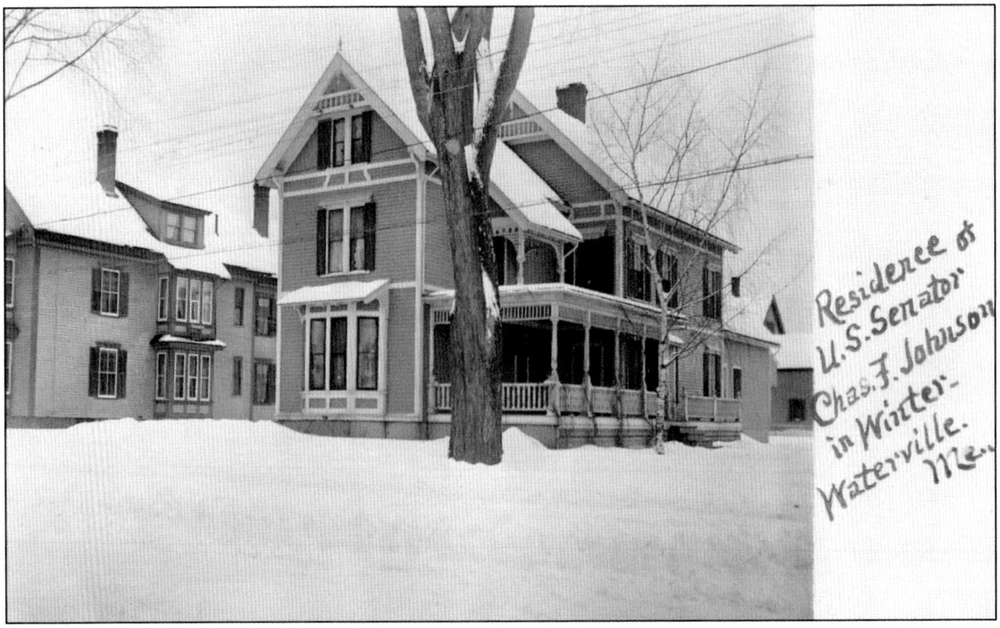

One of Waterville's most prominent political figures, Charles F. Johnson, lived in this house on Silver Street. A local attorney, Johnson unsuccessfully ran for governor as a Democrat in 1892 and 1894. Between those campaigns, he served as Waterville's mayor. In 1910, Johnson was elected to the US Senate, where he served from 1911 to 1917. Later in 1917, Pres. Woodrow Wilson appointed Johnson to a judgeship on the US Court of Appeals for the First Circuit.

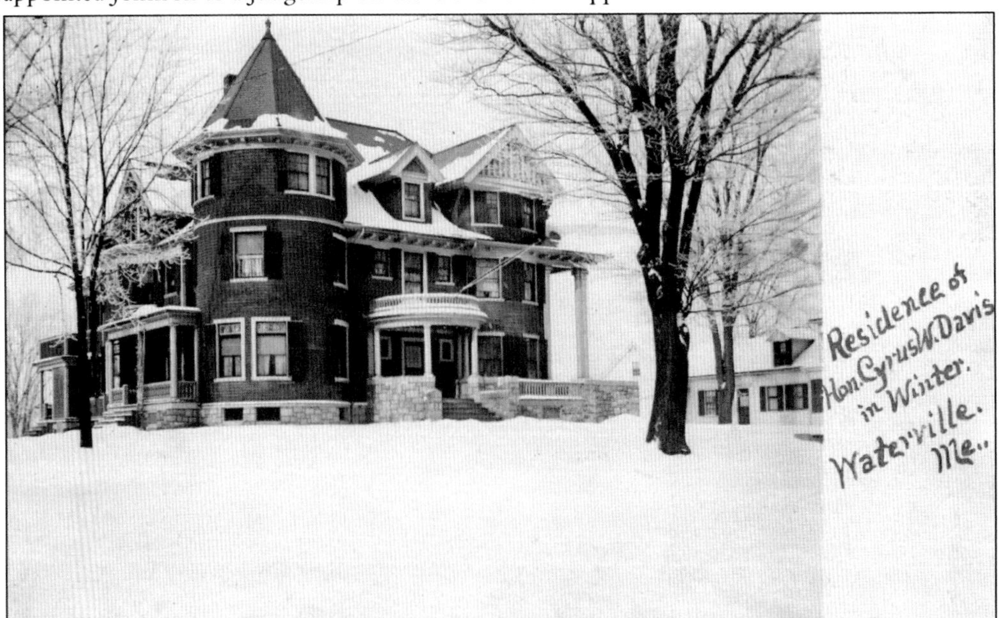

The exuberant Queen Anne style of Cyrus W. Davis's home on Elm Street reflects the career of the man who built it in 1902. In 1890, Davis formed Davis & Smith, a successful investment firm that specialized in mining and electric railroads. A Democrat active in politics, he represented Waterville in the legislature, was elected the city's mayor in 1903 and 1904, unsuccessfully ran for governor in 1904, and served as Maine's secretary of state in 1911 and 1912.

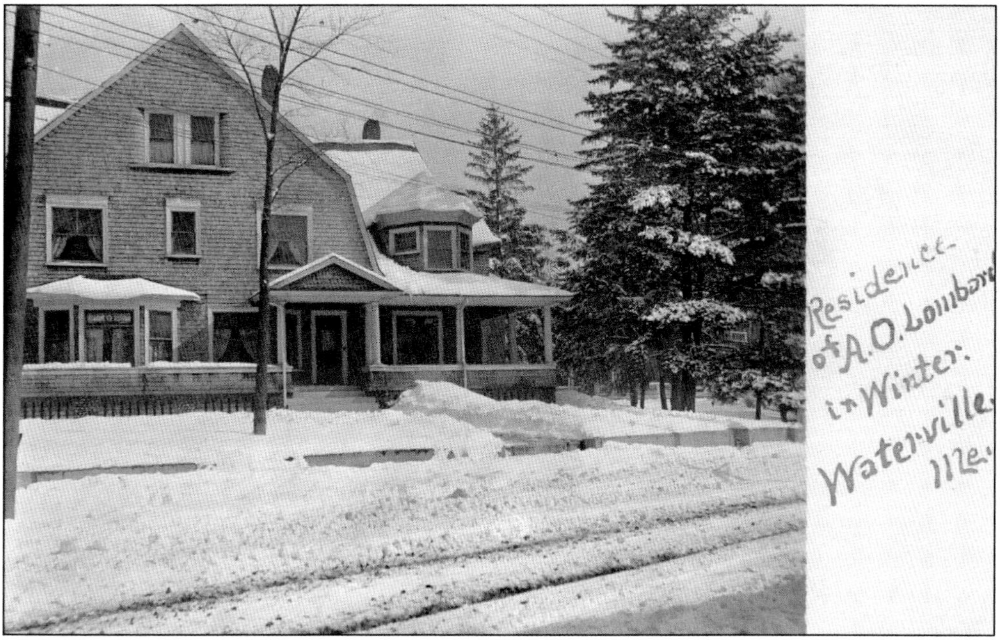

Alvin O. Lombard's spacious 1908 shingle-style house on Elm Street reflected his success as an inventor. Combining his interests in inventing and logging, Lombard created several innovations that helped bring Maine's forest industry into the 20th century. The most well known of these was the Lombard log hauler, which had wheels that ran on an endless track. This endless track, which Lombard patented in 1901, has been a feature of civilian and military equipment ever since.

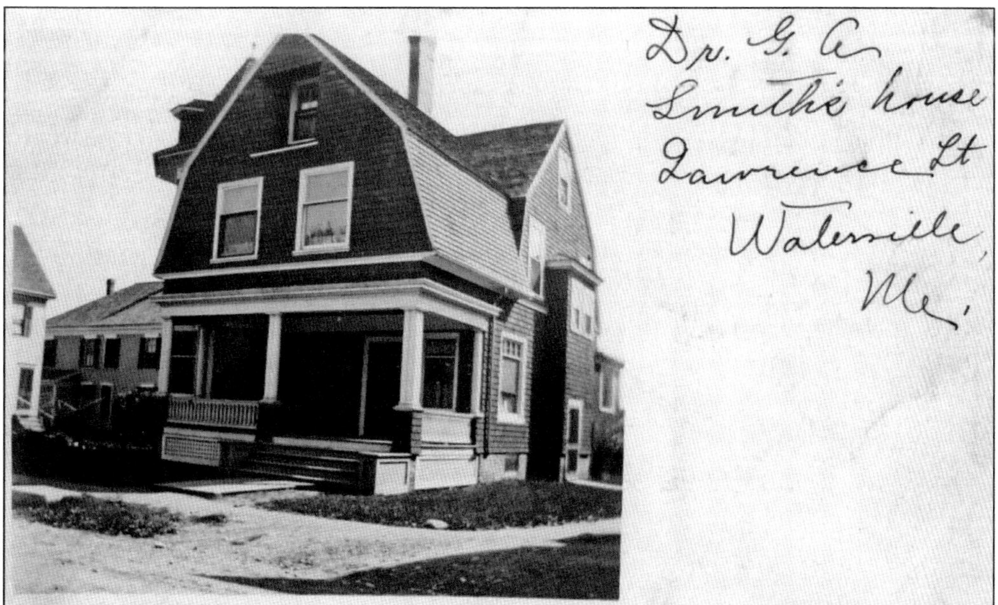

Intersecting gambrel roofs were popular features of shingle-style homes such as this one built by Guy A. Smith on Lawrence Street around 1906. A local dentist, Dr. Smith lived in this fashionable suburban residence with this wife, Tina, until about 1914.

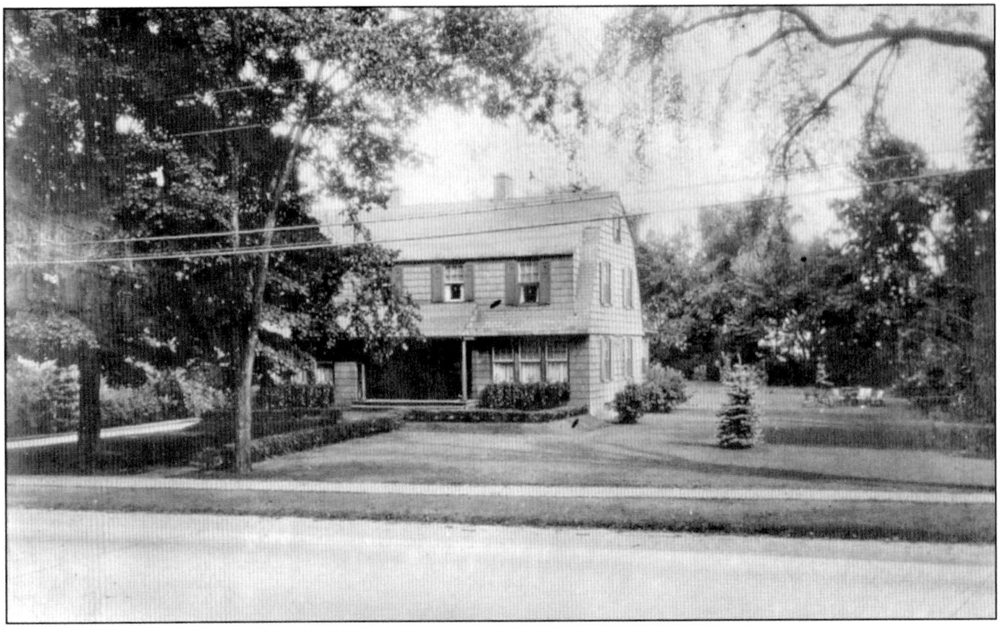

Stanley F. Marr, a mechanical engineer at the Hollingsworth & Whitney Company in Winslow, built this attractive shingle-style house on Silver Street in 1925; he shared it with his wife, Leora. Marr commissioned Maine's leading architects, John Calvin Stevens and John Howard Stevens, to design this home. (Waterville Historical Society.)

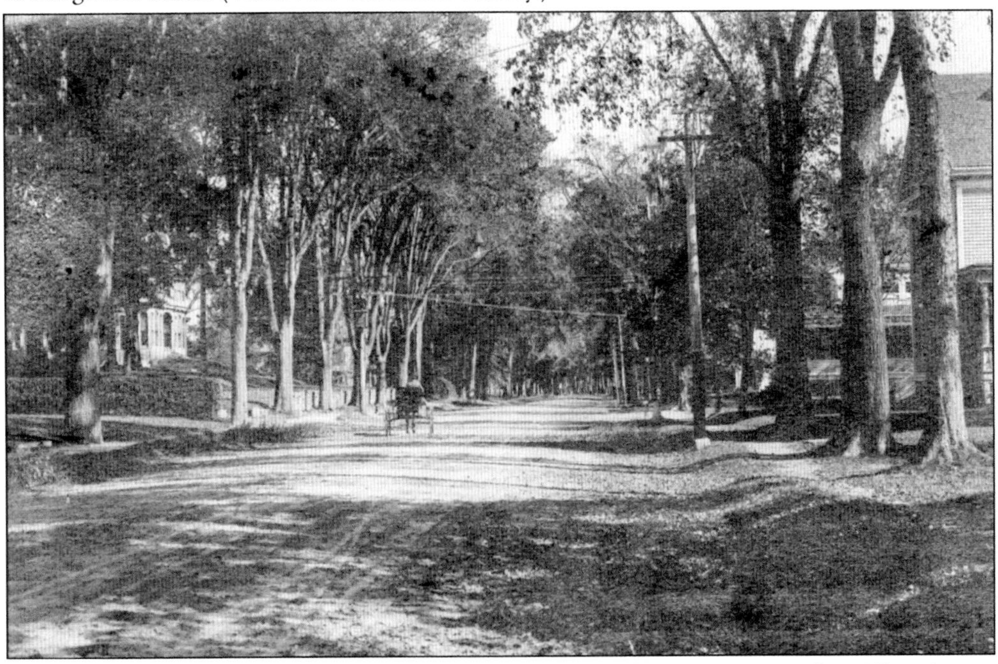

Many of Waterville's finer homes were built on broad, tree-lined avenues such as Silver Street, shown here, looking north, in a 1907 real-photo postcard made by Belfast photographer Charles A. Townsend. Tall, graceful elms like the ones on Silver Street gave Waterville the nickname "Elm City." In the mid-20th century, Dutch elm disease destroyed these beautiful trees, altering the city's appearance.

Five

INDUSTRIES

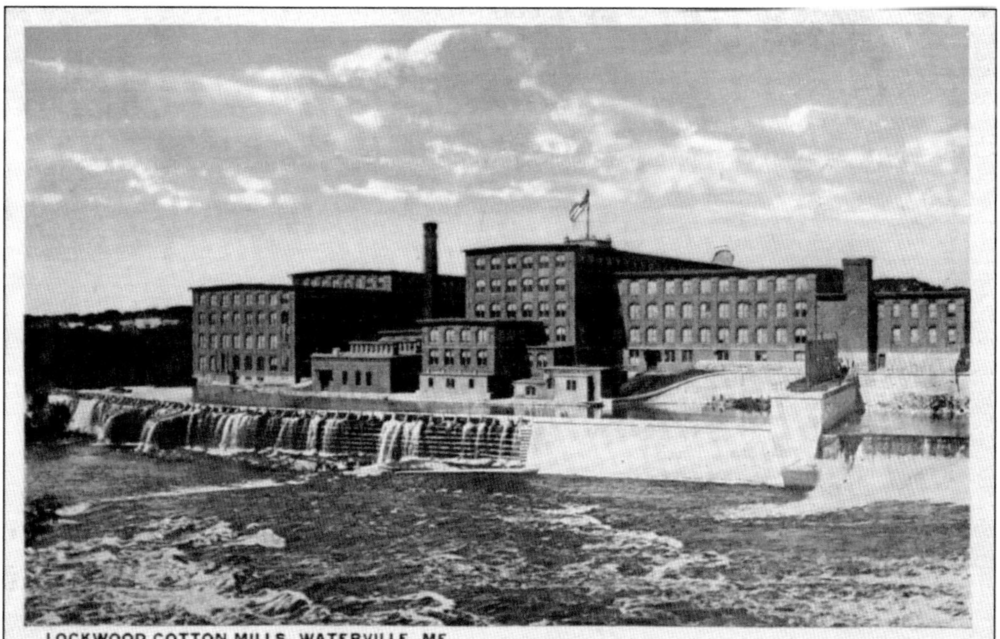

In 1873, the noted mill engineer and developer Amos D. Lockwood proposed the construction of a cotton mill on the Kennebec River at Waterville. Working with Reuben B. Dunn and other local businessmen, Lockwood moved forward on his plan for a 33,000-spindle mill, and workers wove the first cloth in Mill No. 1 in February 1876. Mill No. 2, added in 1882, contained 55,000 spindles.

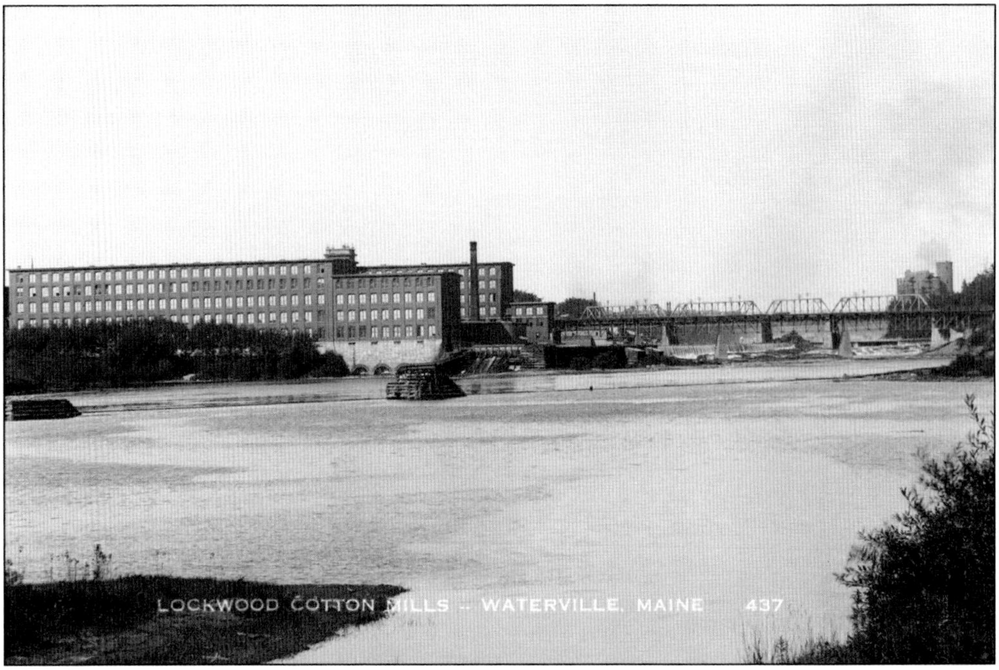

By the early 20th century, the Lockwood Mill had become Waterville's largest employer. In 1911, the mill's 1,150 employees made 17 million yards of cloth on 85,000 spindles. The mill's annual payroll was $400,000. Many workers were French Canadian and had come to the area to work in the mills when they opened in the 1870s. (Penobscot Marine Museum.)

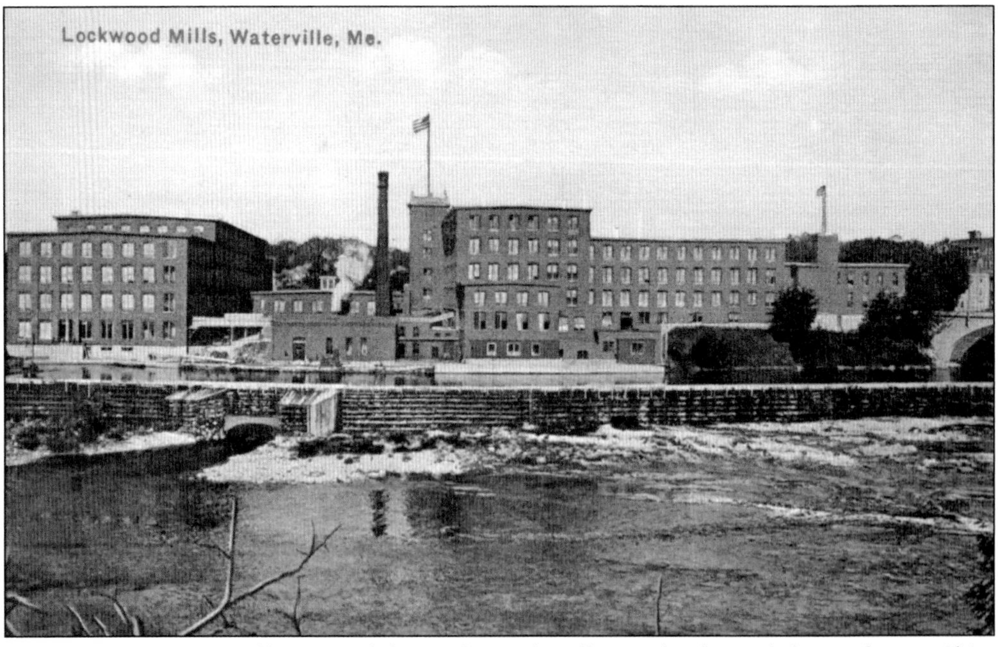

From 1957 to 2002, Mill No. 2 of the Lockwood Mill complex housed the Hathaway Shirt Factory. In 2006, the former shirt factory was transformed into the Hathaway Creative Center, a multifaceted adaptive-reuse project that is helping breathe new life into downtown Waterville. Mills No. 1 and No. 3 currently await adaptive reuse.

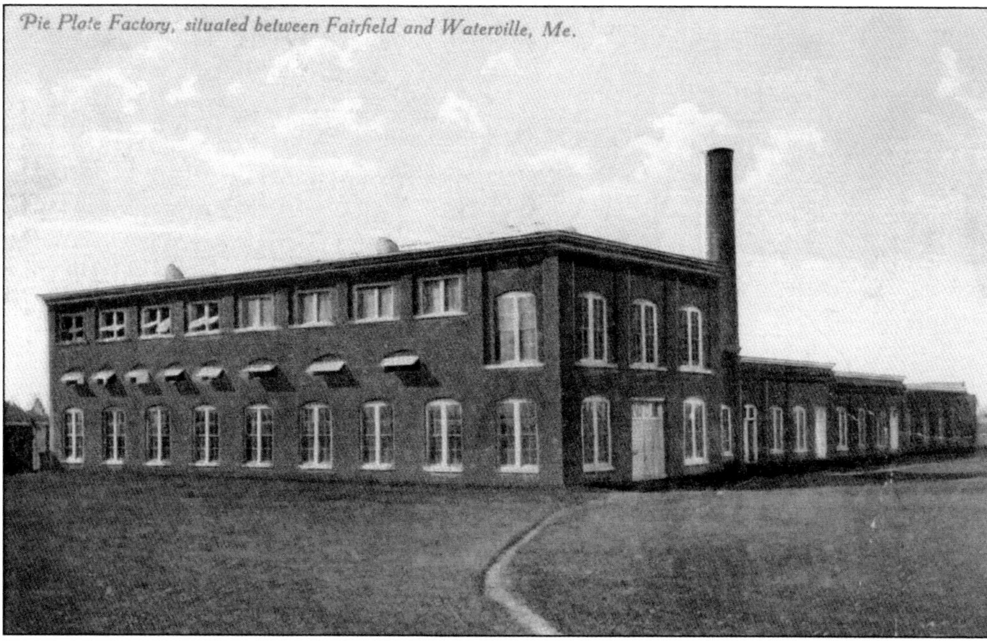

One of Maine's great industrial success stories of the early 20th century is the Keyes Fibre Company. In 1901, Martin L. Keyes invented a machine that could make pie plates and butter dishes from spruce fiber. Production on what would become known as the paper plate began in Shawmut in 1904, but by 1908, all manufacturing operations had been moved to this brick plant on College Avenue at the Fairfield town line.

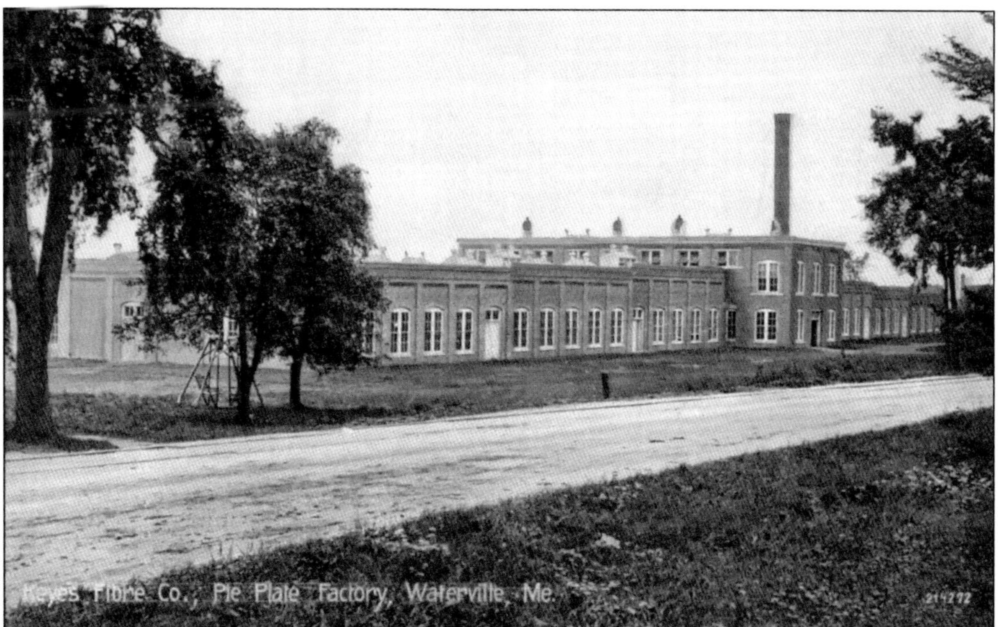

Between 1908 and 1911, the Keyes Fibre Company added the large new wing in the foreground to its factory. By 1911, the plant was running 24 hours each day—in three eight-hour shifts—to make one million pie plates every day (300 million plates per year). That year, Keyes estimated that he needed to produce another 100 million plates annually to meet demand.

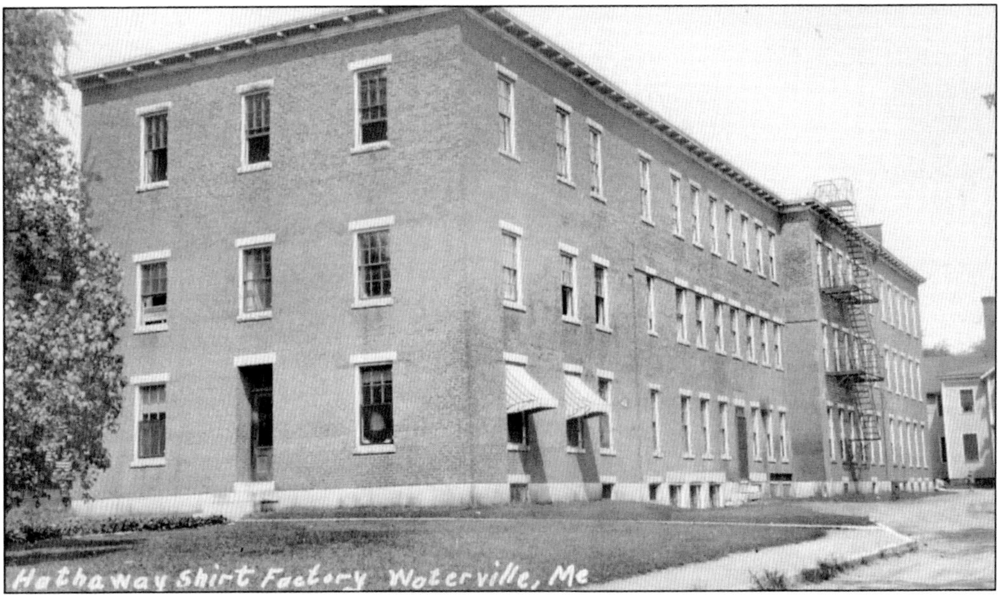

From 1853 until his death in 1893, Charles Foster Hathaway operated Hathaway Shirt Factory, which provided shirts to the Union army during the Civil War, on Appleton Street. For much of the 20th century, Hathaway shirts were manufactured in a factory that was part of the Lockwood Mill. A famous advertising campaign created by Ogilvy & Mather in 1951 featured the eyepatched "Hathaway man." The company ceased production in 2002. (Waterville Historical Society.)

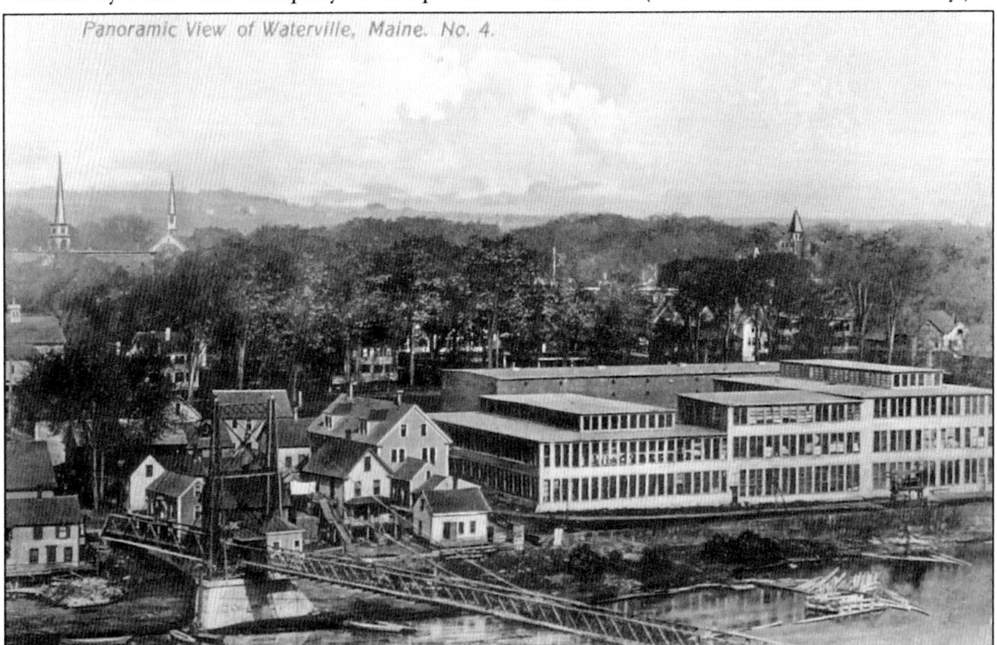

This factory started in 1900 as the Riverview Worsted Mill on the banks of the Kennebec River, producing fine cloth for menswear. In 1909, the plant was acquired by the Wyandotte Worsted Company, which significantly increased production. In 1911, the company employed 200 workers who operated 100 looms and worked in dyeing and finishing departments in the factory's 185,000 square feet of space. (Waterville Historical Society.)

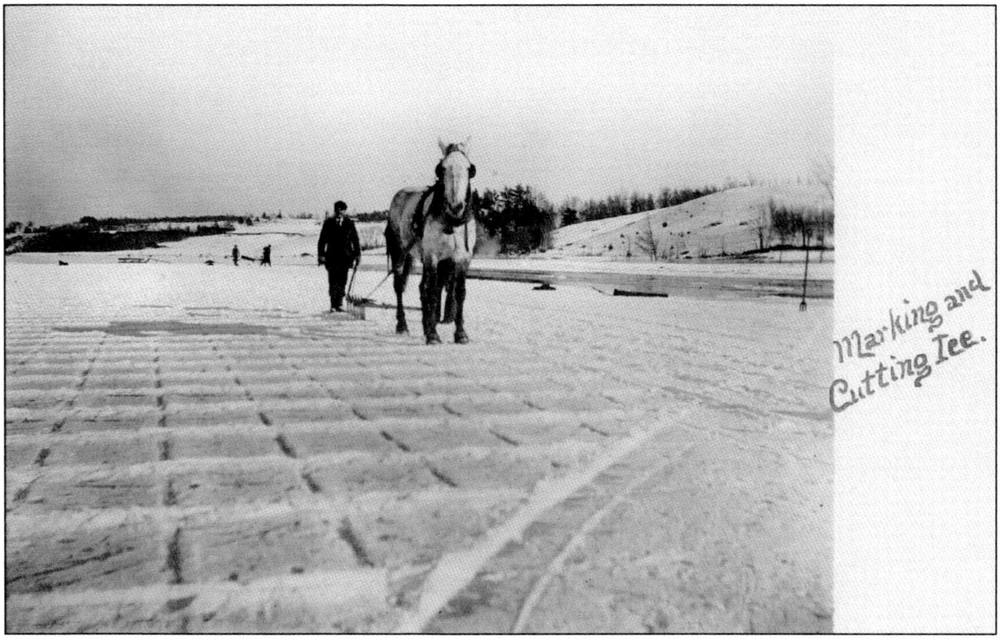

For more than a century, this winter scene was repeated countless times along the Kennebec River. In 1806, Boston businessman Frederic Tudor (aka the "Ice King") began harvesting ice, storing it in icehouses on the riverbanks, and shipping it (in sawdust) to warm climates via his Tudor Ice Company. His efforts led to an ice boom in the area that began in the 1860s. Here, a workman guides a horse to mark pieces of ice for cutting on the Kennebec River near Waterville.

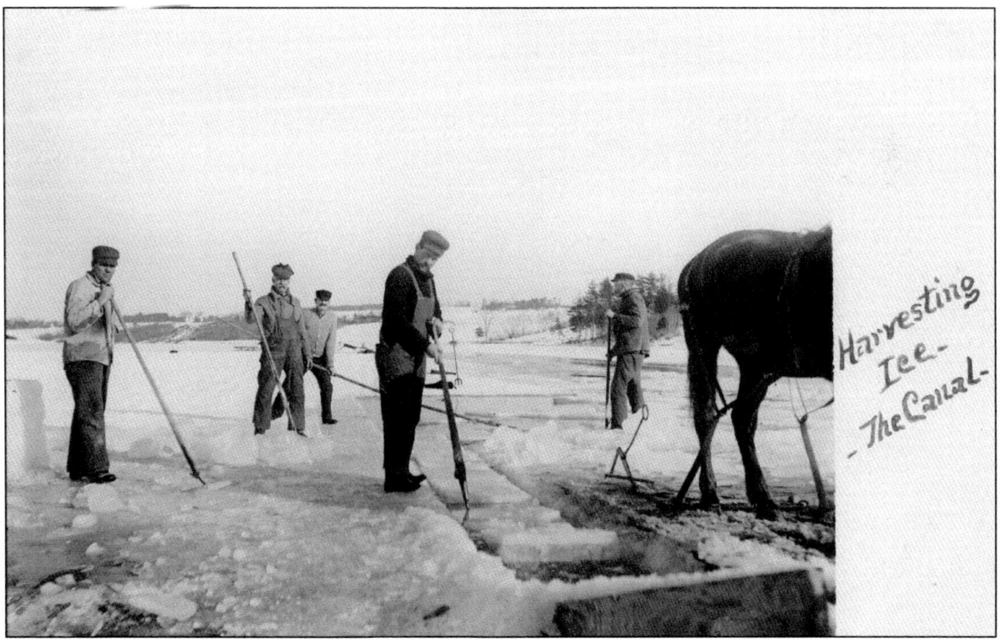

In this c. 1910 image, workmen cut blocks of ice from the Kennebec River for transport to a nearby icehouse. During the post–Civil War period, as many as 25,000 men worked in ice harvesting operations on Maine rivers and lakes. A decade after this picture was taken, the invention of mechanical ice-makers and electric refrigerators heralded the end of the ice industry.

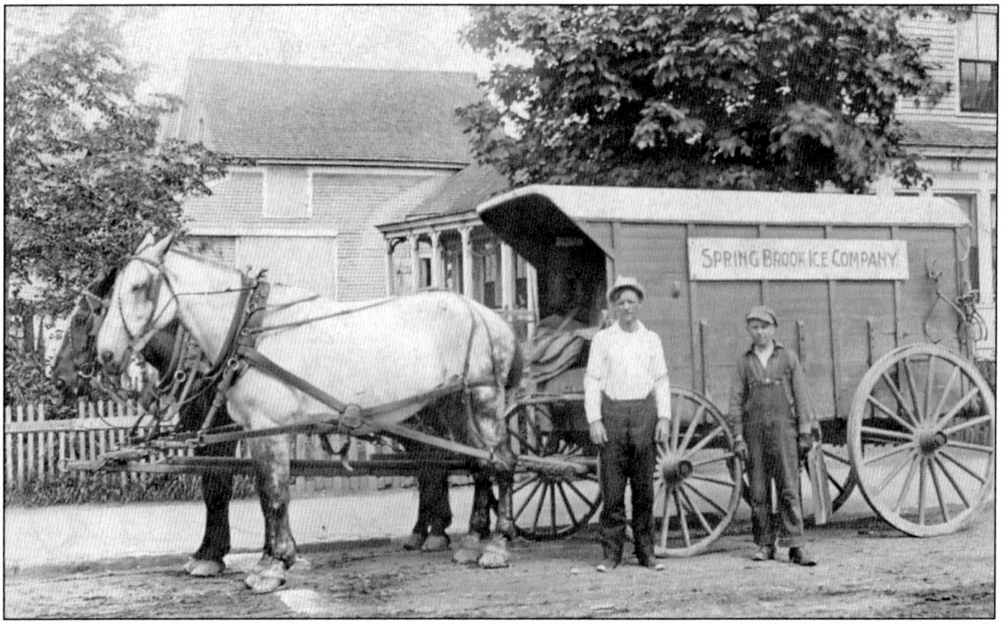

A century ago, horse-drawn wagons delivered ice, milk, bread, and other household staples door-to-door. In this c. 1920 photograph, two unidentified employees of the Spring Brook Ice Company pause during their daily rounds to pose in front of their delivery wagon. The company, which started in 1918, added fuel delivery to its services in 1921 after recognizing the need to diversify as the use of electric refrigerators expanded. (Waterville Historical Society.)

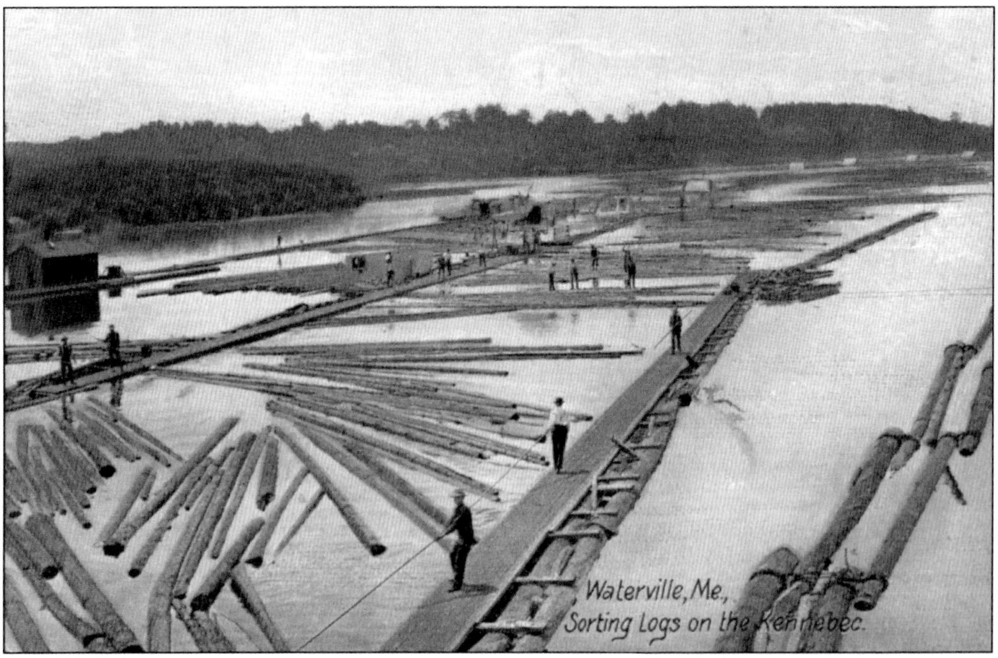

The Kennebec River was an avenue of travel, a source of ice in winter, and a means to deliver thousands of logs from forested areas to sawmills in Skowhegan, Fairfield, Waterville, Winslow, Augusta, and Gardiner. In this Waterville scene, logs are being sorted into different companies' booms before being processed into lumber.

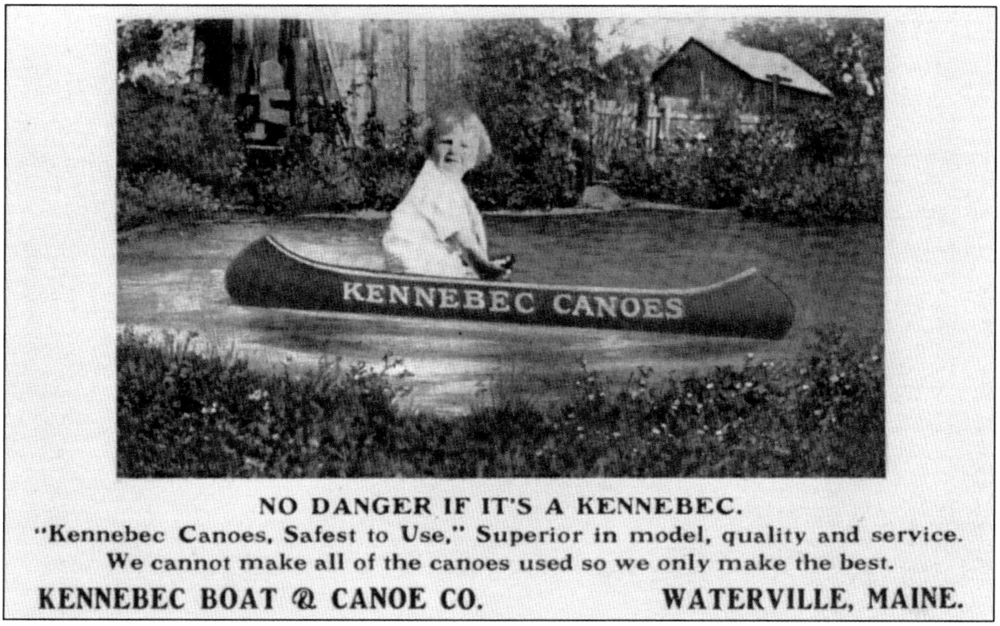

After the Civil War, canoeing became a popular pastime. The popularity of canoeing on the Messalonskee Stream and nearby lakes created a demand in the Waterville area for locally manufactured canoes. In 1909, S.N. Annis and G.F. Terry established the Kennebec Boat and Canoe Company on Chaplin Street. A description of the firm in the March 1911 *Board of Trade Journal* declared, "Their sailing canoes, motor canoes and motor speed boats are rapidly increasing in popularity."

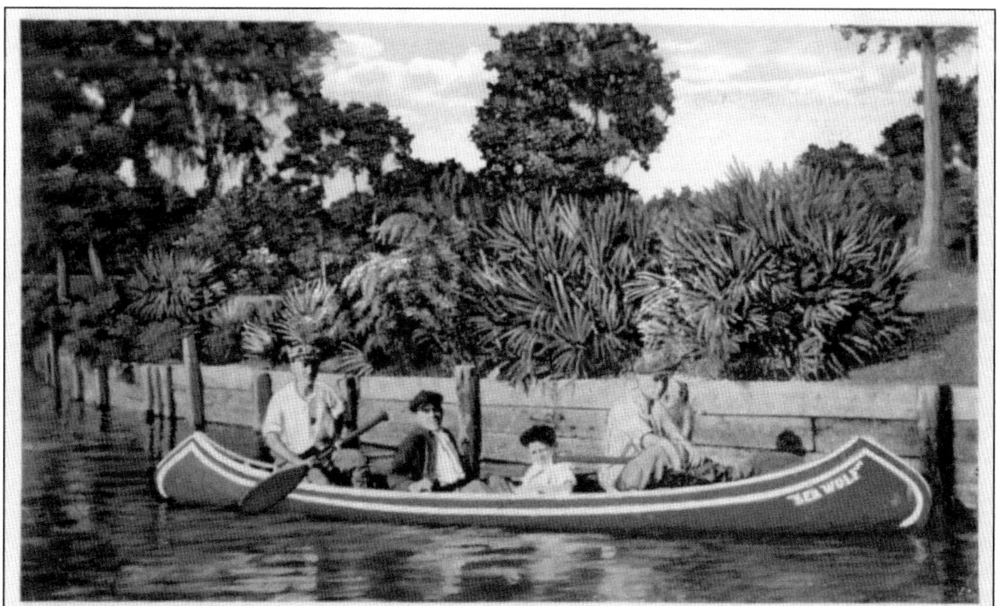

Emphasizing the safety of its product, the Kennebec Boat and Canoe Company sent the following message to its customers on the back of this advertising postcard: "We build canvas covered canoes 12 feet to 35 feet long. Light wooden boats for rowing or use with outboard motors. Before purchasing a canoe or boat, get our free catalogue."

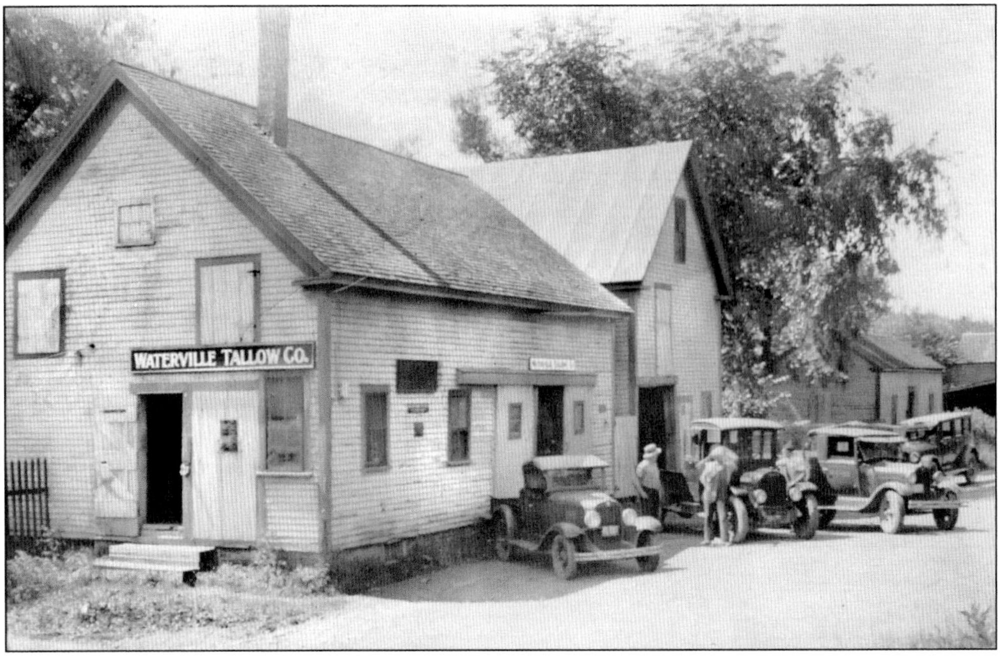

Prior to World War II, many traditional small industries flourished in Waterville. This c. 1930 image shows the Waterville Tallow Company, which processed beef fat into candles and soap in this building located on Middle Street.

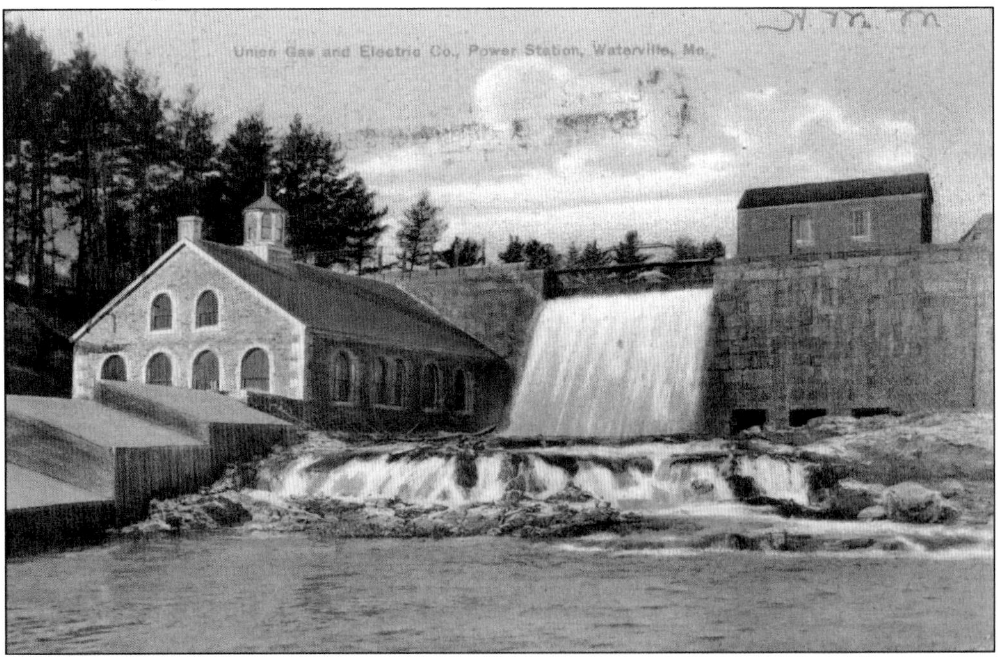

By 1900, many industries relied upon electricity generated by hydropower facilities such as the Union Gas and Electric Company, shown here in 1908. The company built the 40-foot-high stone dam and its adjacent plant on the Messalonskee Stream in 1899 to provide power for electric lighting and motor-driven machinery. The company was based in Boston but locally managed by the Waterville and Fairfield Railway and Light Company.

Six

TRANSPORTATION

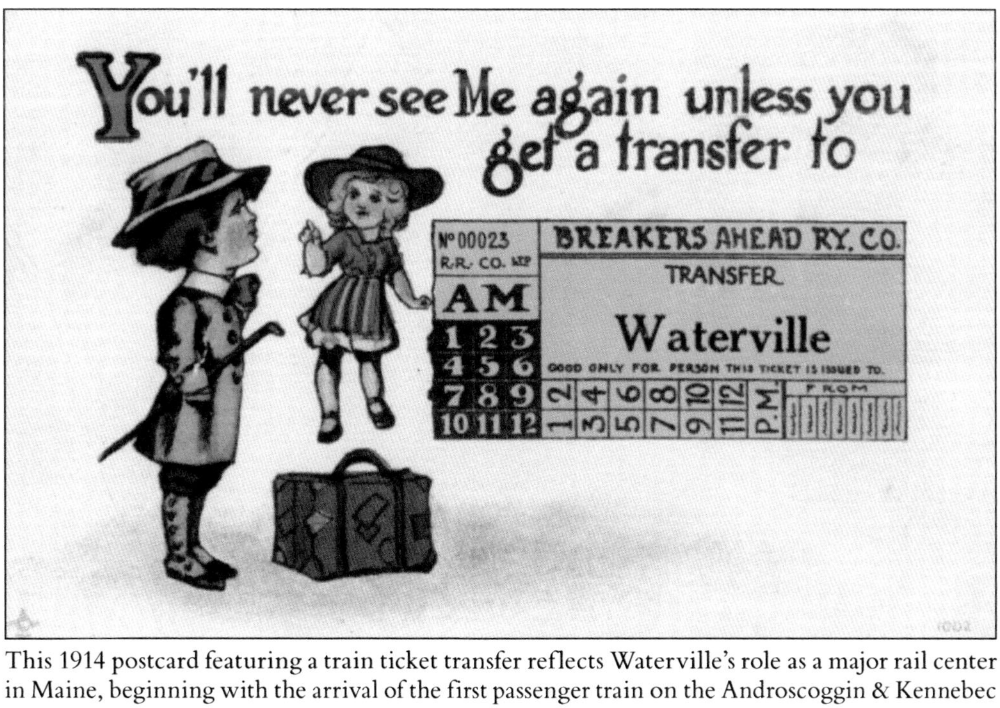

This 1914 postcard featuring a train ticket transfer reflects Waterville's role as a major rail center in Maine, beginning with the arrival of the first passenger train on the Androscoggin & Kennebec Railroad on December 5, 1849. Passenger service to Waterville lasted for more than a century before ending in 1960—a victim of competition from the automobile.

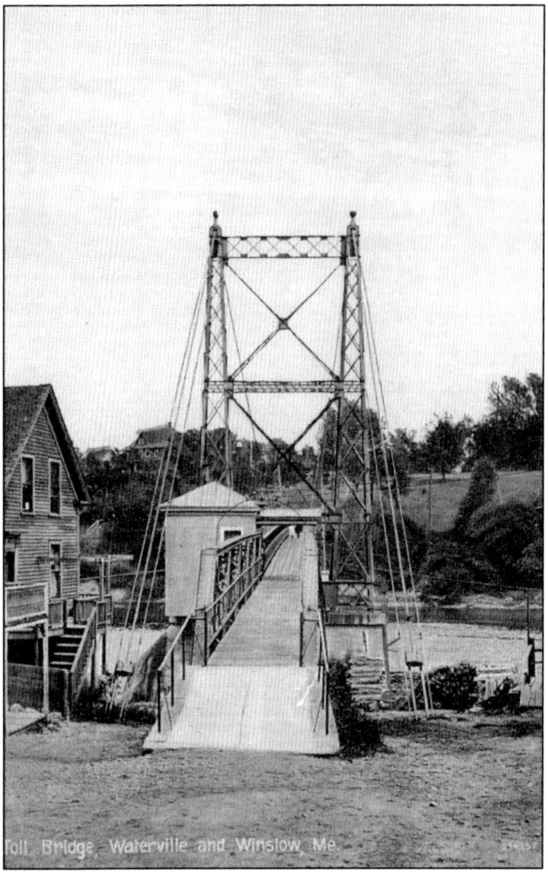

After the Hollingsworth & Whitney Company established a paper mill in Winslow in 1892, workers from Waterville needed a way to easily cross the Kennebec River on foot. This need was addressed with the 1899 incorporation of the Ticonic Footbridge Company, which erected its first bridge in 1901. The contractor was the Berlin Construction Company of Berlin, Connecticut, which built bridges throughout the Northeast. A flood destroyed that bridge in 1902; in 1903, it was replaced with the bridge pictured here.

The new bridge, which opened in 1903, charged a toll of 2¢ per crossing to its 500 daily users, which was collected at a tollbooth attached to the bridge. This view from the Waterville side of the Kennebec River shows the Two Cent Bridge with the Hollingsworth & Whitney mill in the background. The bridge, a local landmark, has been preserved by the City of Waterville through a recent restoration project.

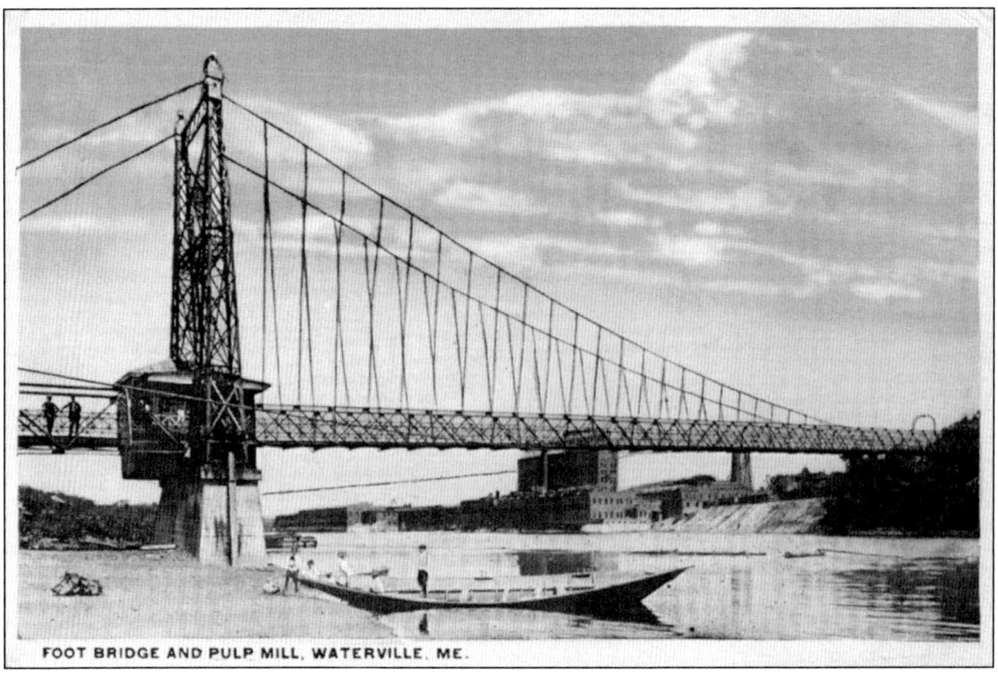

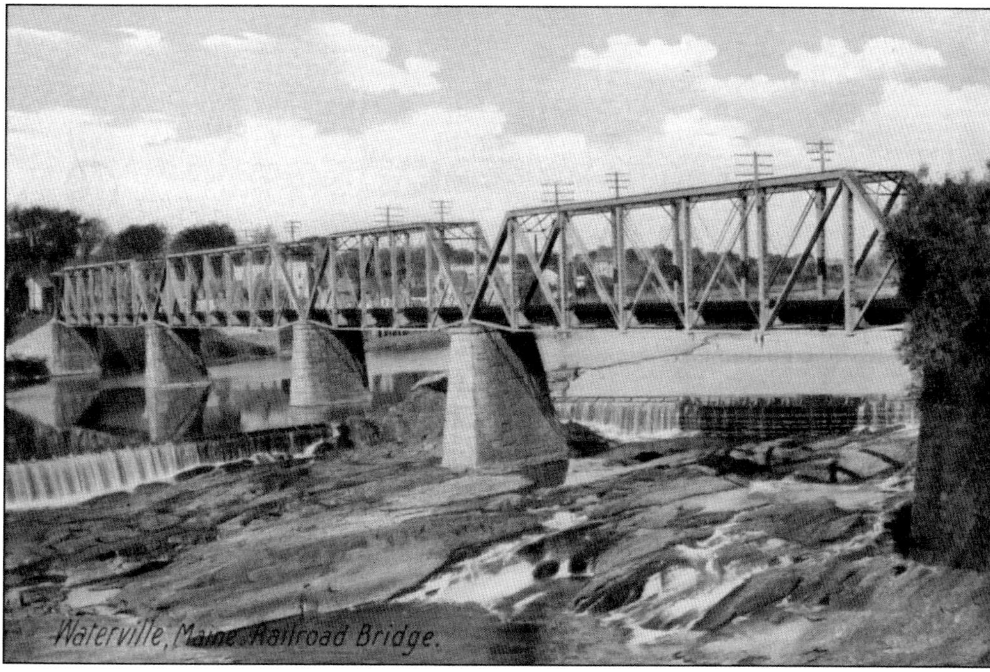

In 1874, Maine Central Railroad built the first iron railroad bridge connecting Winslow and Waterville across the Kennebec River; that structure was later replaced by the four-span steel Ticonic Bridge shown on this c. 1905 postcard. The superstructure of the Ticonic Bridge was rebuilt by the Maine Central Railroad in 1924 and remains in use today.

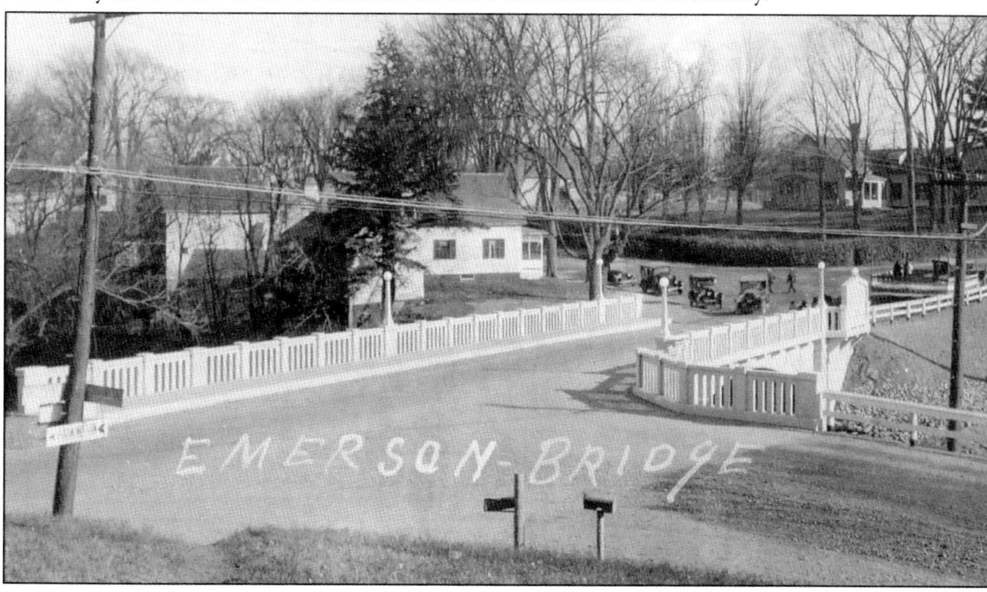

Contractor Green & Wilson built the concrete-arch Emerson Bridge at the foot of Spring Street for $28,710; it replaced an iron bridge that had been in this location since 1895. The new bridge was formally opened on Armistice Day (November 11) in 1924, at which time Mayor Leon O. Tebbetts unveiled a bronze memorial tablet—a gift of the City of Waterville—dedicated to Waterville's World War I veterans. In 1996, the current Emerson Bridge replaced the one shown here. (Waterville Historical Society.)

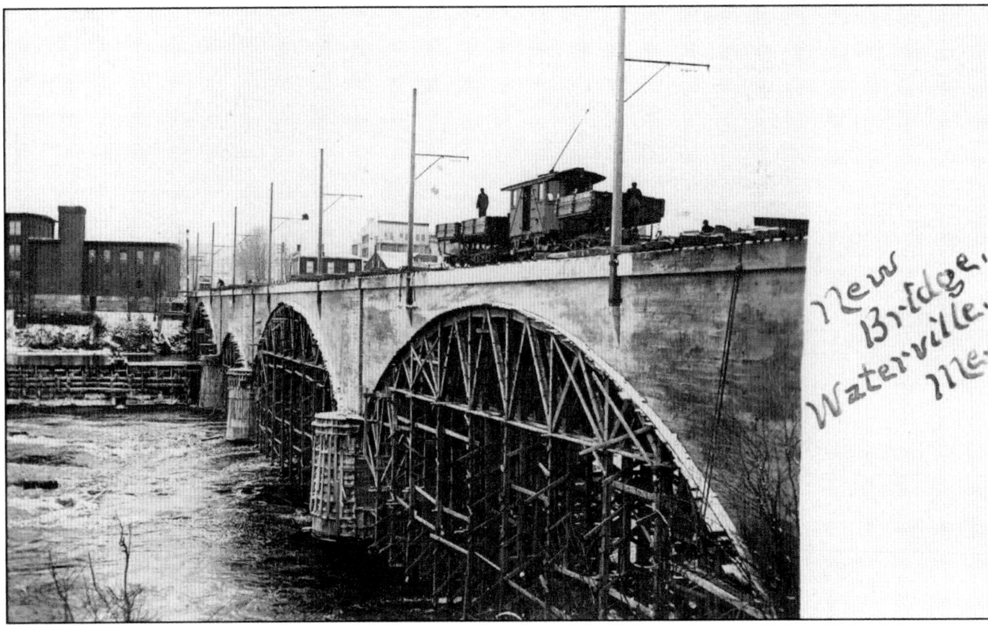

While constructing a line from Augusta to Waterville, the City of Waterville denied Lewiston, Augusta & Waterville Street Railway Company permission to use the highway bridge that spanned the Kennebec River from Winslow to Waterville due to its being structurally inadequate. In 1909, the company built its own four-span concrete bridge, shown here under construction with a work train atop the structure.

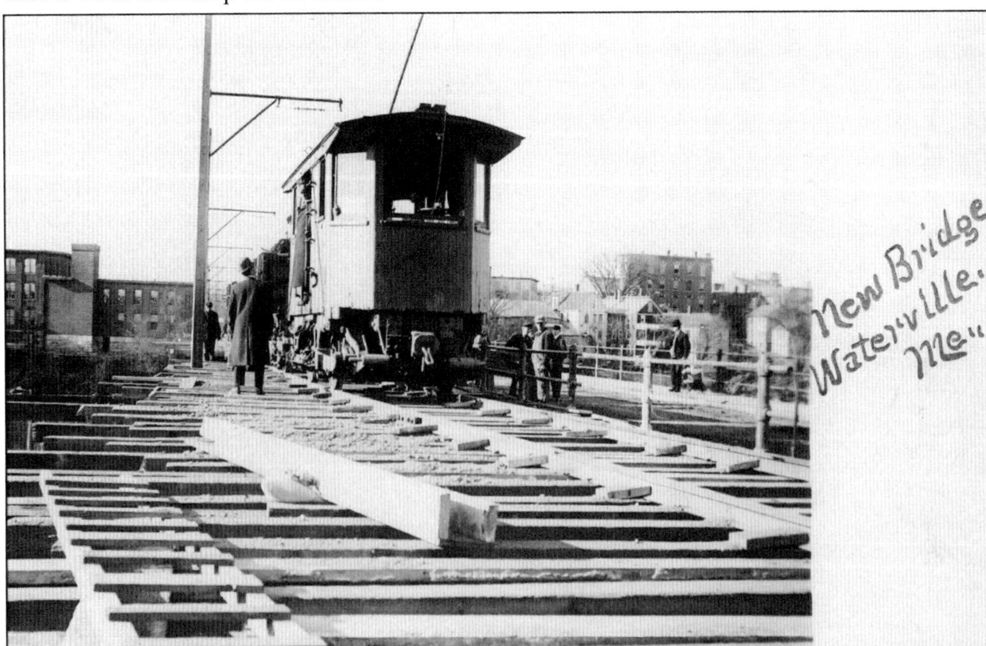

This real-photo postcard offers a closer look at a work train atop the new concrete bridge that was under construction in 1909; workers are placing wooden decking and tracks on the concrete superstructure. D.B. Luten, of the American Bridge Company in Indianapolis, designed the new bridge, and the contractor was Fred T. Ley and Company of Springfield, Massachusetts.

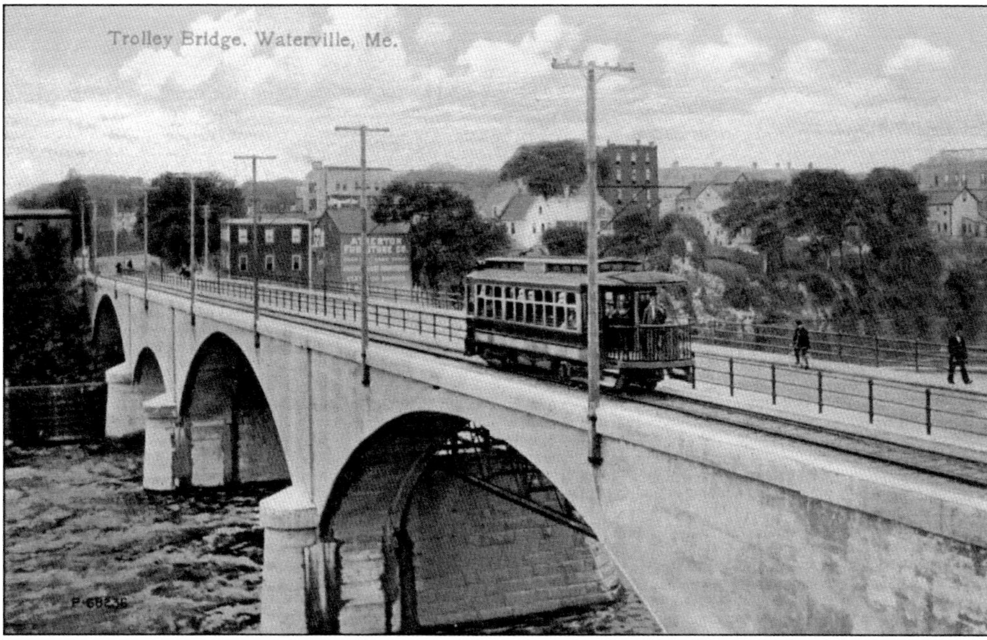

A trolley passes over the new concrete electric railway bridge on its way from Waterville to Winslow. At the time of its completion, this graceful arched structure, at 580 feet long, was the second-longest electric railroad bridge in the country. The four spans were designed to differ slightly in size to counter the effects of the pressure of ice and log jams on the river.

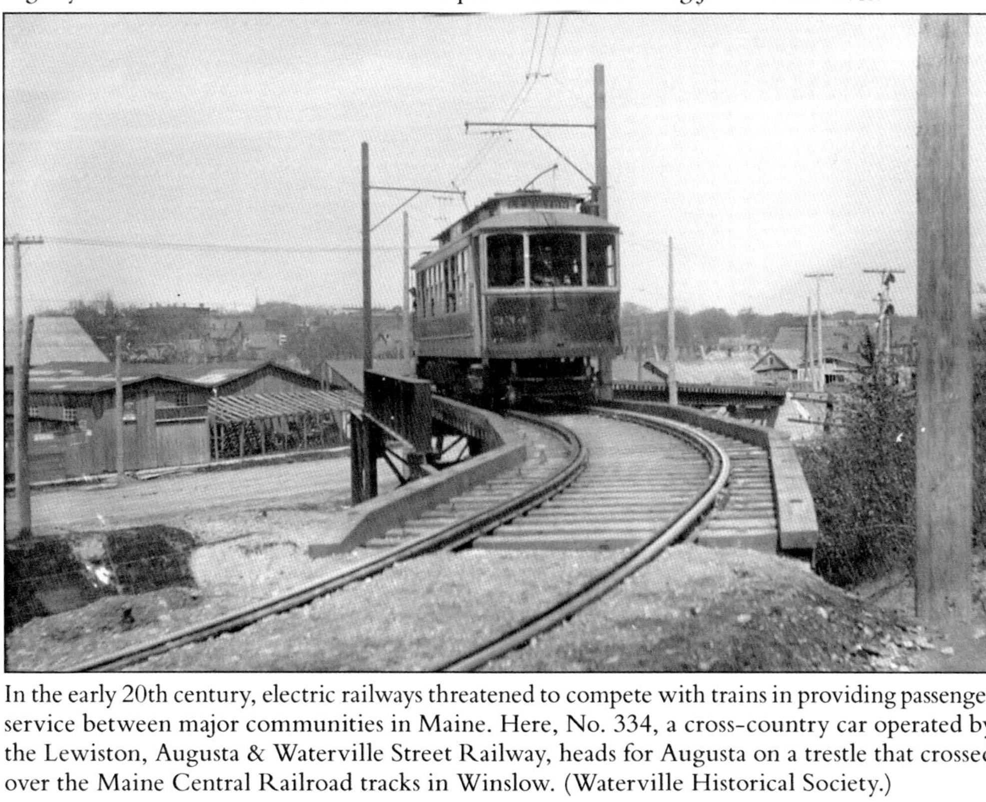

In the early 20th century, electric railways threatened to compete with trains in providing passenger service between major communities in Maine. Here, No. 334, a cross-country car operated by the Lewiston, Augusta & Waterville Street Railway, heads for Augusta on a trestle that crossed over the Maine Central Railroad tracks in Winslow. (Waterville Historical Society.)

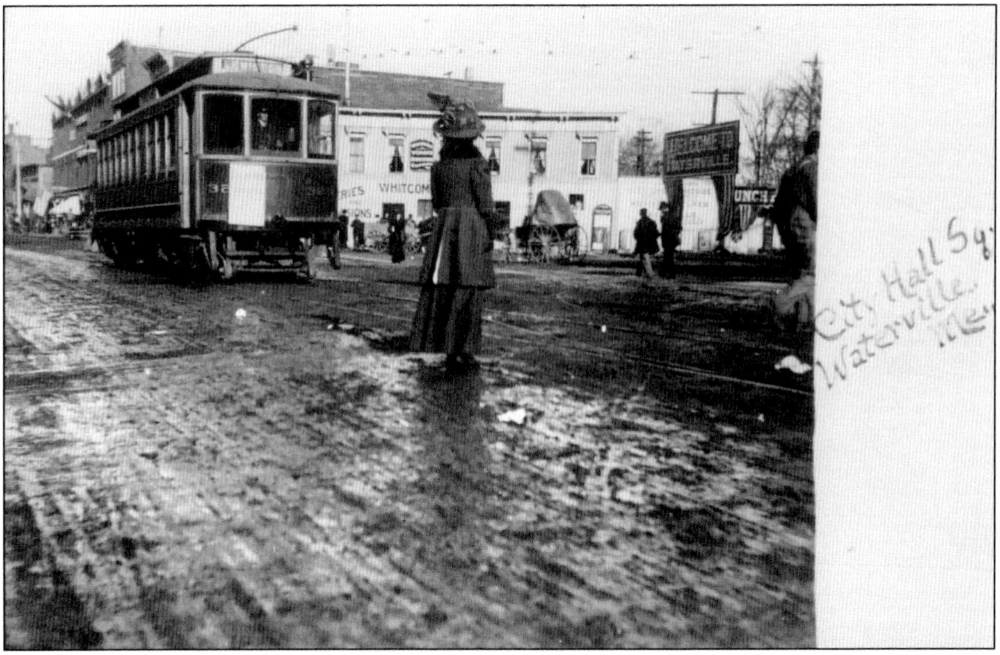

In this 1910 postcard, the Lewiston-bound Car No. 326 of the Lewiston, Augusta & Waterville Street Railway stops for a passenger at Main and Common Streets, near Waterville's city hall.

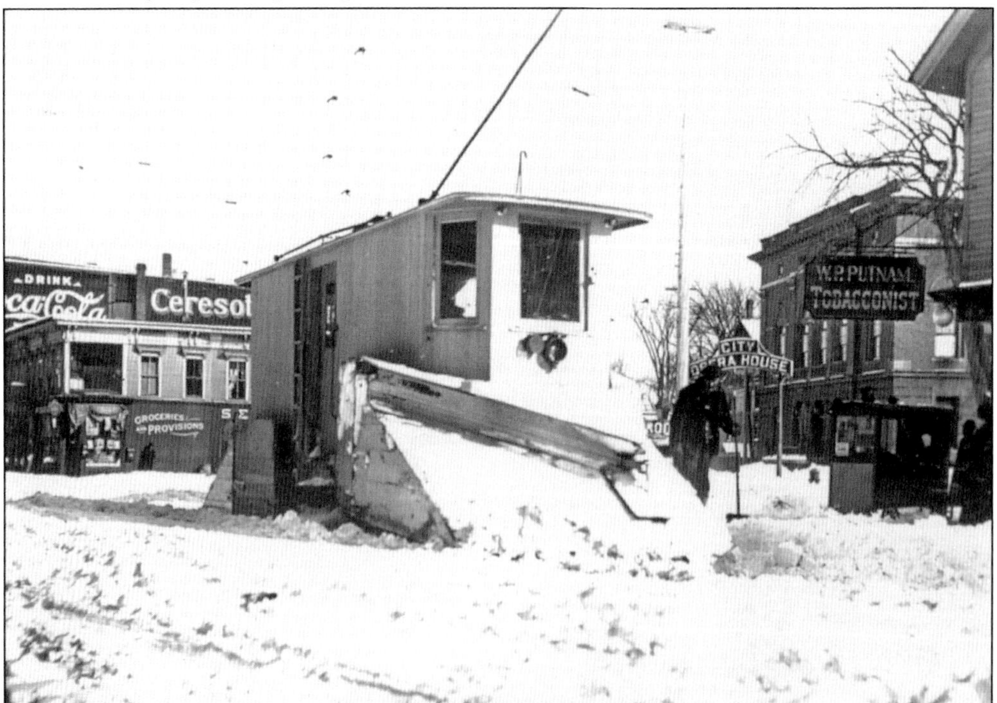

The Lewiston, Augusta & Waterville Street Railway owned electric plows that cleared the tracks after winter snowstorms. In this c. 1910 image, one such plow operates at Main and Common Streets; Waterville's city hall is in the background at right. (Waterville Historical Society.)

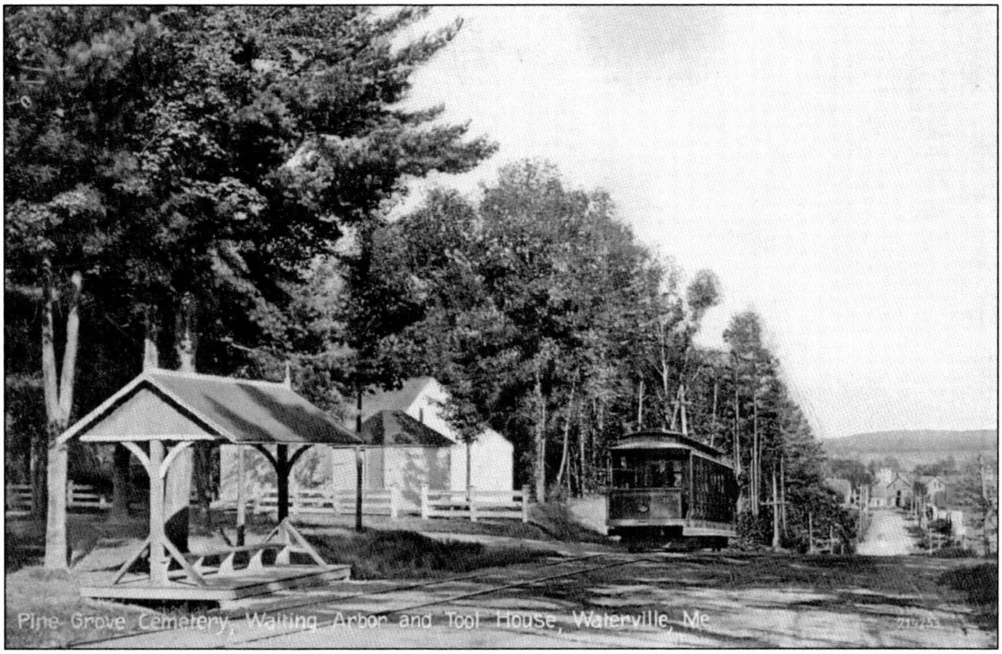

The termination point for one of Waterville's trolley lines was Pine Grove Cemetery, which was established in 1851. Located on the outskirts of the city, the cemetery was an especially popular destination on Memorial Day. Here, an electric car approaches the cemetery entrance; visitors could wait for the trolley in the shelter at left.

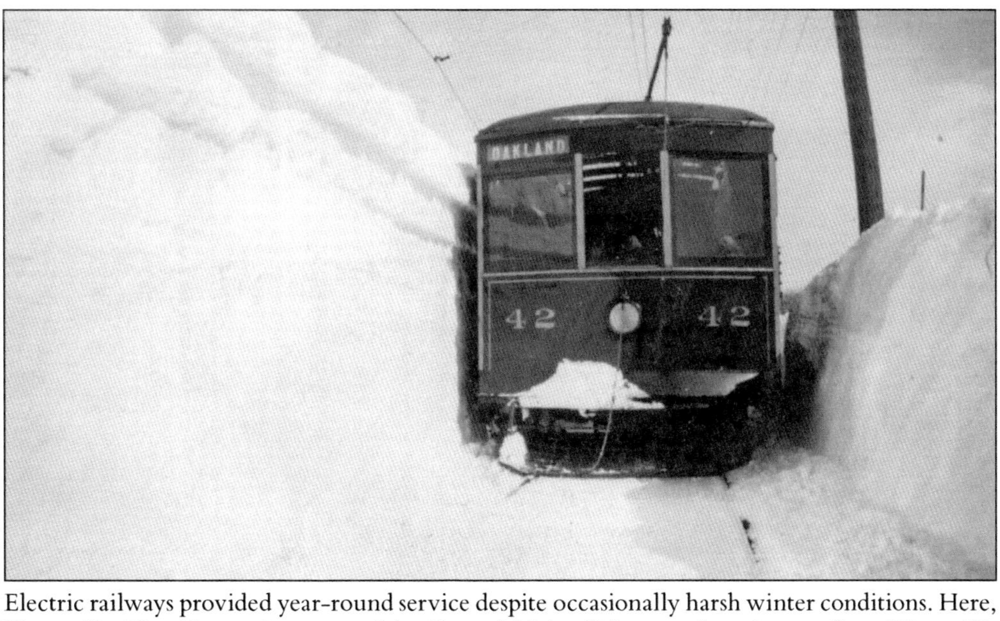

Electric railways provided year-round service despite occasionally harsh winter conditions. Here, Birney Car No. 42 stops just west of the Central Maine Fairgrounds on its way from Waterville to Oakland. (Waterville Historical Society.)

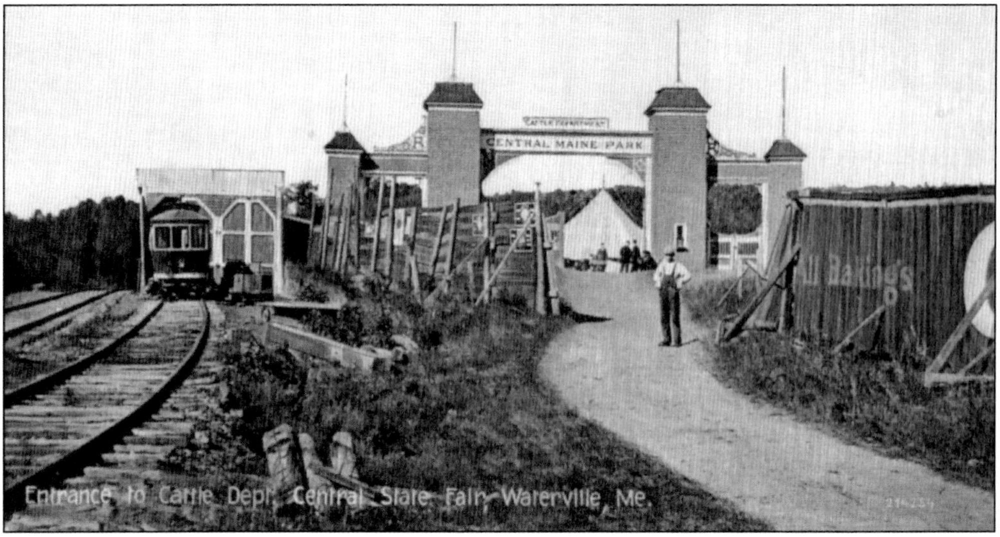

Beginning in 1904, the Waterville and Oakland Street Railway carried thousands of passengers to the Central Maine Fairgrounds located off the present-day Chase Avenue for the Central Maine Fair, which usually took place in early September. In 1911, the *Board of Trade Journal* assured readers that "nothing of a low or degrading nature is allowed on the grounds and the most fastidious may attend without fear of being shocked."

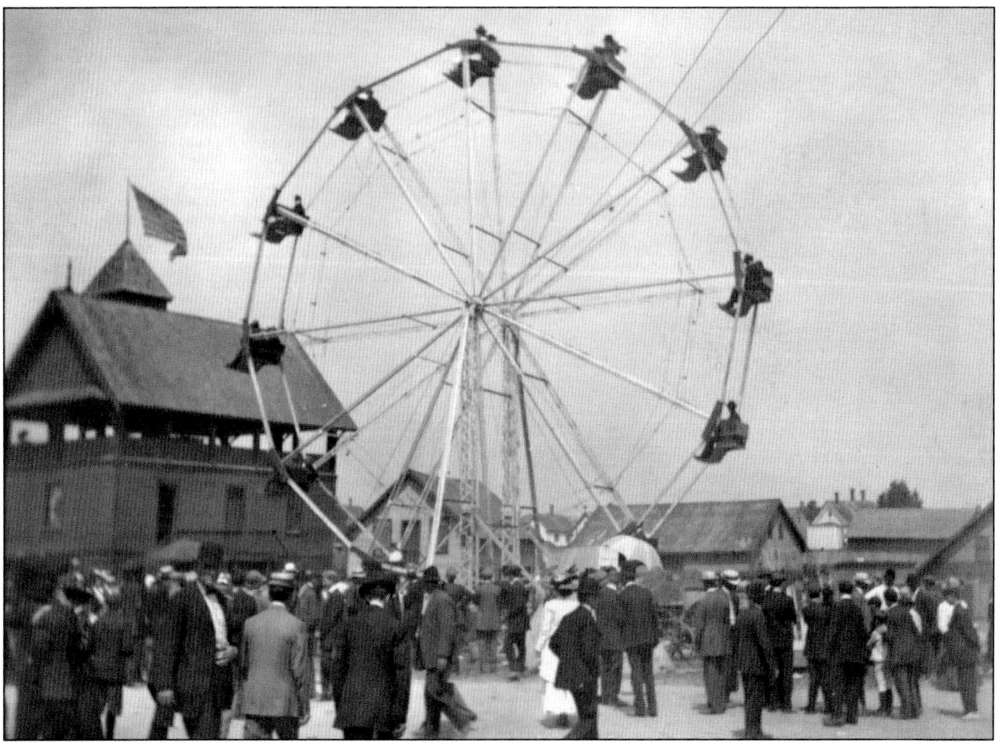

Ferris wheels proved to be popular attractions at fairs across America after the introduction of the first one at the Chicago World's Fair in 1893. In this image from September 2, 1909, visitors enjoy the experience of a Ferris wheel ride on the midway of the Central Maine Fair in Waterville. (Waterville Historical Society.)

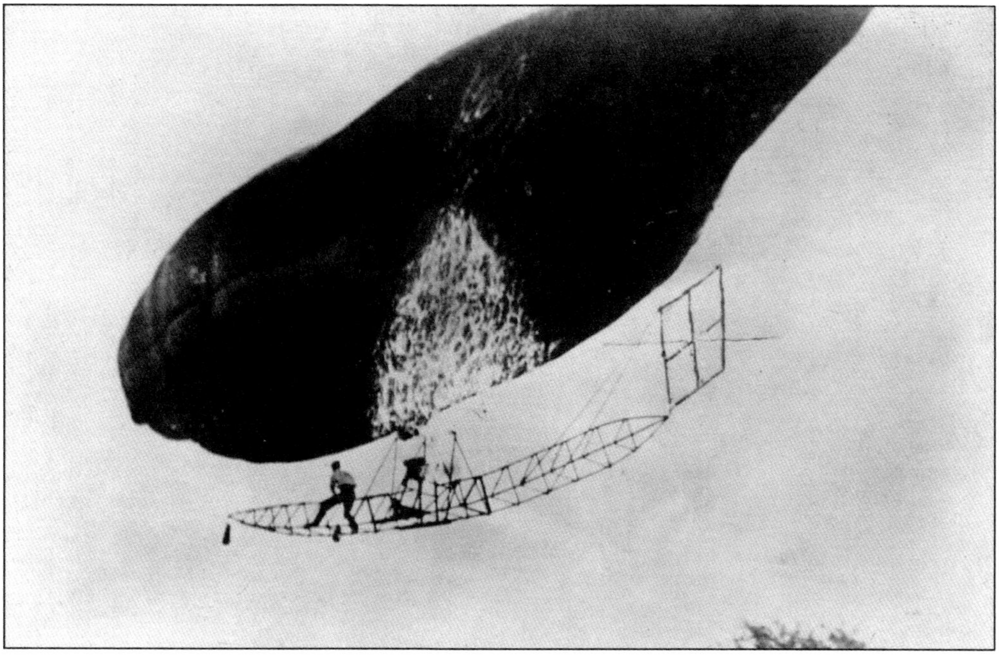

The 1908 Central Maine Fair was the scene of a tragic aviation accident that was captured in this real-photo postcard by a photographer named Voloz. Charles O. Jones of Hammondsport, New York, was demonstrating his dirigible balloon, a Strobel airship called the *Boomerang*, when it caught fire and crashed 500 feet to the ground, killing its pilot in full view of 25,000 spectators.

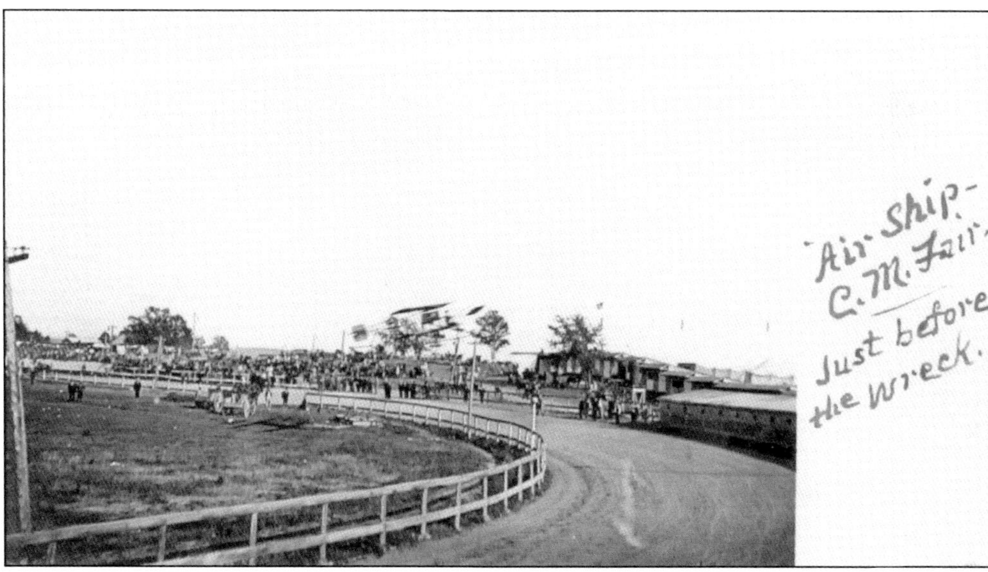

Eight years after the Wright brothers made their first flight in 1903, George Schmitt of Rutland, Vermont, made daily flights at the Central Maine Fair on August 31 and September 1 and 2, 1911. On September 1, Schmitt hit a telephone line with his landing wheels and was thrown uninjured from his plane. Two years later, he was not so fortunate and lost his life in a plane crash in Rutland. (Waterville Historical Society.)

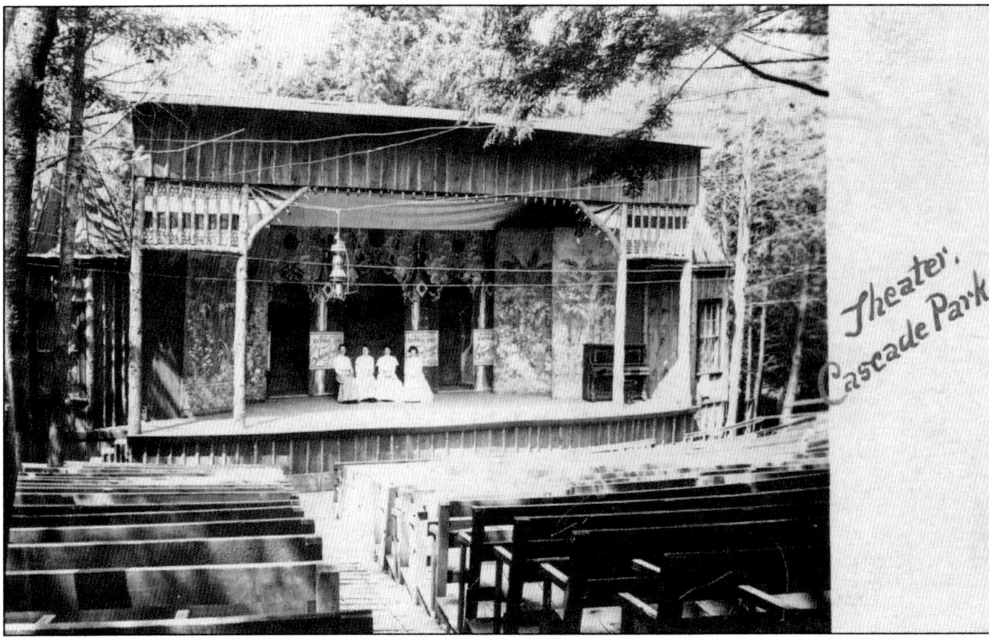

In the early 20th century, street railways frequently built amusement parks to encourage increased ridership on their lines. During this period, the Waterville & Oakland Street Railway operated Cascade Park in nearby Oakland—it featured an outdoor theater that was open from late spring until early fall. Entertainment offered here included vaudeville, pageants, and concerts.

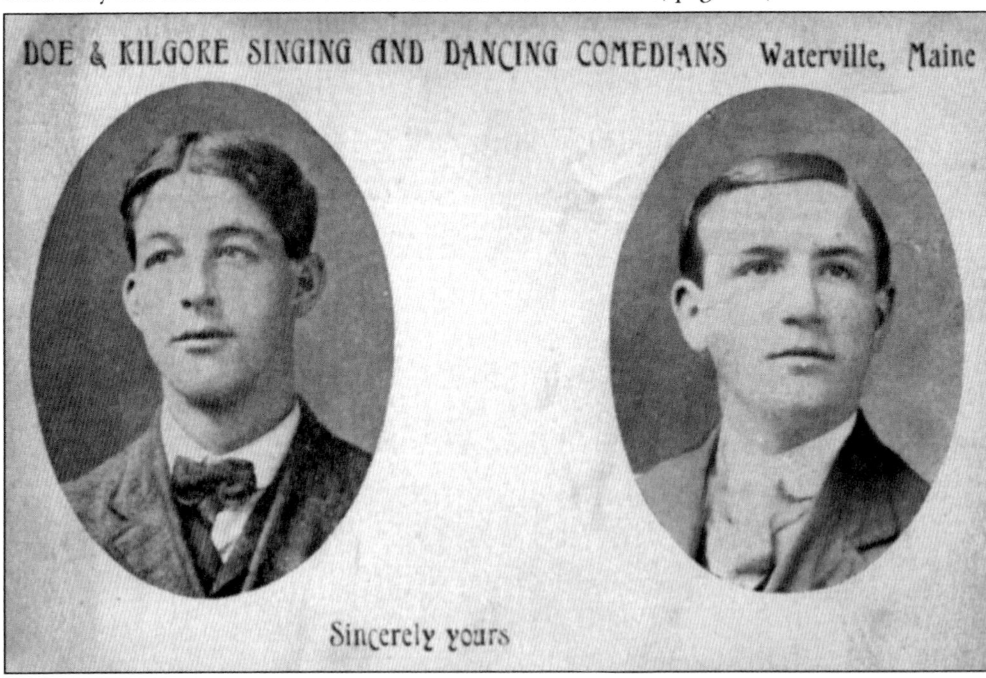

This c. 1905 postcard bills Doe and Kilgore as "singing and dancing comedians" from Waterville. These young men were among hundreds of performers who traveled the state in the early 20th century to entertain audiences in vaudeville theaters and town halls in an era when motion pictures were in their infancy.

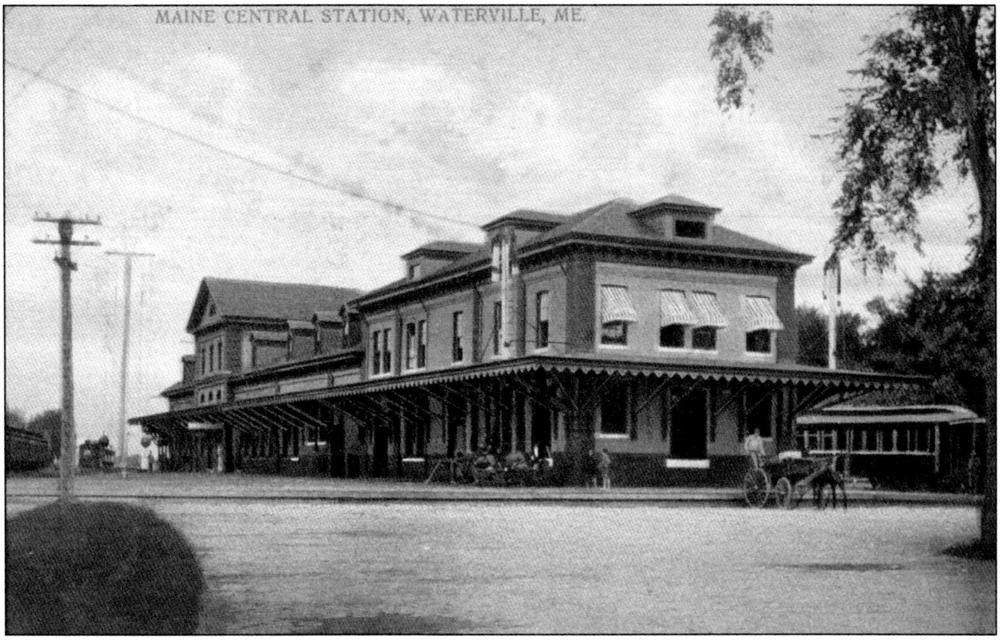

In 1872, the Maine Central Railroad built the left section of its Waterville railroad station on College Avenue, across from Colby College. Gridley J.F. Bryant and Louis P. Rogers of Boston were the architects. The building contained a ticket office, a waiting room, administrative offices, baggage storage, and an American Express office. This station was enlarged in 1906 with the construction of the two-story hipped roof section at right.

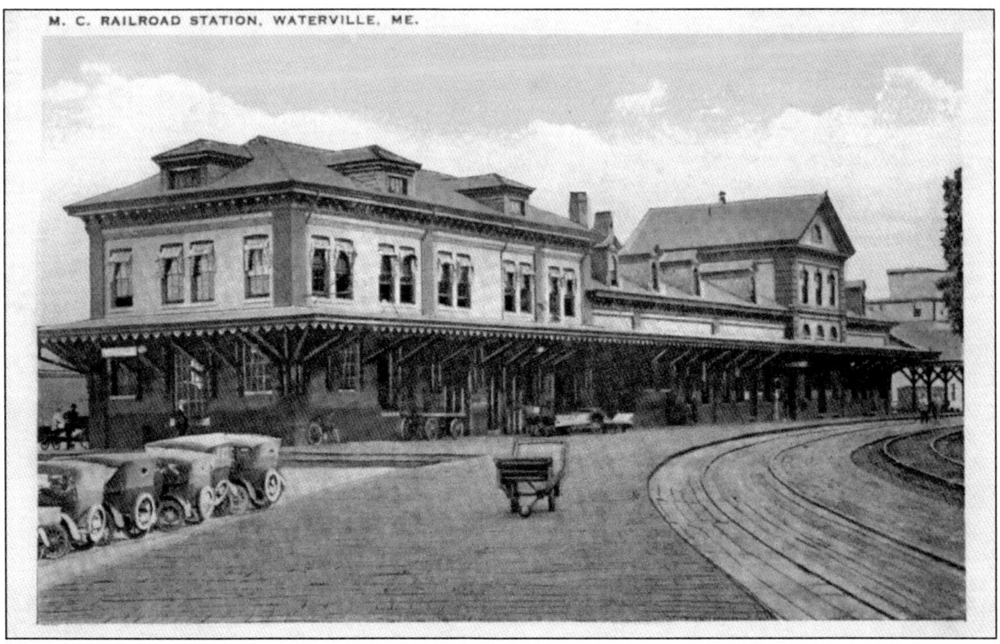

A photograph captured this view of the Maine Central Railroad station from the loading platform; the tracks are at right. The section built in 1872 is at right, with the 1906 addition at left. Like so many stations in Maine, this one was torn down after passenger service ended in 1960.

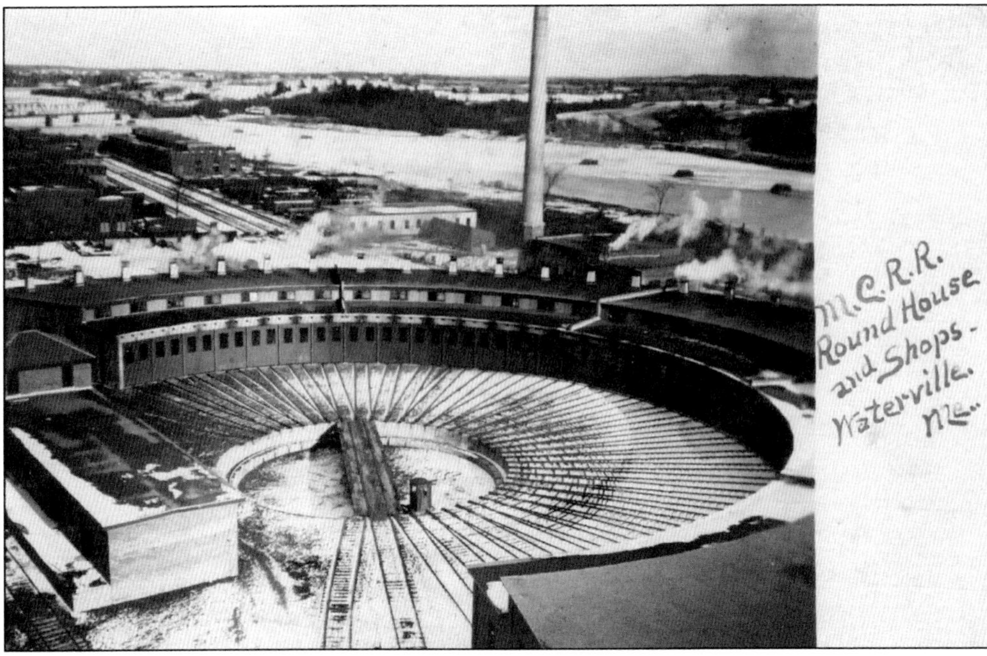

In the 1880s, the Maine Central Railroad decided to locate its machine and repair shops in Waterville, which marked the beginning of the growth of its large railroad yard north of the commercial center of the city. In 1911, the railroad built this 35-unit roundhouse and adjoining brick shops; the new complex was constructed by local contractor Horace Purinton.

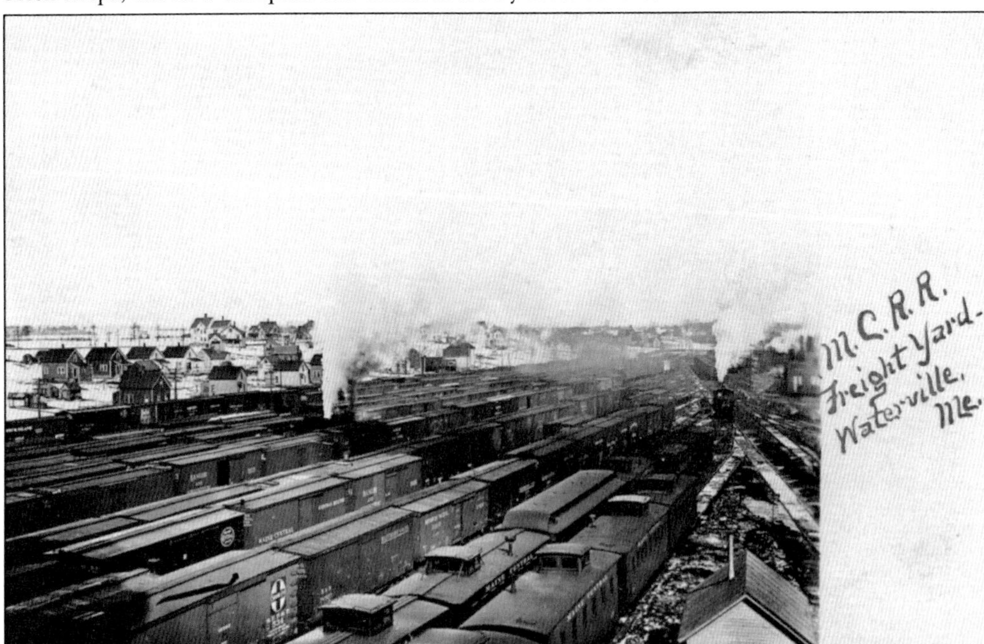

Freight cars extend as far as the eye can see in this view of the Maine Central Railroad freight yard. In 1926, *Sun-Up Magazine* commented, "The freight business handled through this city is enormous. Immense freight trains are brought to the city every day and here broken up into smaller trains to reach various points."

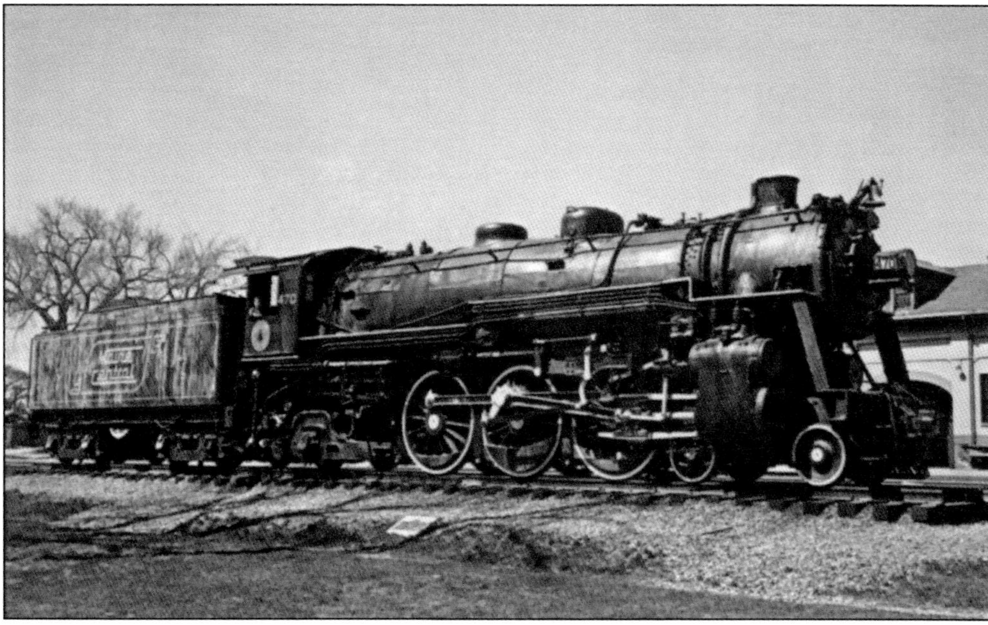

Maine Central Railroad (MCR) engine No. 470, a 4-6-2 or "Pacific" type locomotive, was built by the American Locomotive Company in 1924. Its final run on June 13, 1954, marked the last time that a steam engine operated on Maine Central Railroad. The locomotive is shown here on display after the MCR gave it to the City of Waterville to be preserved as a monument to the steam era.

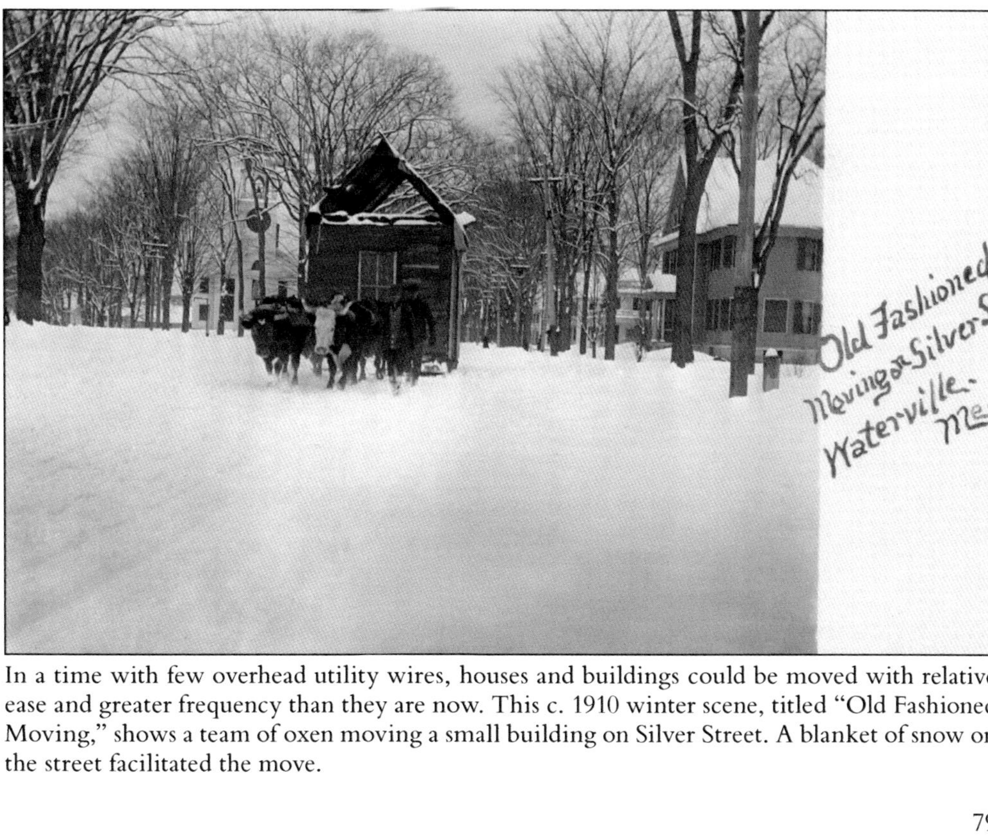

In a time with few overhead utility wires, houses and buildings could be moved with relative ease and greater frequency than they are now. This c. 1910 winter scene, titled "Old Fashioned Moving," shows a team of oxen moving a small building on Silver Street. A blanket of snow on the street facilitated the move.

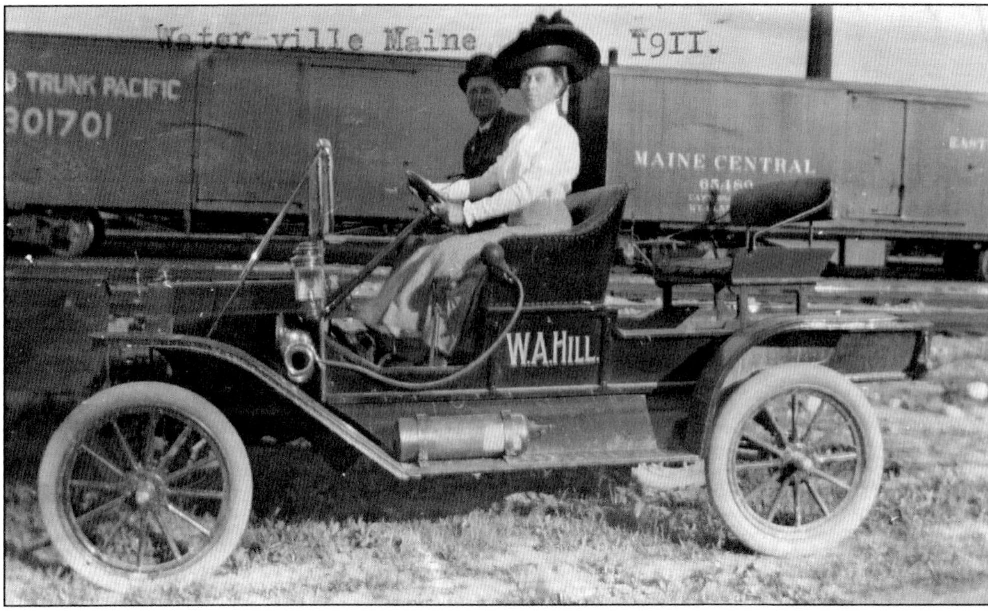

An early Ford Model T photographed in 1911 at the railroad yard in Waterville bears the name W.A. Hill, possibly Wallace A. Hill, a roofing contractor in nearby Fairfield. The inscription on the back of the card indicates it was made by local photographer Ralph W. Atkins.

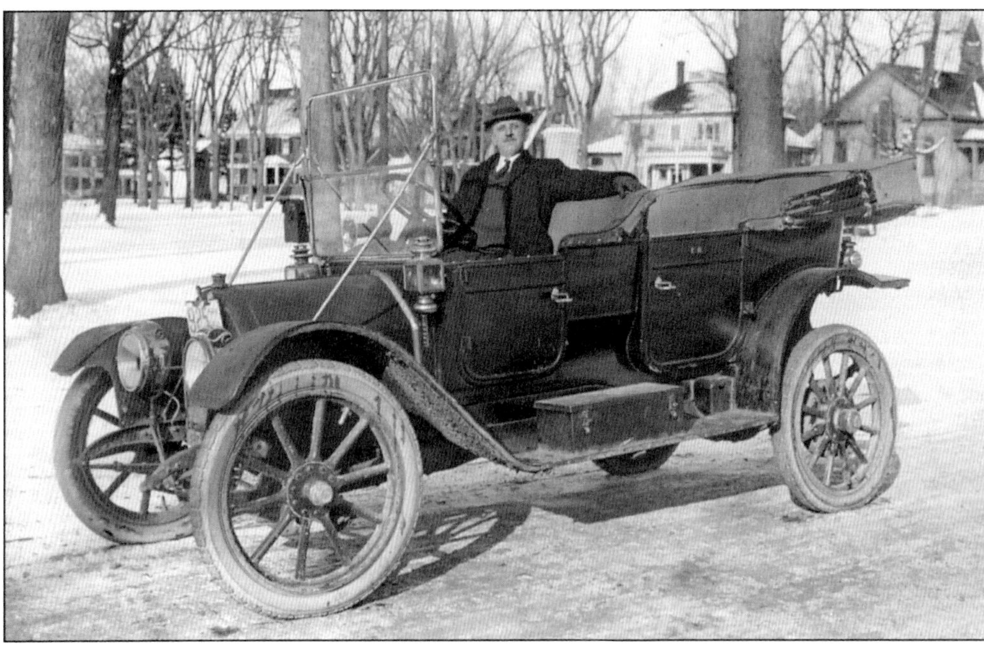

In a period when many motorists put their automobiles up on blocks for the winter, proud car owner Sherman L. Berry stopped on Elm Street for this picture in front of a snowy Monument Park. This real-photo postcard can be dated to 1915 by the style of the Maine license plate attached to the front of the radiator. (Waterville Historical Society.)

Seven

Hotels

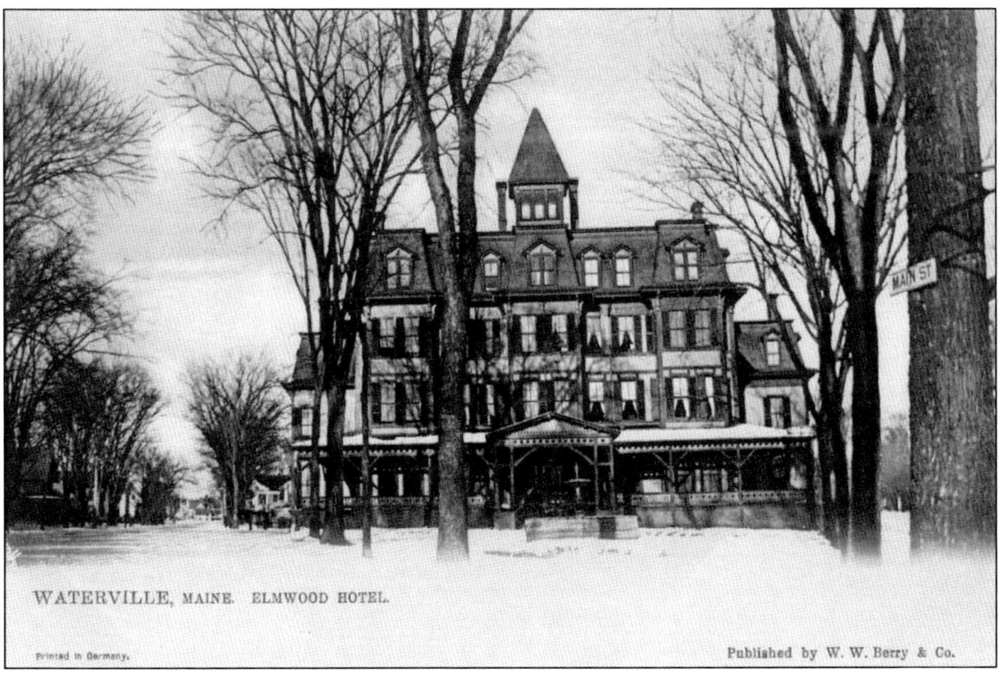

The Elmwood Hotel occupied a highly visible site at the corner of Main Street and College Avenue from 1850 until its demolition in the 1960s. The first Elmwood Hotel burned down in 1878 and was replaced in 1879–1880 by this elaborate four-story wooden hotel designed by Francis H. Fassett of Portland. The Elmwood was large enough to accommodate short-term guests, long-term boarders, local gatherings, statewide conventions, and Colby College events.

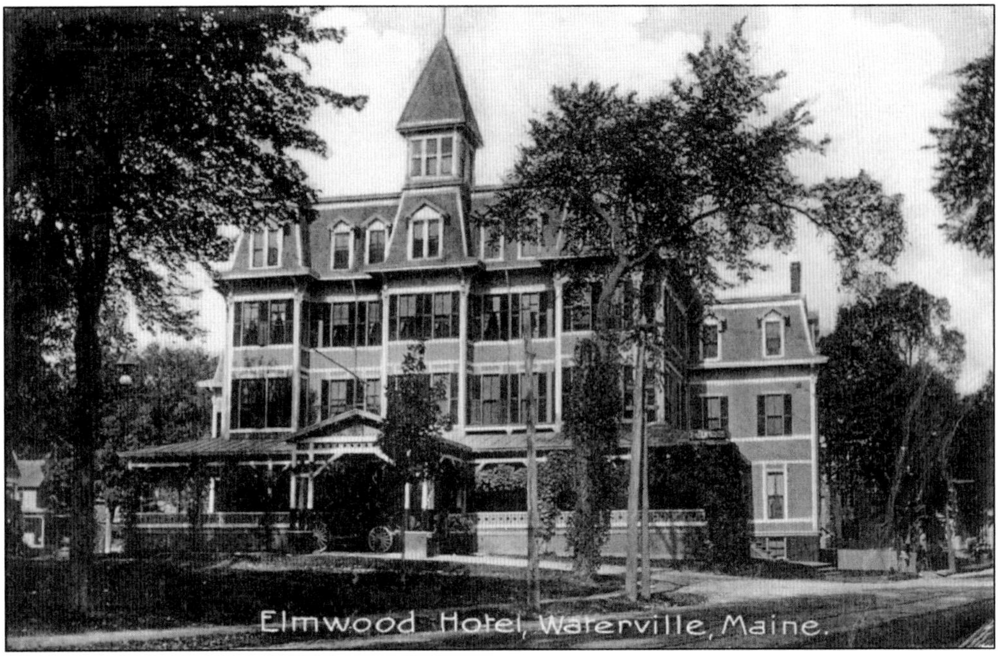

This 1907 view of the Elmwood Hotel shows the three-story College Avenue wing (at right) added in 1890. A corresponding wing was simultaneously constructed on the opposite side of the building. According to the October 3, 1890, issue of the *Industrial Journal of Bangor,* the enlargements were necessary "on account of the excellent patronage the hotel has had this season."

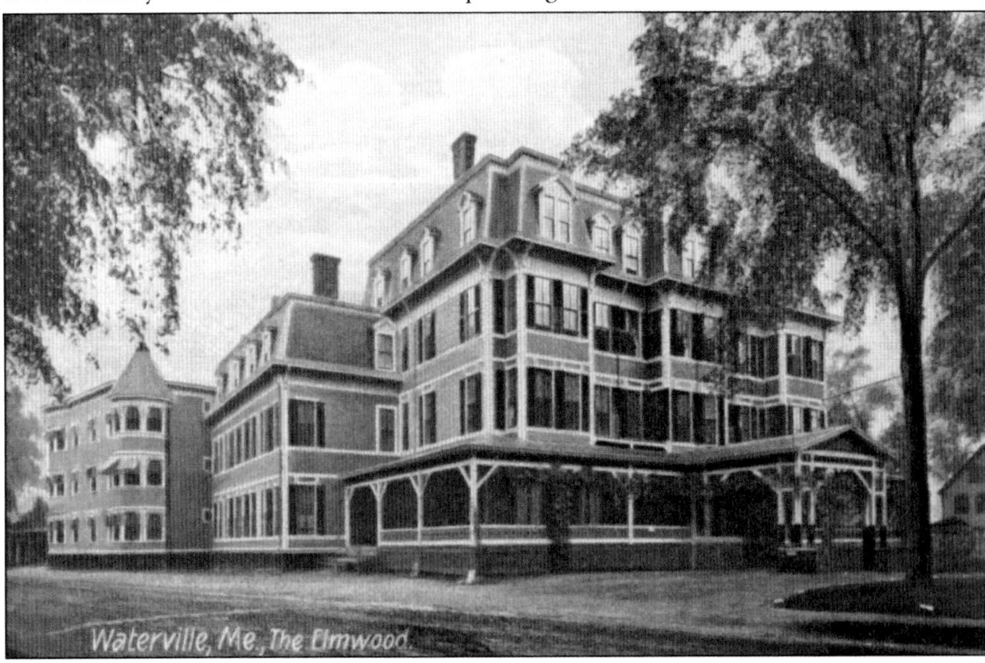

Another 1907 view of the Elmwood shows the Main Street side of the hotel with the 1890 wing and a second three-story wing, added in 1902, at far left. Edwin Whittemore's *History of Waterville,* published that year, commented, "A recent addition made necessary by the increasing business, has made the capacity of the house 150 rooms."

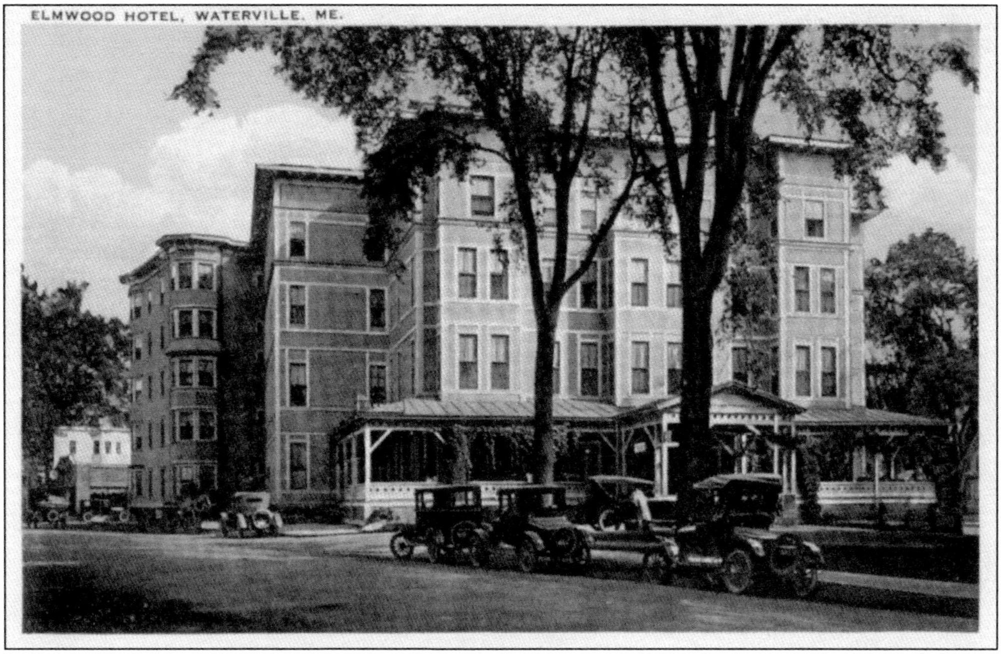

In 1908, the owner of the Elmwood Hotel, George White, and its manager, Henry Judkins, commissioned William H. Butterfield to design a final major expansion of the hotel. That year, one story was added to the 1890 wings and two stories were added to the 1902 wing, creating an additional 50 rooms. The remodeling included passenger and baggage elevators and private baths and telephones in most of the rooms.

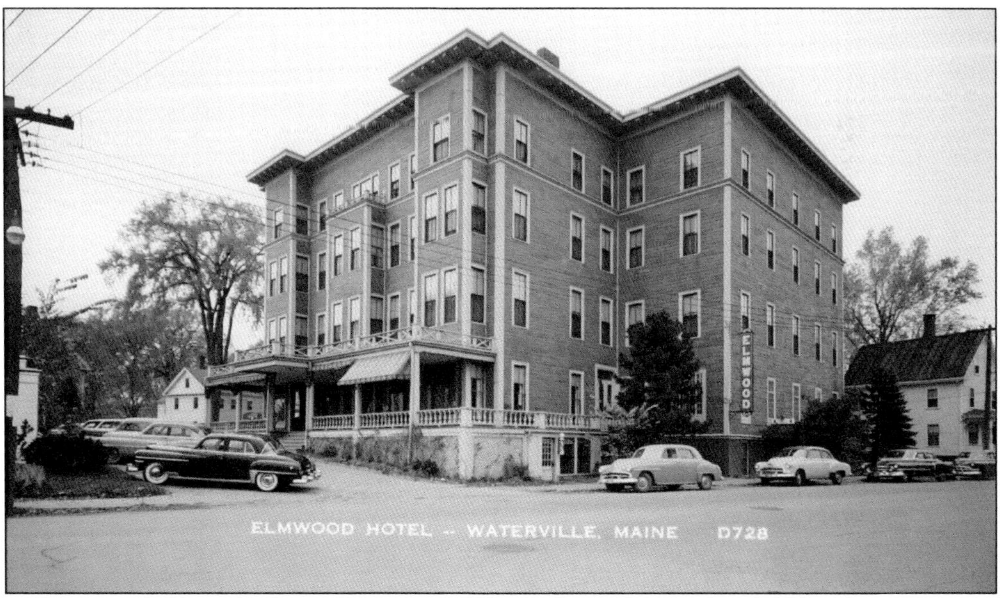

As the popularity of the automobile grew after World War I, the Elmwood advertised as "a headquarters for commercial men and automobilists." By the time this post–World War II postcard was made, the Elmwood was billing itself as a "motor hotel." However, competition from roadside cabins and motels led to the end of "Waterville's premier hotel" in the 1960s. (Penobscot Marine Museum.)

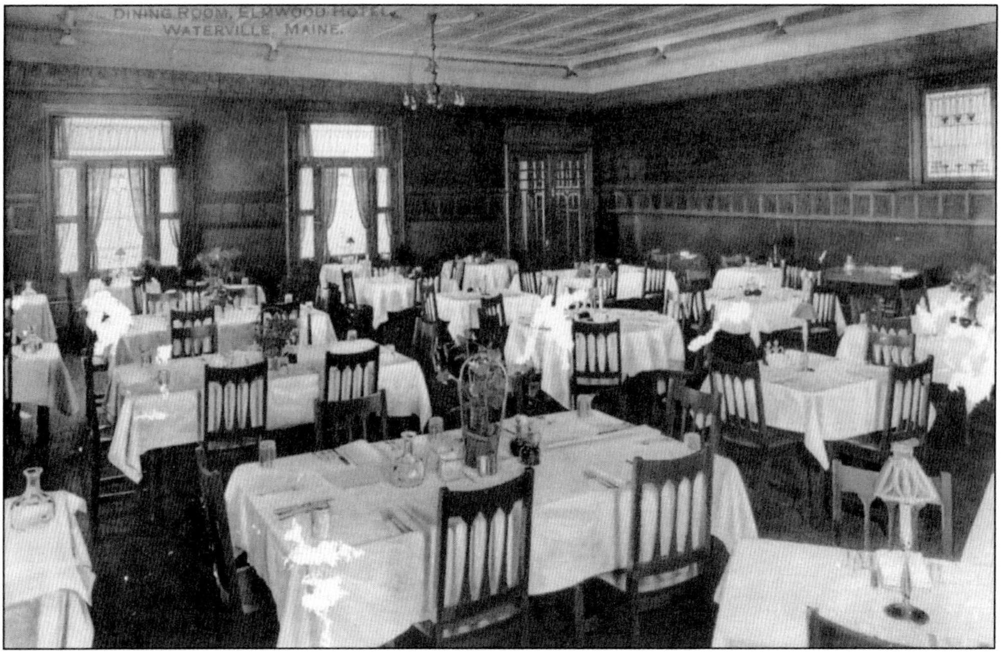

On the evening of Saturday, January 28, 1911, veteran Elmwood Hotel manager Henry Judkins proudly opened this elegant new dining room. The March 1911 *Board of Trade Journal* described the room in glowing terms: "The room has a cheerful appearance as the woodwork and the furniture are done in willow green. The walls are shaded from Pompeian red to brown shades to represent Spanish leather. The ceiling is ivory white." (Waterville Historical Society.)

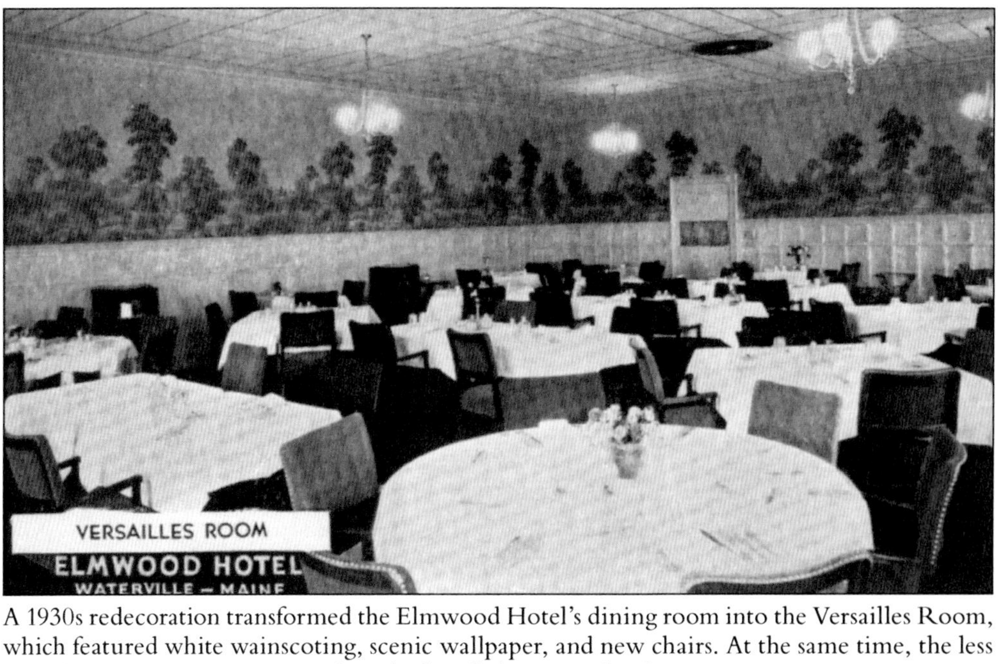

A 1930s redecoration transformed the Elmwood Hotel's dining room into the Versailles Room, which featured white wainscoting, scenic wallpaper, and new chairs. At the same time, the less formal Pine Tree Tavern opened on the hotel's basement level.

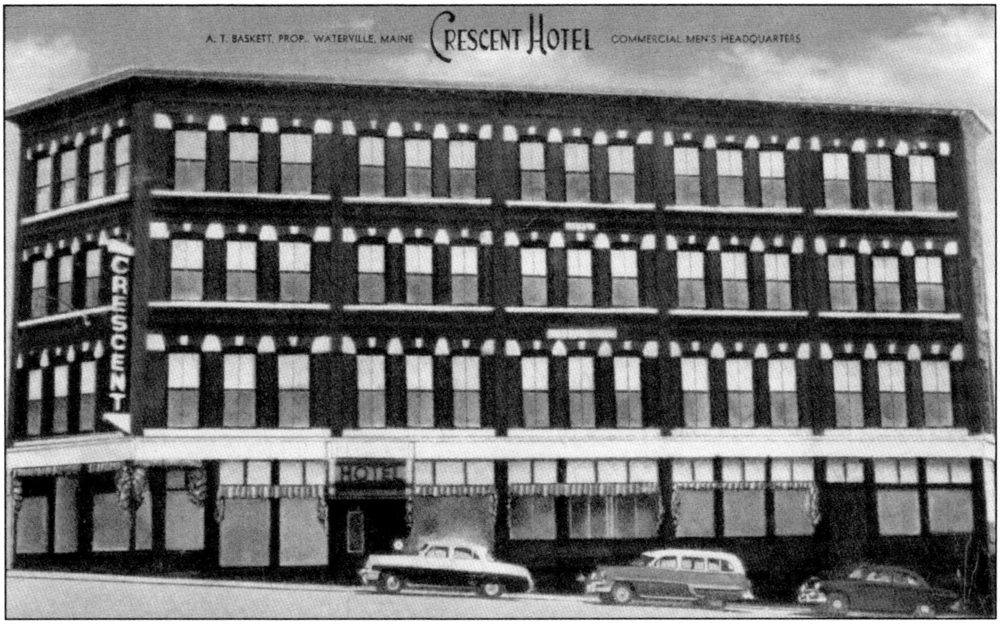

In 1879 and 1880, Reuben B. Dunn erected this large brick building—the Dunn Block—on Main Street. The architect was Francis H. Fassett of Portland. From the 1880s to the 1960s, the Dunn Block housed a series of hotels, starting with the Lockwood House and followed by the Bay View Hotel and the Crescent Hotel (pictured). These commercial hotels catered to the needs of traveling businessmen, salesmen, and theatrical troupes.

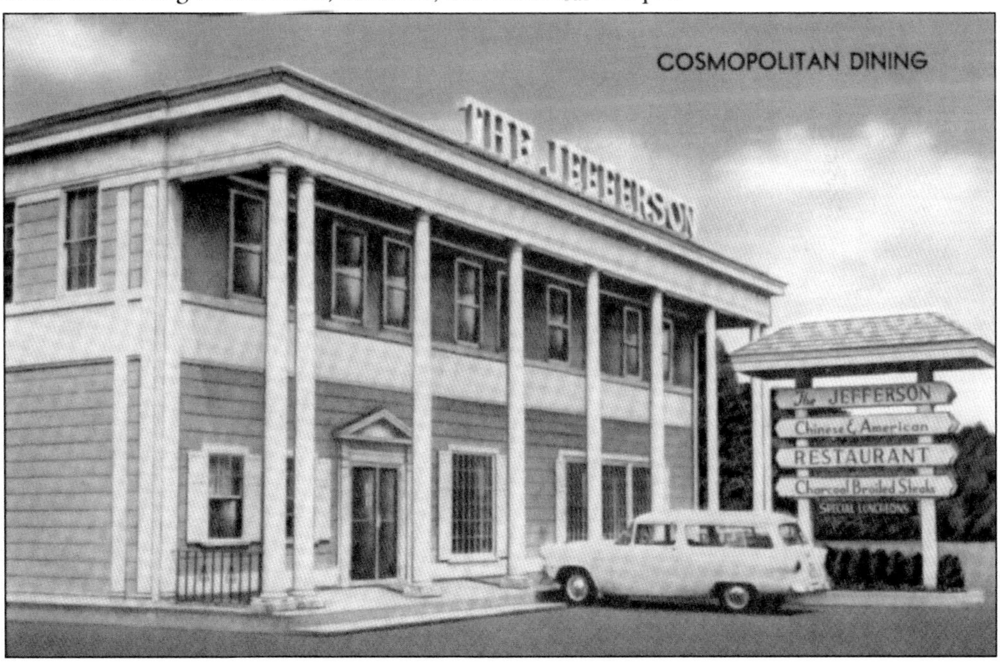

For more than four decades, the Jefferson, located on College Avenue, was a favorite Waterville restaurant serving American and Chinese cuisine. Founded in 1935 by Louis and Celia Shiro as a hotel with a dining room, the original Jefferson burned down in 1945 and was rebuilt as it appears in this 1959 postcard. In 1977, the Jefferson became John Martin's Manor, a popular steakhouse.

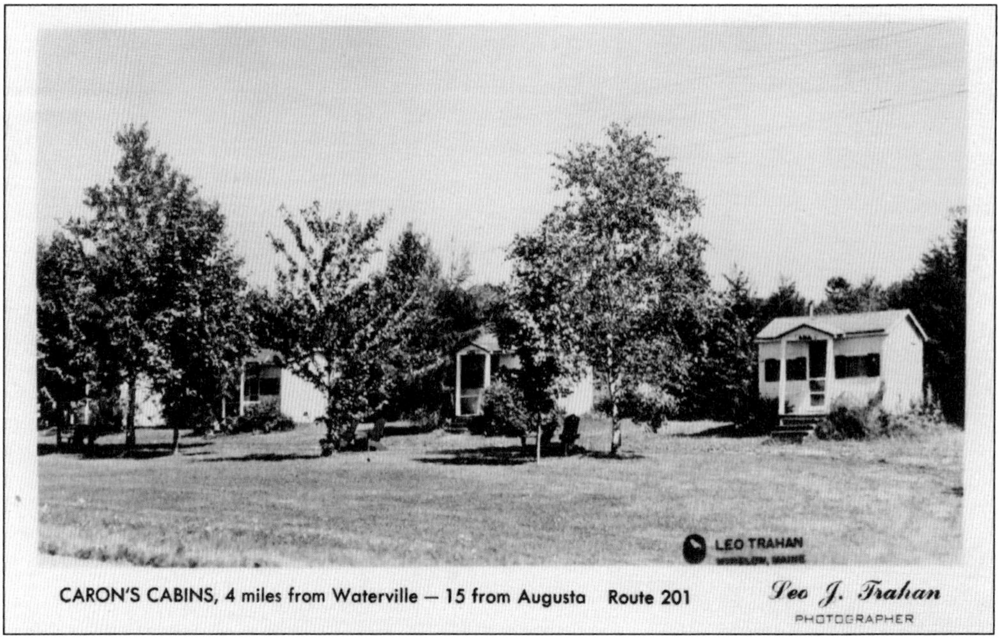

After World War I, the growing popularity of automobile travel—and the improved roads that came with that popularity—created a new form of vacationing. Increasingly, middle-class tourists preferred the ease and affordability of roadside cabins to traditional downtown hotels. Caron's Cabins was located on US Route 201, the main road from Augusta to Waterville.

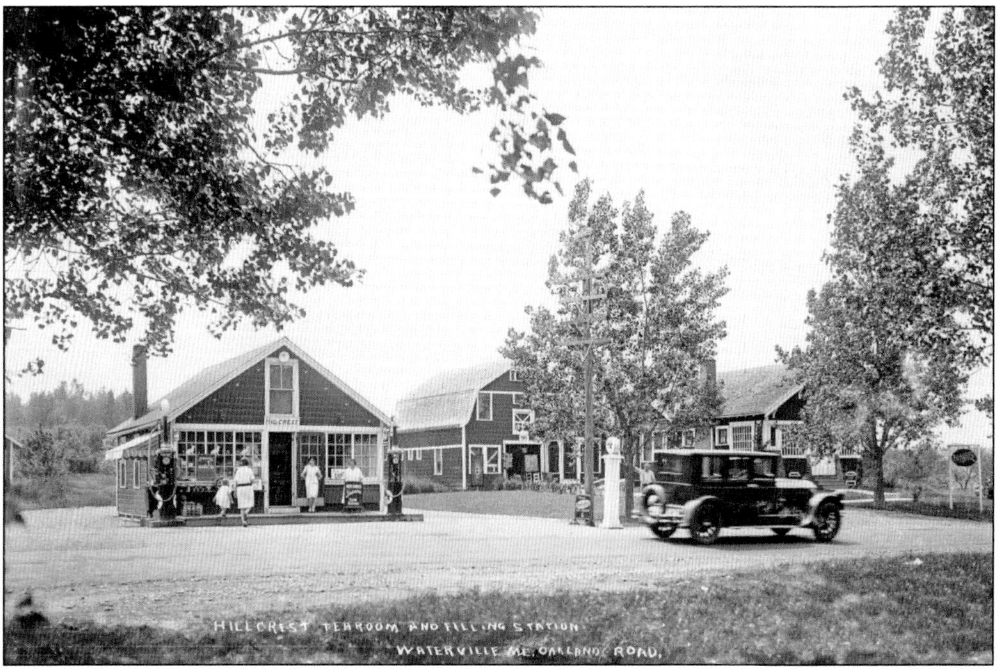

Roadside restaurants and gas stations sprang up along automobile routes in the 1920s. Here, an automobile is stopped for gas at the Hilcrest Tea Room and Filling Station on Oakland Road in Waterville. Whitcomb's Antique Shop, another roadside business, is in the gambrel-roofed barn next to the tea room. (Penobscot Marine Museum.)

Eight

The Old Colby Campus

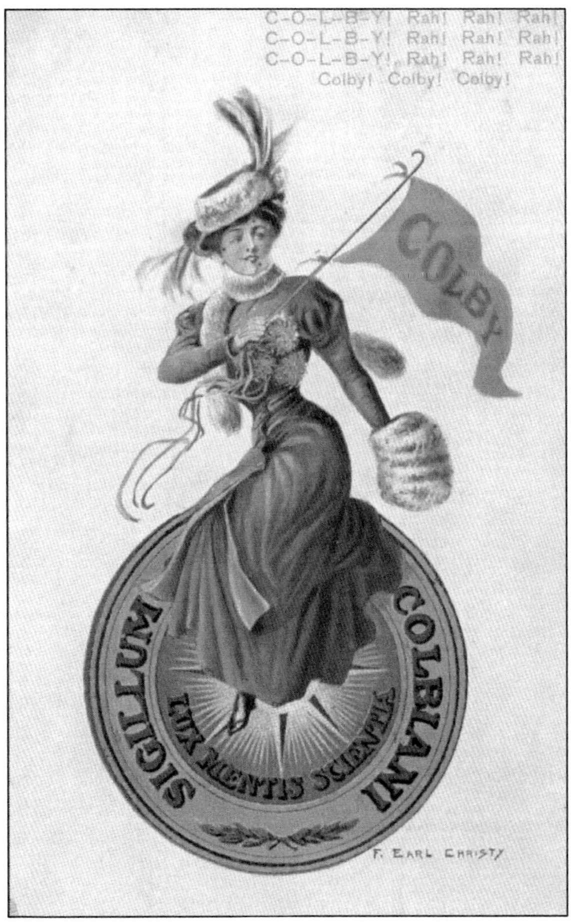

In 1813, Maine Baptists founded the Maine Literary and Theological Institution—the school now known as Colby College. Classes began in 1818, and in 1820, the Maine Legislature gave the college the authority to grant degrees. School trustees voted to change its name to Waterville College in 1821. In 1864, threatened with closure due to the economic impact of the Civil War, the college was saved by a $50,000 gift from Boston merchant (and Waterville native) Gardner Colby. In 1866, Waterville College trustees voted to rename the school Colby University in honor of Colby, and the Maine Legislature approved the change in 1867. (Waterville Historical Society.)

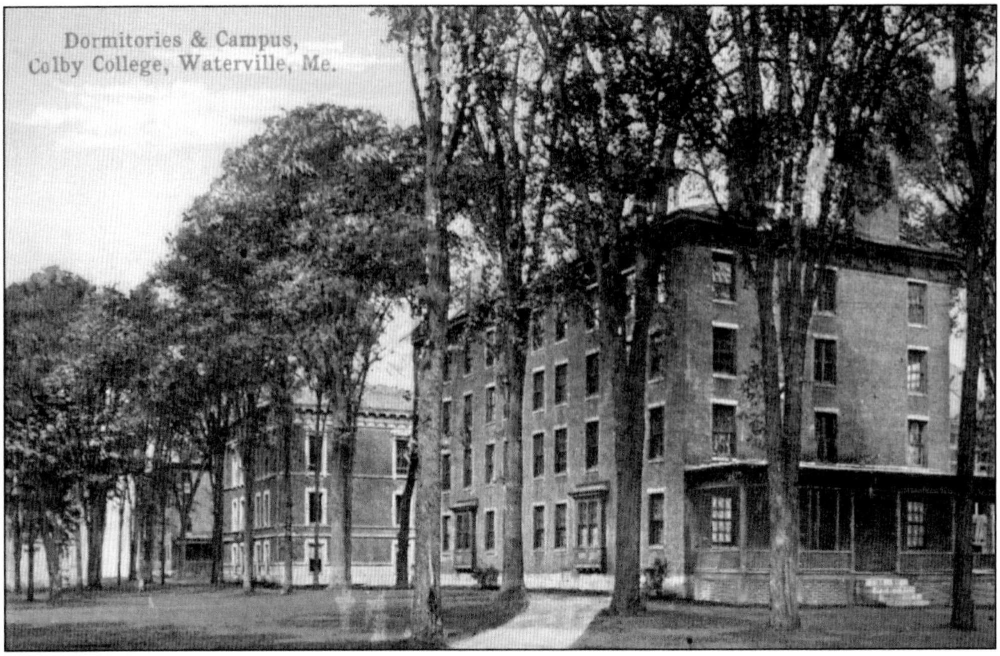

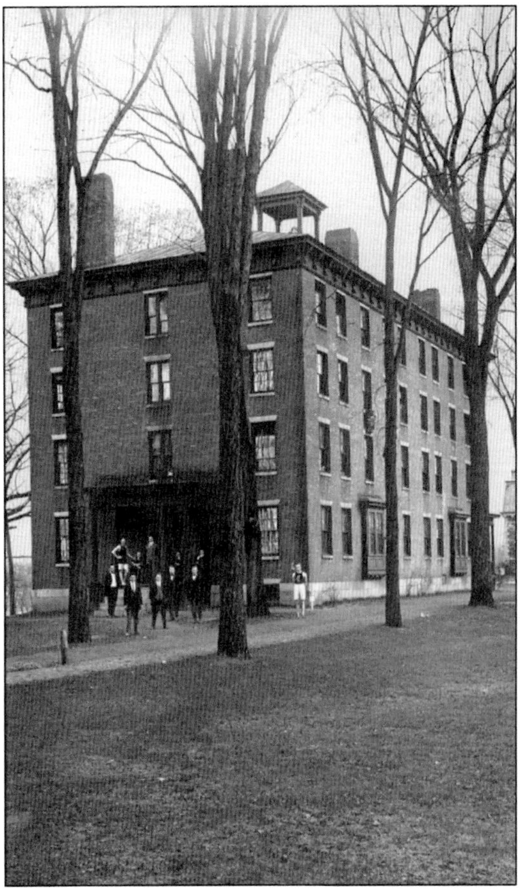

In 1821, the school built South College (at right). This four-story brick building contained 32 double student rooms, recitation rooms, a library, and a chapel. Albert W. Paine, an early graduate, recalled in 1885 that "upon completion of South College, the event was celebrated by a complete illumination of it, every square of its seven-by-nine glass windows having a lighted candle behind it."

Two local contractors, brick mason Peter Getchell and carpenter Lemuel Dunbar, constructed South Hall in a late Federal style similar to that of dormitories at other New England schools. After nearly 80 years, South College was remodeled in 1899 under the direction of Portland architect John Calvin Stevens, who introduced bathrooms with showers and improved ventilation. The *Colby Echo* declared on June 2, 1899, that "these changes will be heartily welcomed by the students." The postcard at left shows the remodeled South Hall. (Waterville Historical Society.)

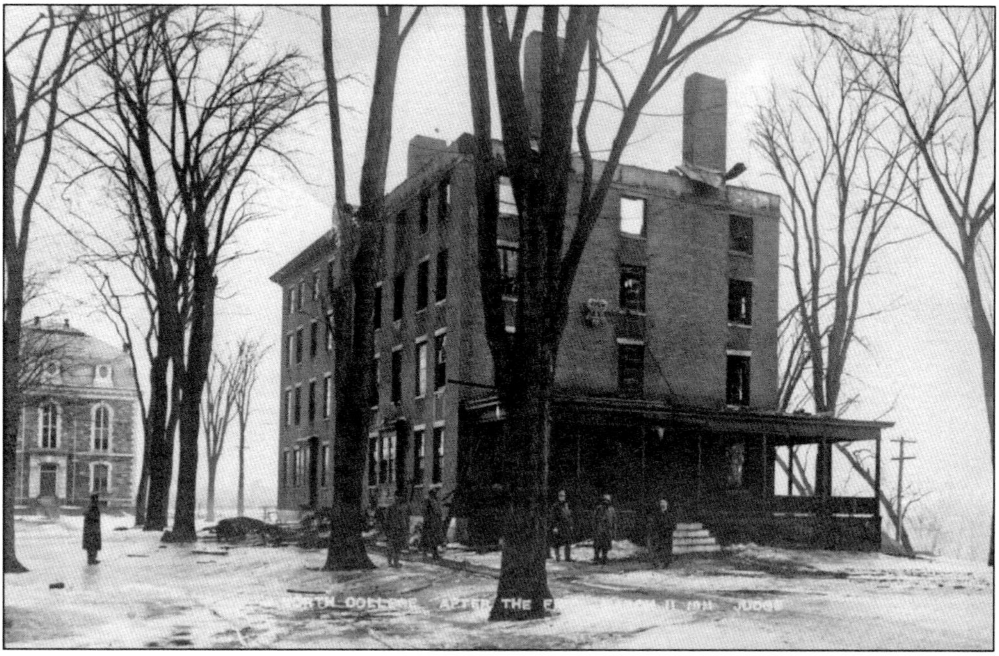

In 1822, Peter Getchell and Lemuel Dunbar constructed North College, which was identical to South College, for $3,000. It was renamed Chaplin Hall in 1872 for the school's first president, Rev. Jeremiah Chaplin. In 1903, John Calvin Stevens remodeled Chaplin Hall. This postcard shows the building after a fire that occurred in March 1911. The building was repaired and remained in service as a dormitory until the college moved to a new campus in the early 1950s.

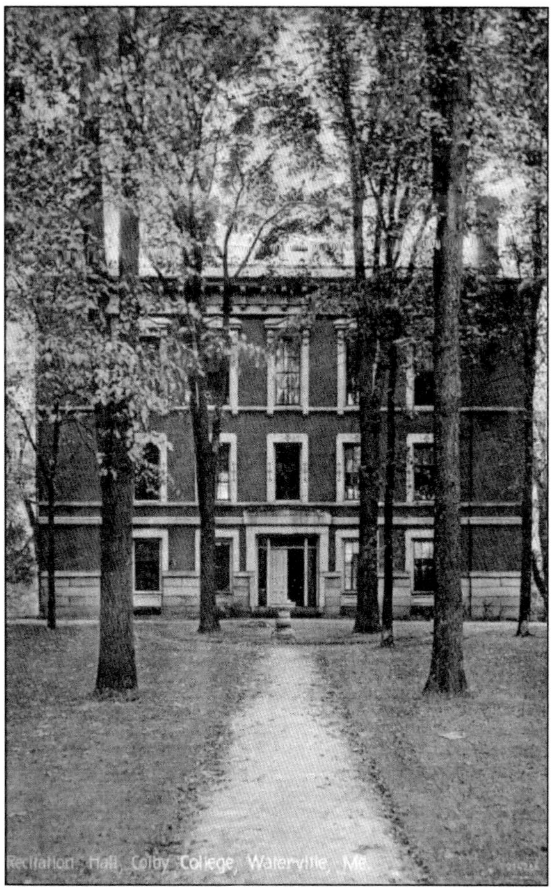

Between 1836 and 1837, Recitation Hall was built between South and North Colleges to create a New England college row. Designed by Thomas U. Walter of Philadelphia, this Greek Revival–style building housed classrooms and the chapel. Between 1870 and 1872, Recitation Hall was remodeled in the Italianate style by Boston architect Alexander R. Esty and was renamed Champlin Hall for Pres. James Champlin.

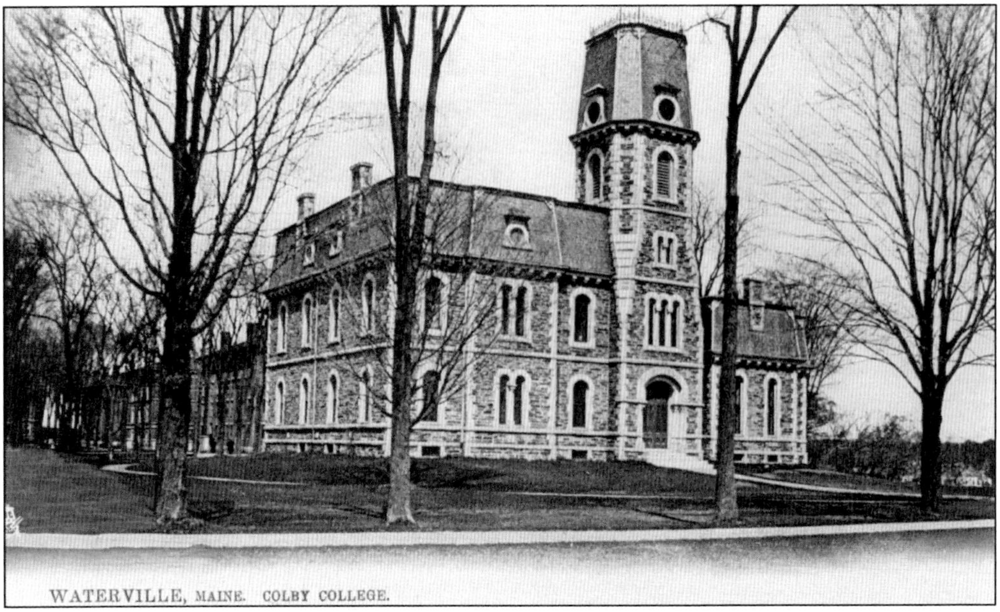

In 1866, college trustees voted to construct a building containing a library, a chapel, and an alumni hall to honor the 27 Colby alumni who lost their lives in the Civil War. Memorial Hall was built between 1867 and 1869 adjacent to South College on the former site of the president's house, which was moved to make way for the new structure. Using local stone, architect Alexander Esty and contractor J.P. Blunt fashioned a stately building in the French mansard style.

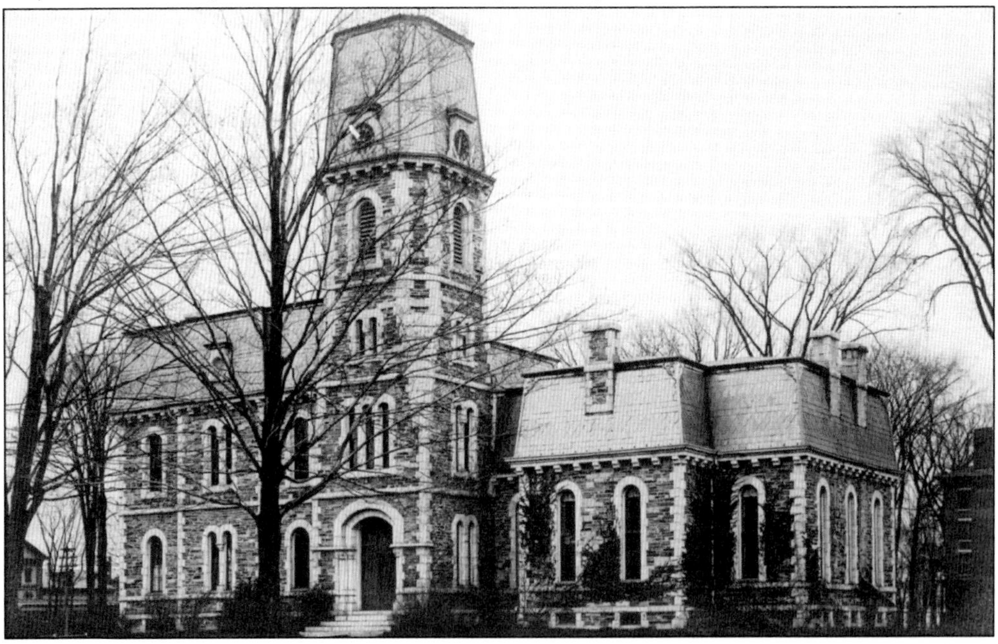

Often referred to as the first building in the North meant to commemorate Civil War casualties, Memorial Hall embodied the college's commitment to preserving the Union. Shortly after the hall was completed, a marble statue, *The Weeping Lion* by Martin Milmore, was installed in the alumni hall room on the second floor, along with a plaque listing the names of those from the college who died in the war.

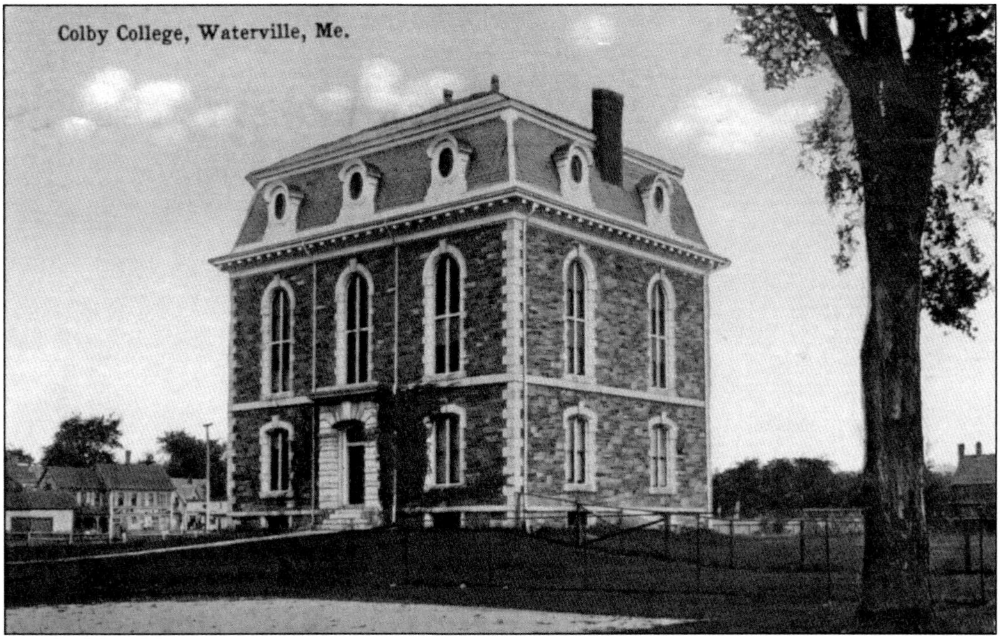

Maine governor Abner Coburn, a wealthy lumberman from Skowhegan, gave the college $10,000 towards a new science building for chemistry, geology, and natural history. Constructed north of North College (Chaplin Hall) in 1872, Coburn Hall was the work of architect Alexander Esty and echoed the local stone and the French mansard style he used in designing Memorial Hall.

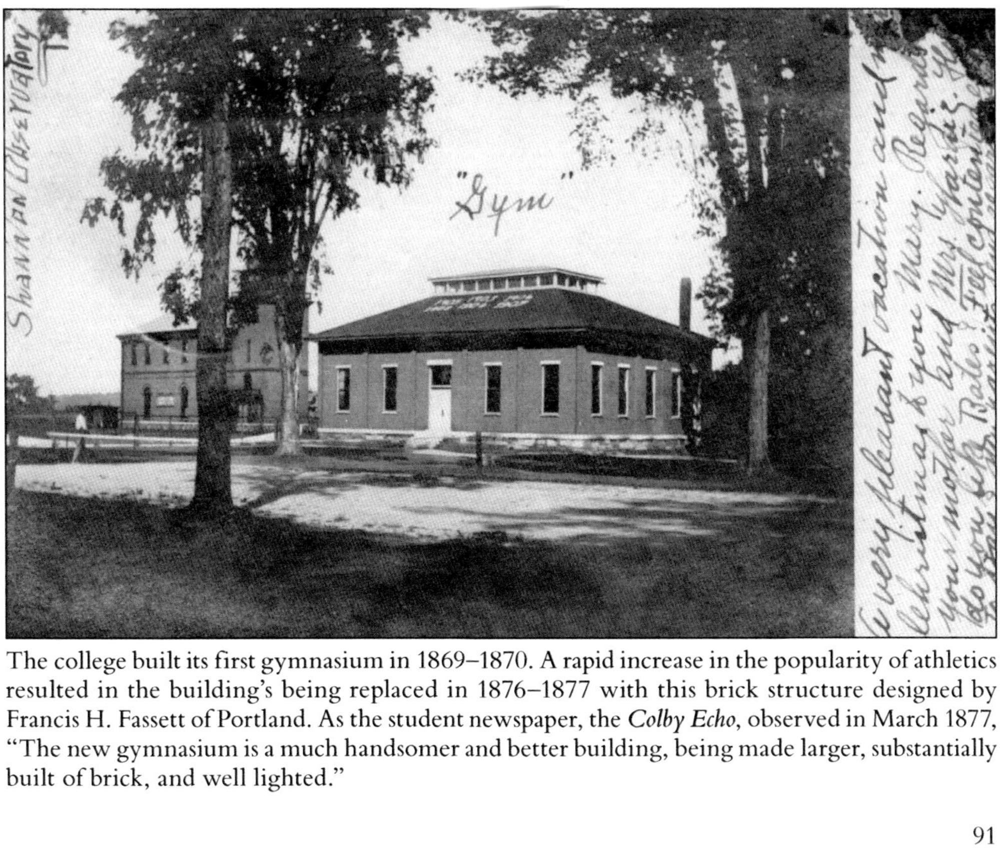

The college built its first gymnasium in 1869–1870. A rapid increase in the popularity of athletics resulted in the building's being replaced in 1876–1877 with this brick structure designed by Francis H. Fassett of Portland. As the student newspaper, the *Colby Echo*, observed in March 1877, "The new gymnasium is a much handsomer and better building, being made larger, substantially built of brick, and well lighted."

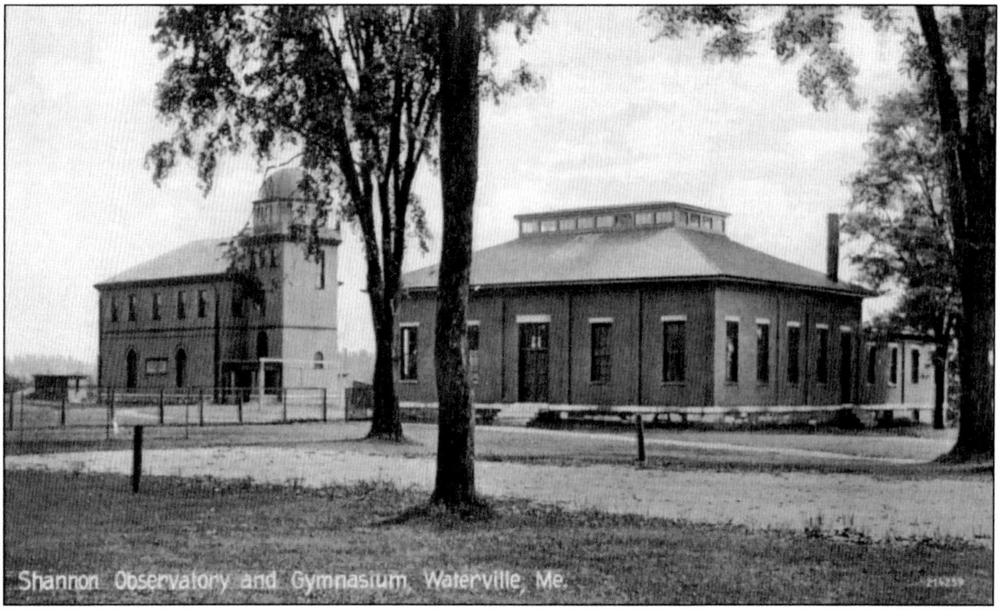

The Shannon Observatory and Physical Laboratory (at left) was named for Richard Shannon (class of 1862), who gave $15,000 in 1889 to build this brick scientific facility from designs by John Calvin Stevens and Albert Winslow Cobb. The first story housed a large room for electrical experiments, while the second floor served as a physics lecture hall and laboratory. The tower contained an astronomical observatory.

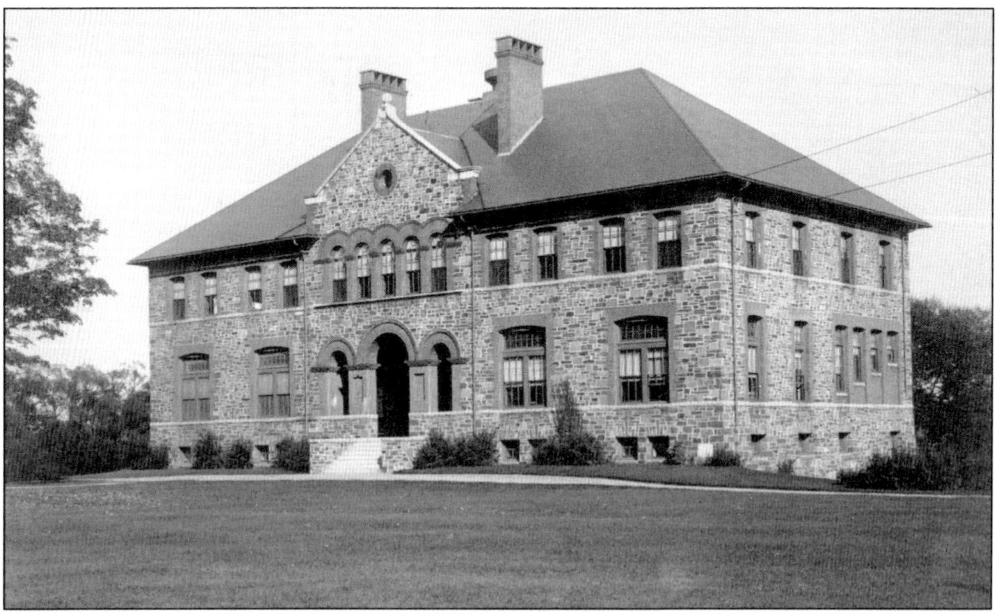

As construction began on Shannon Observatory in 1889, Colby aspired to build a chemical laboratory planned by Stevens and Cobb. This project did not materialize until 1898, when the college committed $50,000 to construct the Stevens-designed Chemical Hall south of Memorial Hall. This handsome Romanesque Revival structure used the same local stone as Memorial Hall and Coburn Hall. Upon completion in 1899, the *Industrial Journal* deemed the building "ideal in all its particulars."

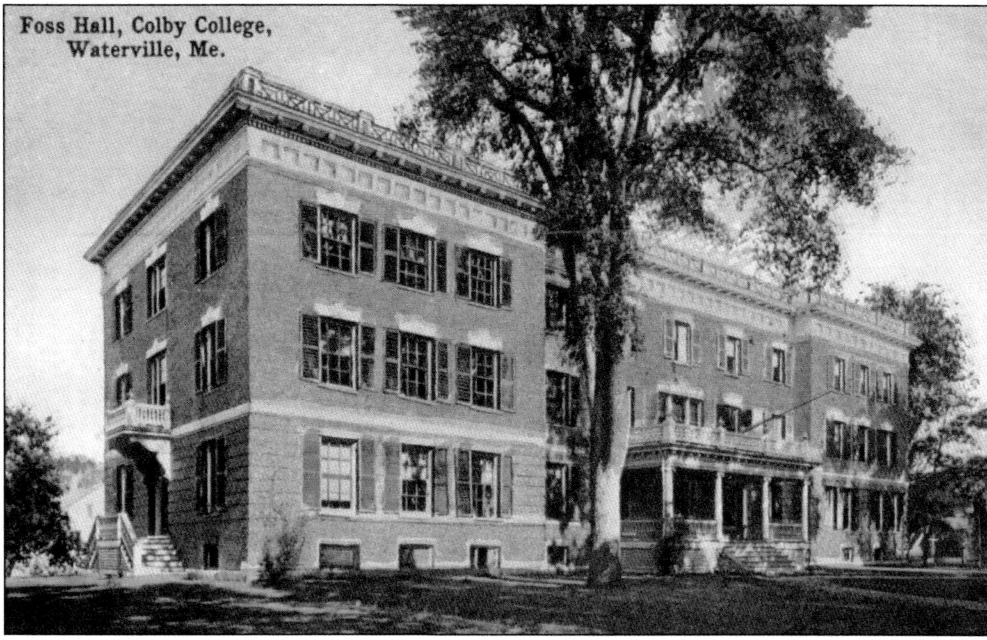

Colby's longstanding need for a women's dormitory was fulfilled in 1904 with the gift of $40,000 from Eliza Foss Dexter to build Foss Hall on College Avenue. John Calvin Stevens and John Howard Stevens designed this three-story brick Colonial Revival building to include two floors of rooms for female students and a 200-seat dining room. Construction began in September 1904, and Foss Hall was dedicated in June 1905.

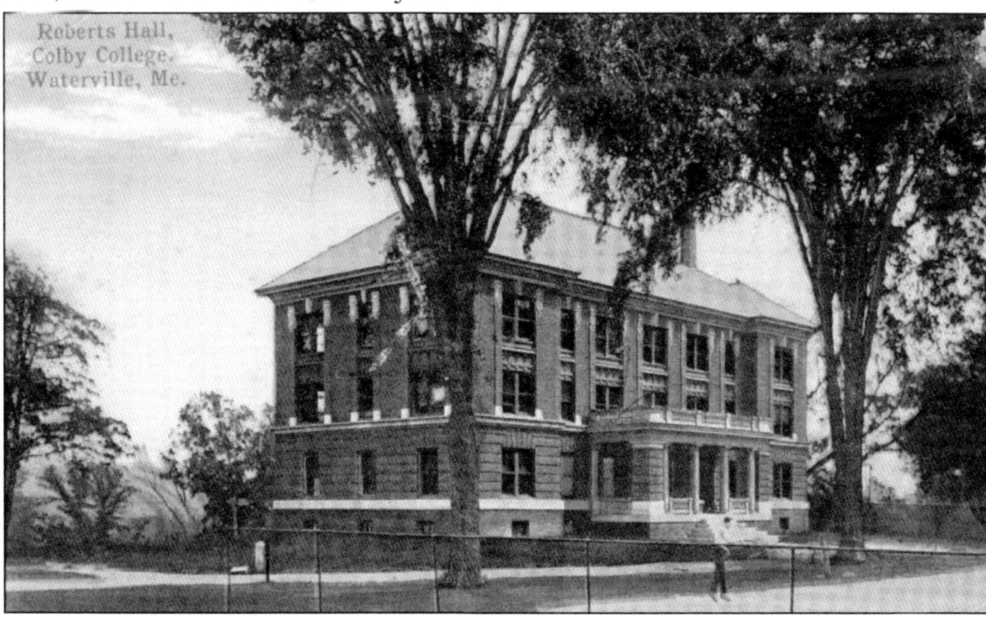

The growth of Colby under Pres. Arthur J. Roberts's leadership resulted in the construction of a new men's dormitory in 1911. Named for the man who led the college from 1908 to 1927, Roberts Hall was built northeast of Chaplin Hall from plans by Miller and Mayo, a Portland-based architectural firm. This three-story brick Colonial Revival building was designed to house 45 students in 17 suites and 5 individual rooms.

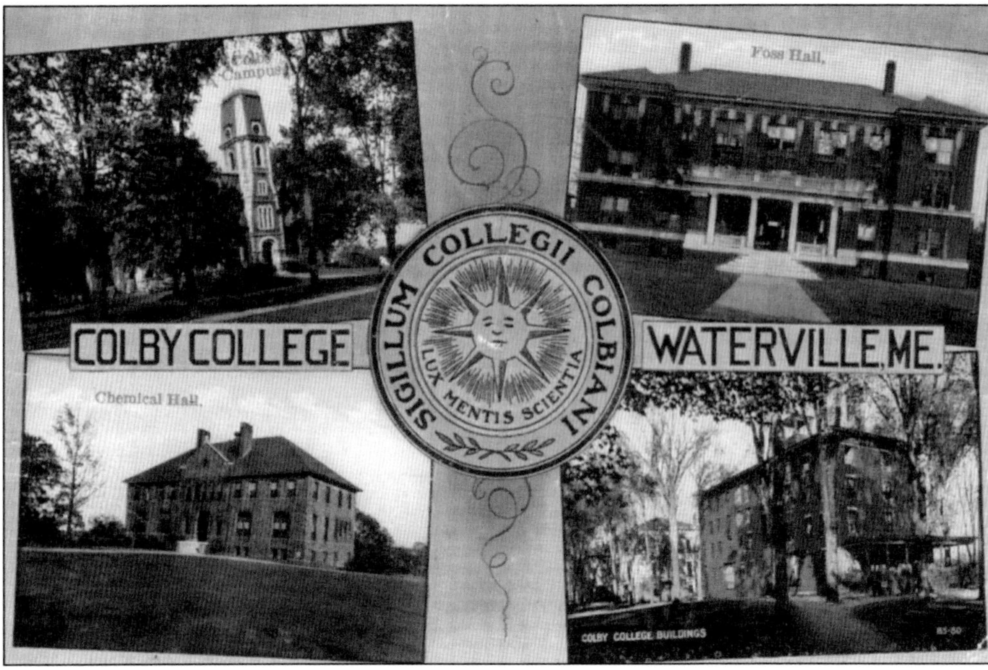

This 1918 postcard features views of four prominent Colby College buildings: Memorial Hall (upper left); Roberts Hall, incorrectly labeled as Foss Hall (upper right); Chemical Hall (lower left); and South College (lower right). At the center are the Colby seal and the college motto, *Lux Mentis Scientia*, or "Knowledge is the Light of the Mind."

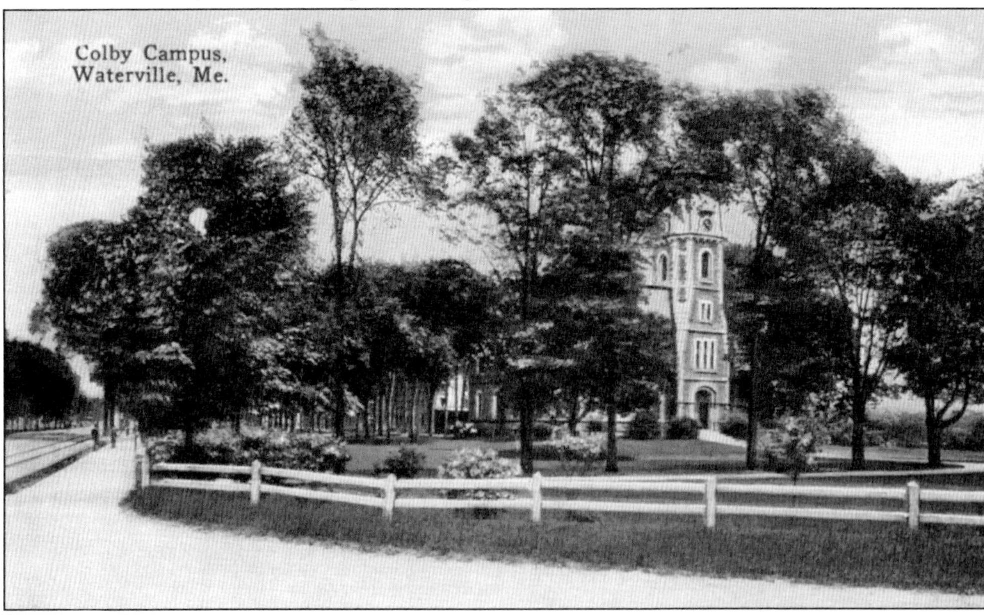

Upon approaching Colby from the south, a viewer's first glimpse showed the landscaped campus and the tower of Memorial Hall. A description of the school in the March 1911 *Board of Trade Journal* stated: "Memorial Hall, the most conspicuous building on the campus and standing at the southern end, contains the college library and the chapel. It was erected in 1869, and the academic atmosphere is given to the exterior of the building as well as its interior."

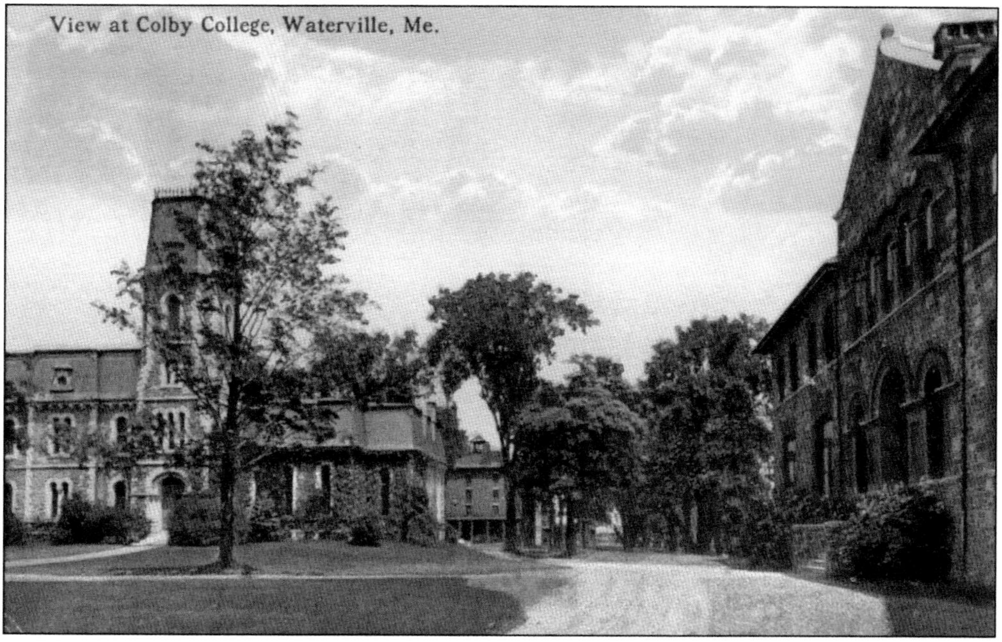

The southern end of the college is shown in this view, with Memorial Hall at left and Chemical Hall at right, framing the road that traveled through the campus parallel to the Kennebec River. An 1898 Colby brochure listed a chemistry laboratory as one of the school's most pressing needs and correctly predicted that it would be built that year.

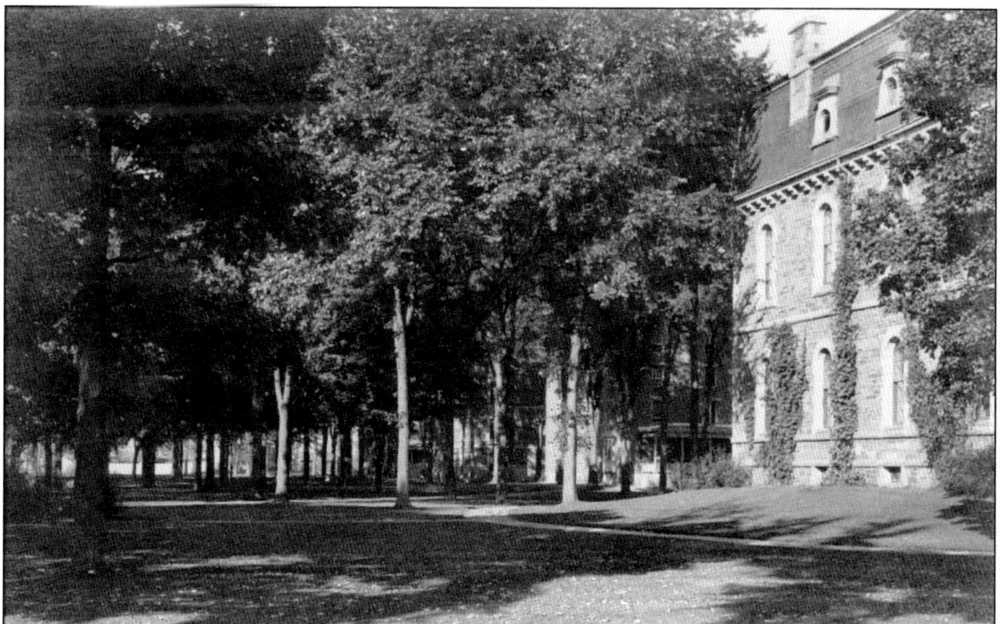

The dense foliage of the Colby campus was captured in this real-photo postcard looking north with Memorial Hall at right. Belfast photographer Charles A. Townsend published this postcard in 1907. The scene is reminiscent of an 1898 statement in *Souvenir of Waterville* that said, "Colby has one of the most commanding and beautiful situations in Maine with its extensive campus environed by magnificent old trees with their wealth of foliage."

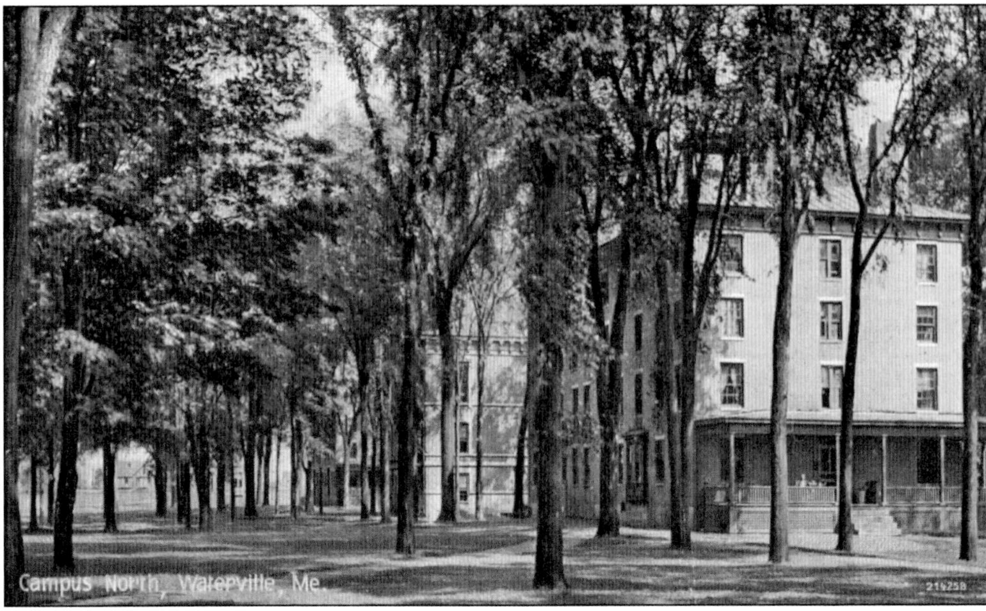

When this postcard was made in 1912, the center of the campus was this row of three original buildings—South College (at far right), followed by Champlin Hall and Chaplin Hall. As Bryant Tolles wrote in *College Buildings in New England Before 1860*, "The row at Colby, known as the Bricks, was one of New England's more handsome collegiate building groups. Situated in a grove of hardwoods, this simple symmetrical trinity dominated the rolling terrain around its campus."

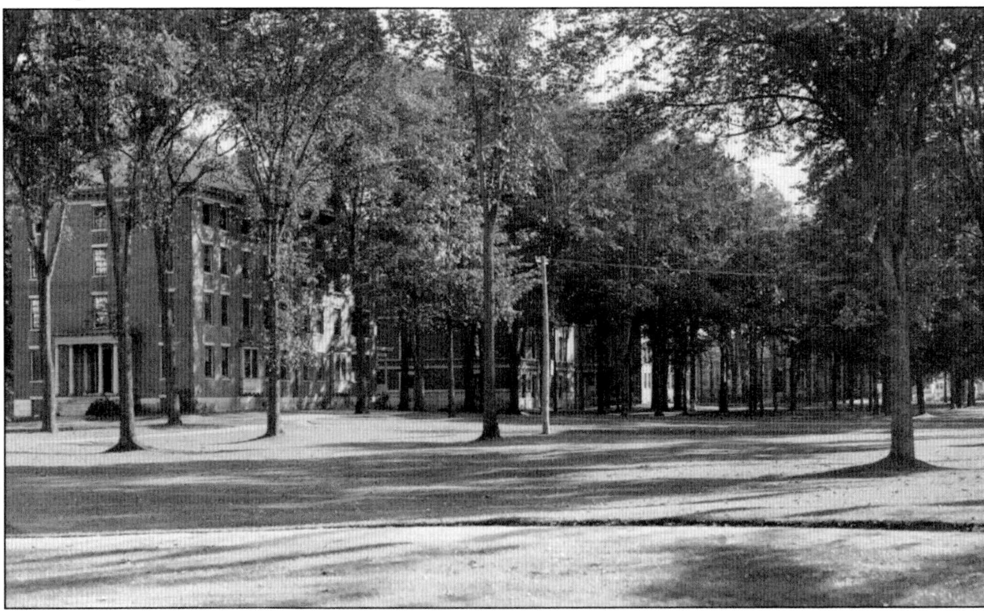
Charles A. Townsend created this 1909 real-photo postcard of the campus, a view looking south with Chaplin Hall at left. Two years later, the March 1911 *Board of Trade Journal* described Colby as such: "The campus of the college, terraced by nature and covered with large shade trees, occupies 26 acres in the northern part of Waterville and is located between College Avenue and the west bank of the Kennebec."

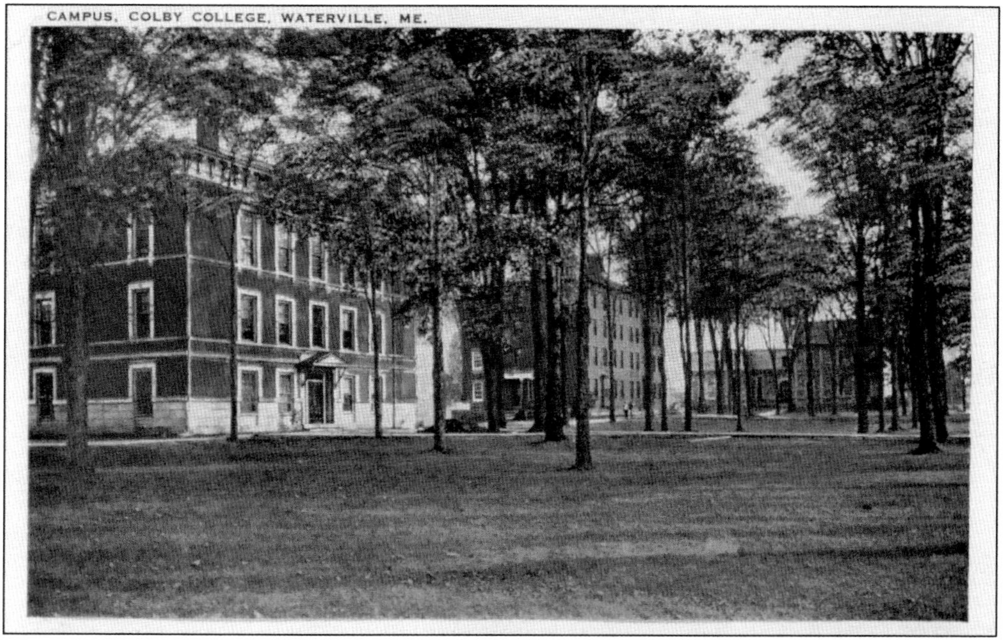

Champlin Hall (left) and South College (right) are the focus of this 1926 southward-facing view of the campus. A visitor to Colby observed in the March 1911 *Board of Trade Journal* that "the college buildings stand upon rising ground, with ample space assigned to each one, and they are beautified with well-kept lawns and connected walks shaded by tall and stately elms."

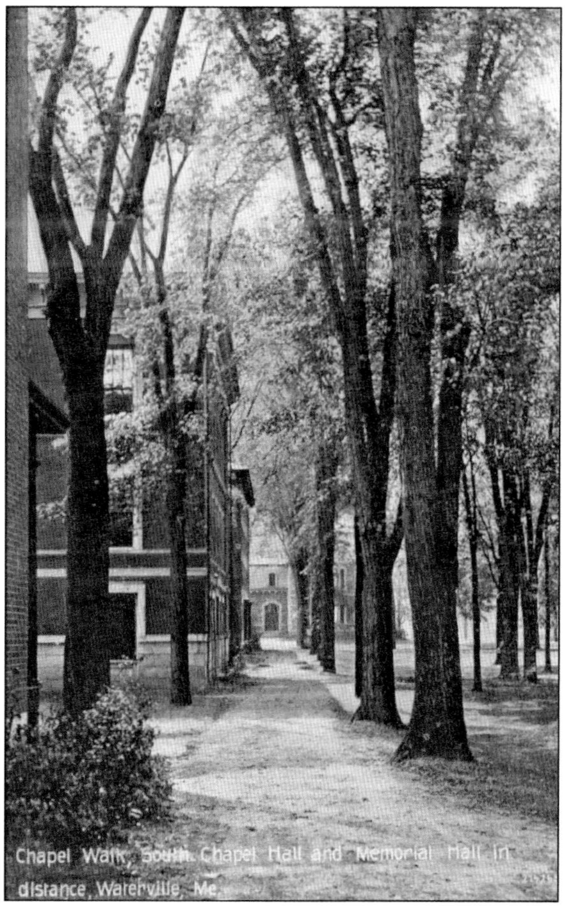

This postcard shows Chapel Walk as it leads south to Memorial Hall, passing Chaplin Hall, Champlin Hall, and South College along the way. According to the March 1911 *Board of Trade Journal*, "It was a May Day custom of students in the [1850s and 1860s] to plant trees upon the campus, and this accounts for the beautiful willows and locusts as well as the maples and elms that students of today are enjoying."

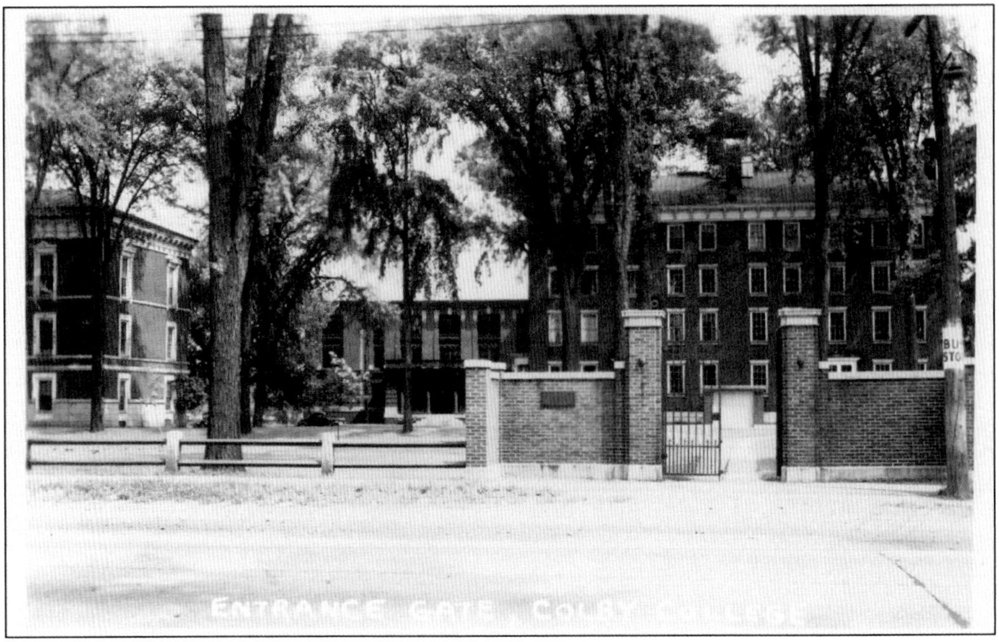

When this real-photo postcard of the college was produced in 1941, construction was already underway on the new Mayflower Hill campus. A 1916 study by Boston landscape architect Franklin A. Robinson resulted in the construction of this brick entrance gate on College Avenue. Pictured here are, from left to right, Champlin Hall, Hedman Hall, and South College.

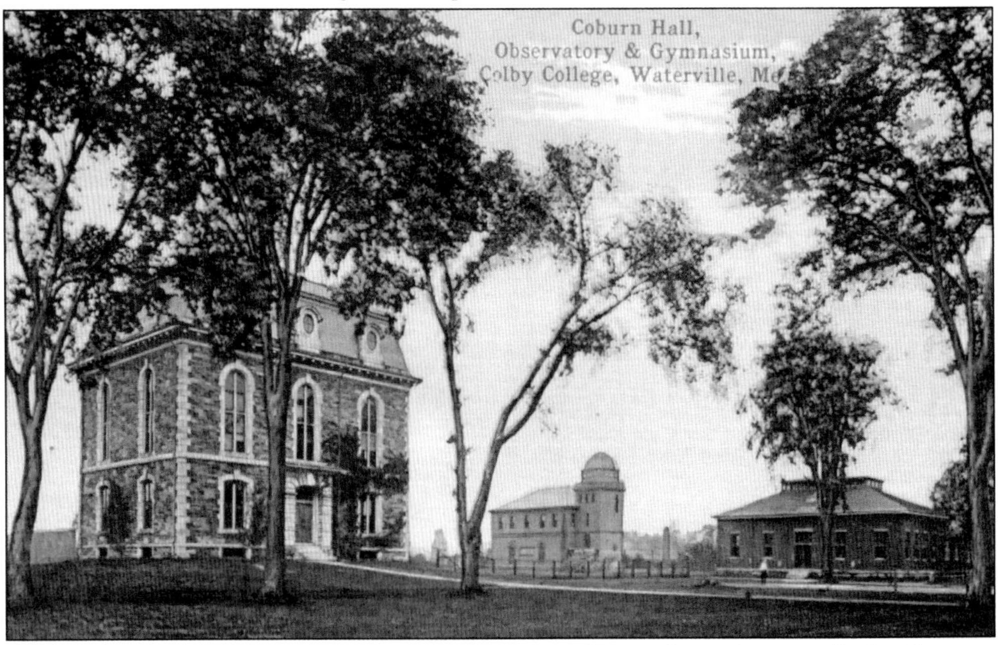

The north end of the campus was defined by, from left to right, Coburn Hall, the Shannon Observatory, and the gymnasium. The observatory was built in 1889 to the specifications of Prof. William A. Rogers, an internationally known physicist who served on the Colby faculty from 1886 until his death in 1898. Rogers came to the Colby from the Harvard College Observatory, where he was an assistant professor of astronomy.

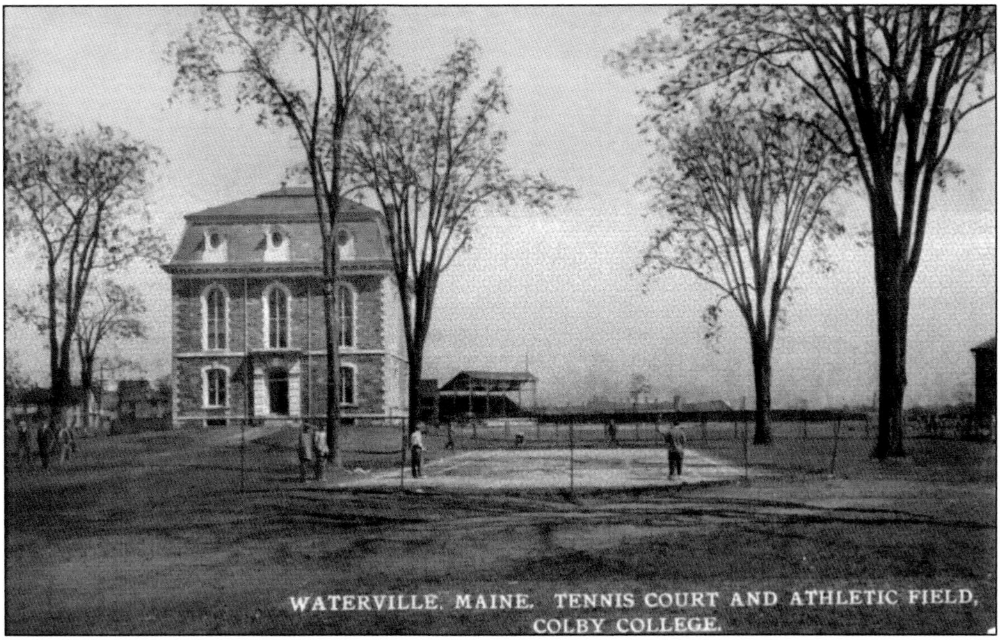

By 1900, the campus had six clay tennis courts, including the two shown here outside of Coburn Hall. Beyond these courts was the athletic field, which included a baseball diamond, a football field, a quarter-mile-long track, and a grandstand. The original grandstand, which was built in 1885, was replaced in 1904 by the one shown in the background of this image; William M. Butterfield designed this 1904 grandstand.

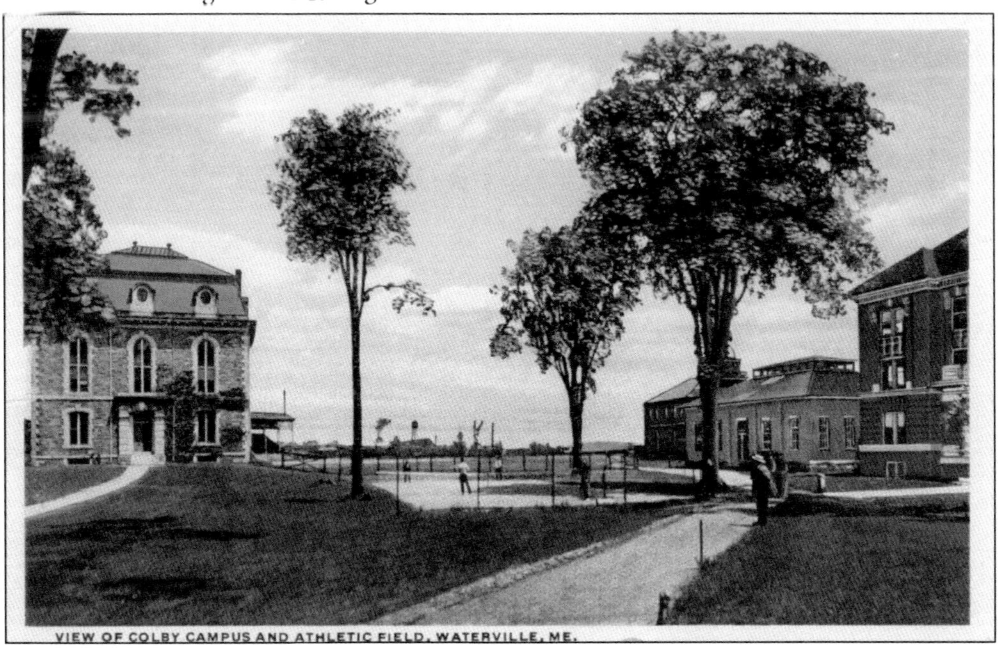

This 1921 view of the north end of the campus includes, from left to right, Coburn Hall, two tennis courts and the athletic field, the Shannon Observatory, the gymnasium, and Roberts Hall. A year earlier, the college had rebuilt the clay tennis courts at Coburn Hall to a standard that enabled Colby to participate in the Maine Intercollegiate Tennis Tournament.

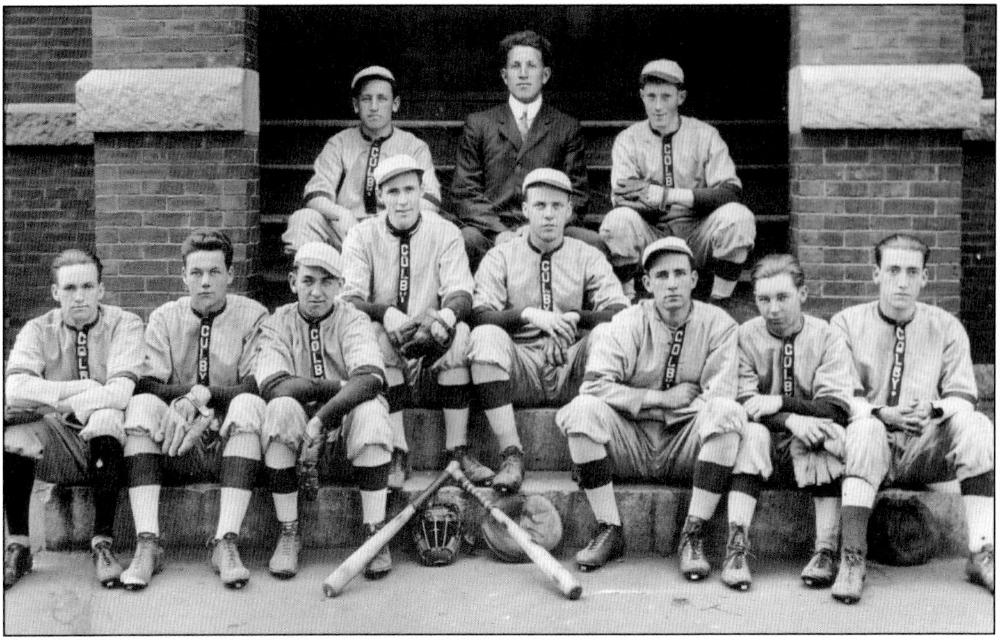

Although baseball was played at Colby as early as 1865, the first ball club was not organized until 1867. The college has fielded an official baseball team from 1875 to the present, except for two years during World War II. The uniforms in this early-20th-century postcard displayed the college colors—blue and gray—with the word "Colby" adorning the front of the shirts.

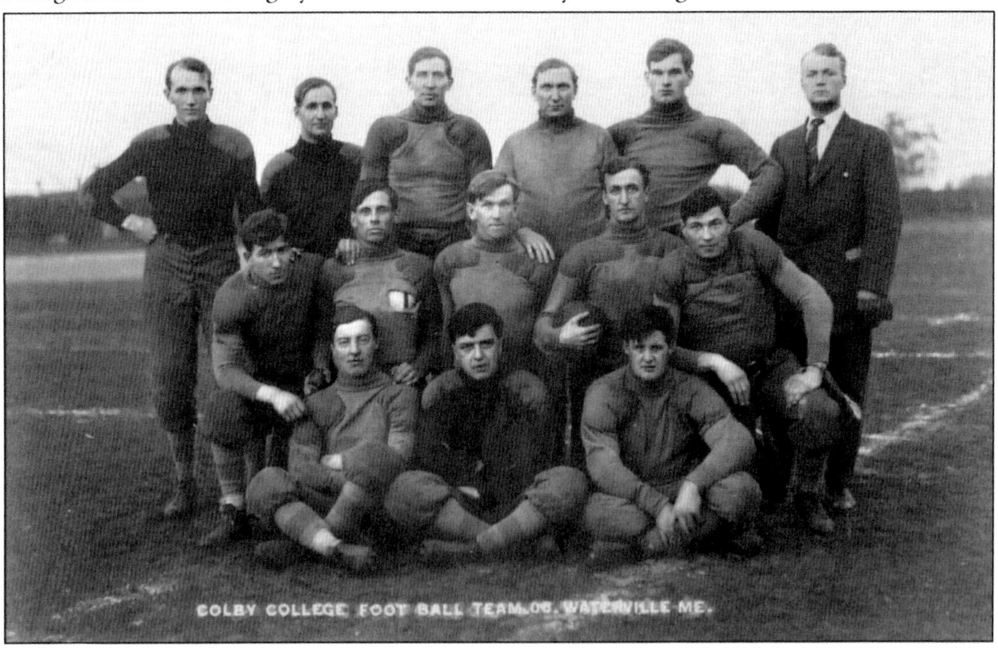

In 1886, when football was first discussed at Colby, the sport was referred to in the *Colby Echo* as "a rough and dangerous game, and even our stalwart men shrink from a football contest." The first varsity team formed in 1892. By 1908, the year that this team played, the sport had become a college fixture. This 1908 Colby College team tied Bowdoin College for the state championship, and Colby won the title the next year.

Healthy athletic rivalries developed in the late 19th century among Colby, Bowdoin, Bates, and the University of Maine. A Saturday-afternoon football game, such as this one between Colby and Maine that was played in Orono on November 4, 1911, could attract 2,500 fans. Colby supporters watched in disbelief as their team lost this game to Maine 20-0. According to the *Waterville Morning Sentinel*, "Colby was outplayed in every department of the game."

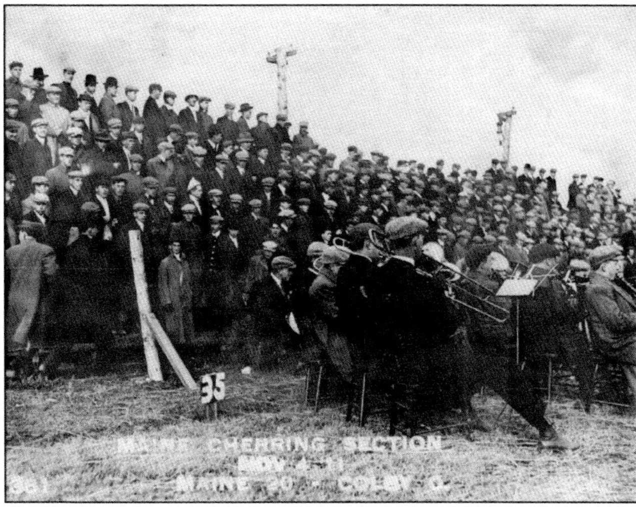

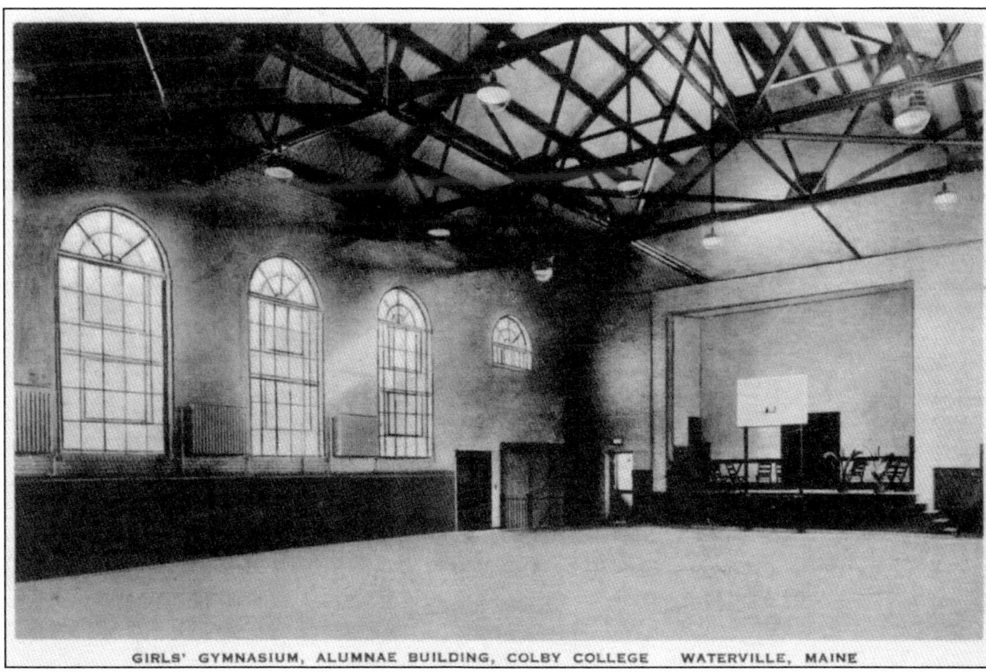

The Alumnae Building was constructed in 1928–1929 as a physical education and recreational facility for female students. In large part, Colby alumnae provided the $96,000 needed to erect the building from plans by Horace T. Muzzy; contributions included $25,000 from Florence Dunn of Waterville and $10,000 from Louise Helen Coburn of Skowhegan. Colby admitted the school's first female student, Mary Low, in 1871, followed by Coburn, who began her studies at Colby in 1873.

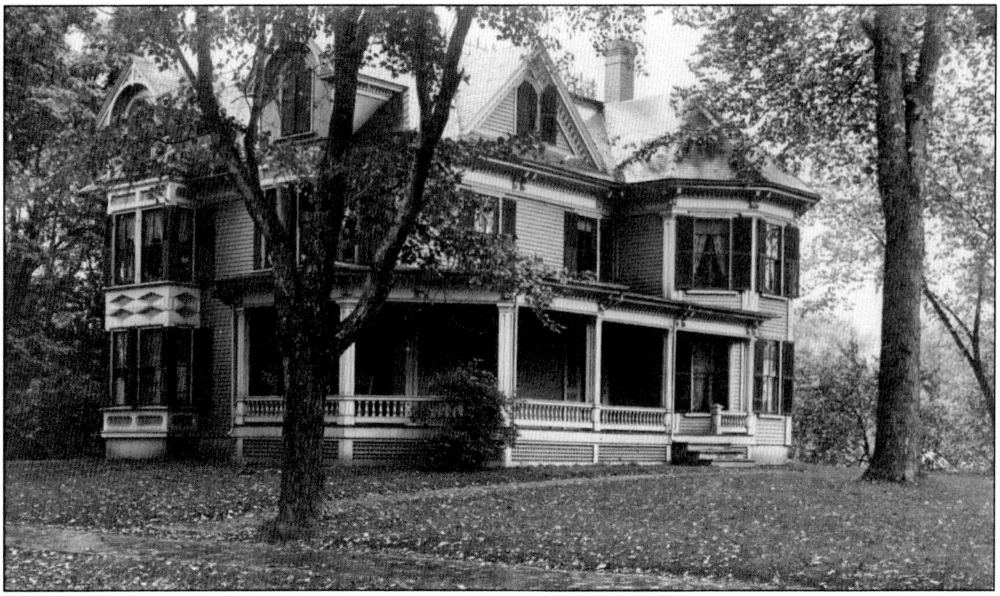

Colby's chapter of Delta Kappa Epsilon, the college's first fraternity, was founded in 1845. In 1898, DKE became the first fraternity to have its own house when it purchased the Bunker residence on College Avenue for $6,000. DKE converted the home to a fraternity house under the supervision of architect John Calvin Stevens. In 1945, the DKE house became home to the American Legion Department of Maine.

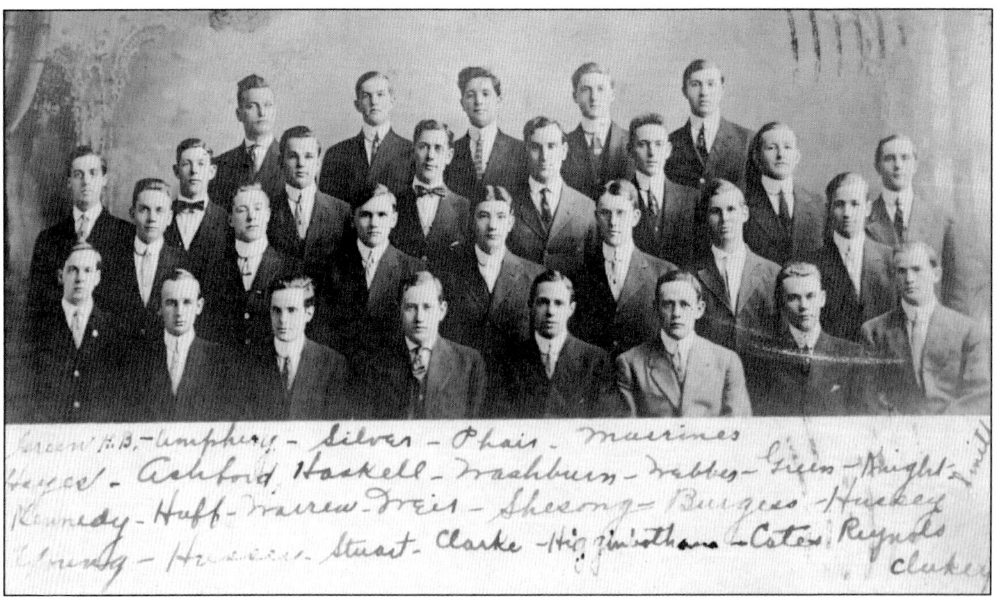

The Colby chapter of the Alpha Tau Omega fraternity began in 1892; ATO members assembled for this group picture in 1911. Ernest Cummings Marriner (class of 1913) is at far right in the fourth row—Marriner served the college for 37 years in various roles as librarian, professor, dean of men, and dean of faculty. His 1963 book, *The History of Colby College*, is a major source of information about the school. (Waterville Historical Society.)

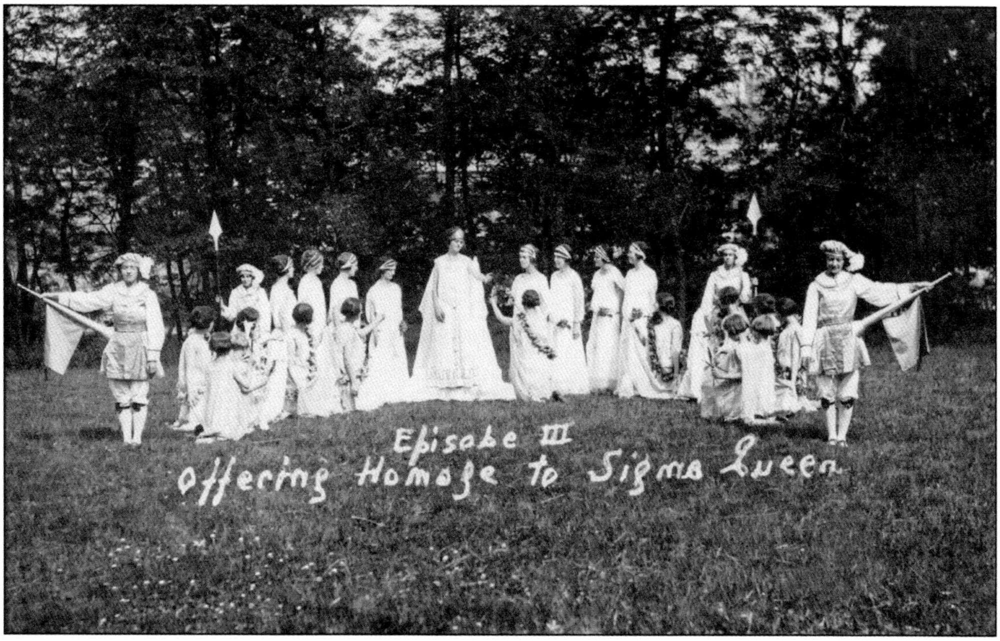

In 1874, four women in the class of 1877 founded Sigma Kappa, Colby's first sorority. In 1924, the sorority celebrated its founding with an elaborate pageant staged on campus. This is a scene from Episode III, "Offering Homage to Sigma Queen." The heralds standing at either side were dressed in lavender costumes.

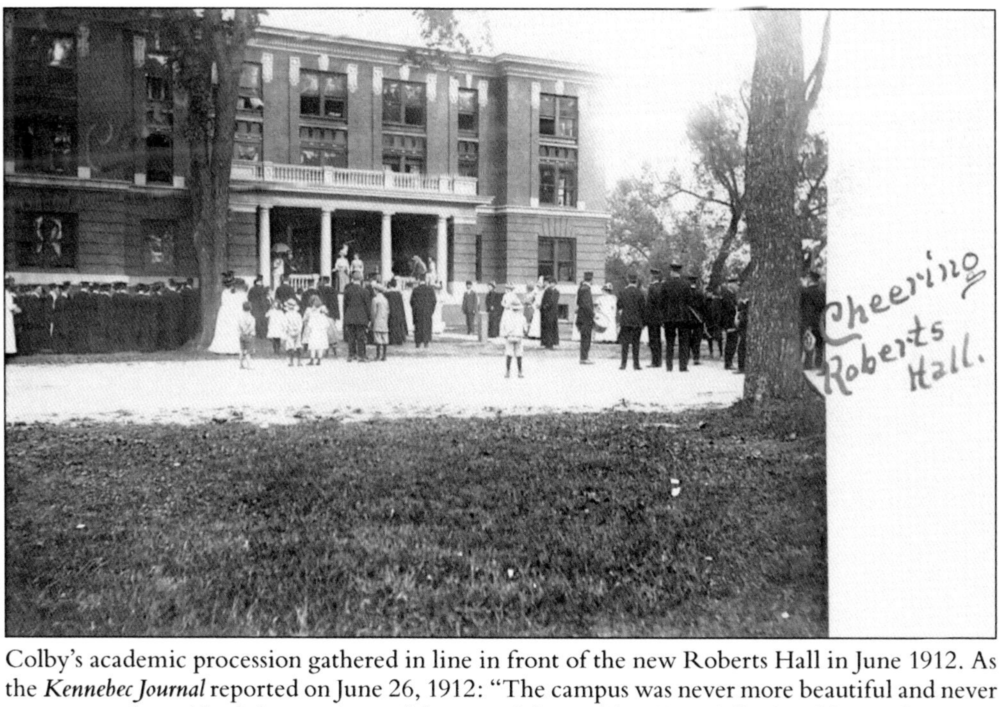

Colby's academic procession gathered in line in front of the new Roberts Hall in June 1912. As the *Kennebec Journal* reported on June 26, 1912: "The campus was never more beautiful and never were more alumni back for reunions of classes and fraternities. Especially the older graduates are surprised and perhaps saddened, for they have not found the old Colby, but the Colby of today." (Waterville Historical Society.)

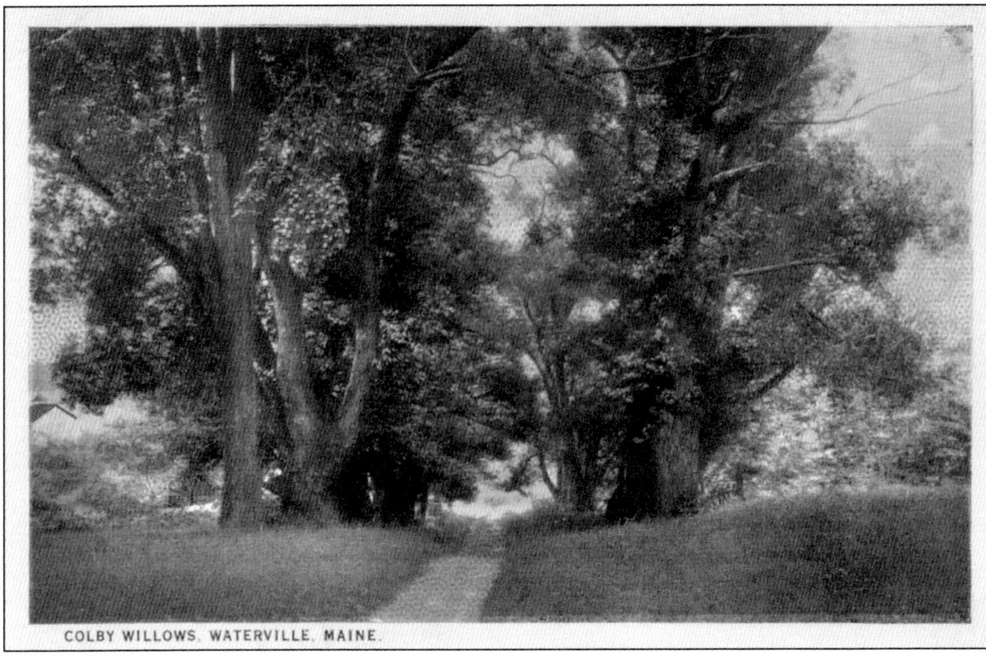

The Colby Willows, which extended on either side of a path from South College to the Kennebec River, were one of the most beloved features on campus. Freshman and sophomores planted the first willows on campus in 1832. In 1880, the *Colby Echo* asked of the willows, "How many men through all these years have delighted to leave their study tables and books and to seek rest beneath their cooling shade?"

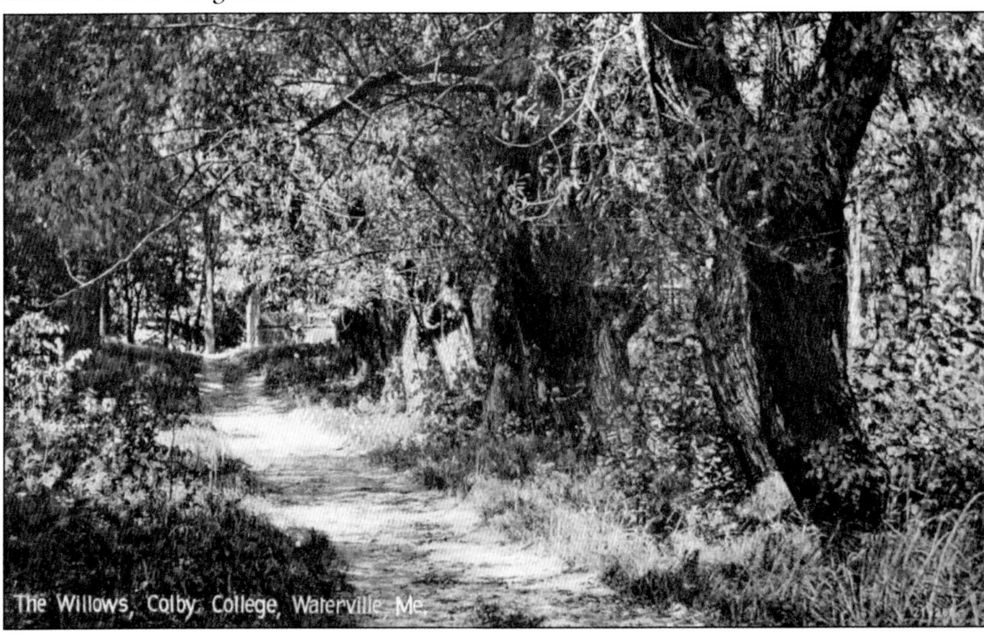

Willow Day became a graduation tradition in which new trees were planted to preserve the path to the river. In 1927, the author's mother, Esther Knudsen, a graduating senior, began the Willow Day address with these words: "About us lean the willows clad in their cloaks of green and wrapped in a veil of tradition. It is with a keen sense of pride that we view them."

Nine

The New Colby Campus

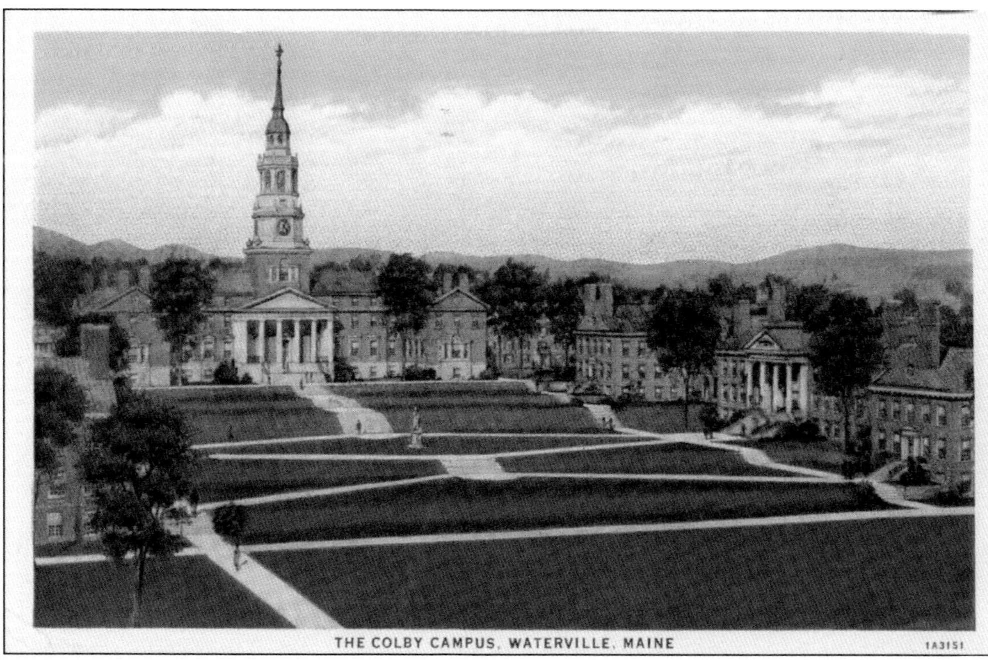

In 1930, the Colby College Board of Trustees voted to build a new campus. In 1931, Jens Frederick Larson, a noted college architect who favored using the Georgian Revival style, drew the plans for the new campus and its buildings. In an echo of Thomas Jefferson's vision for the University of Virginia, Larson made the library the focal point with a long lawn in front framed by buildings on either side.

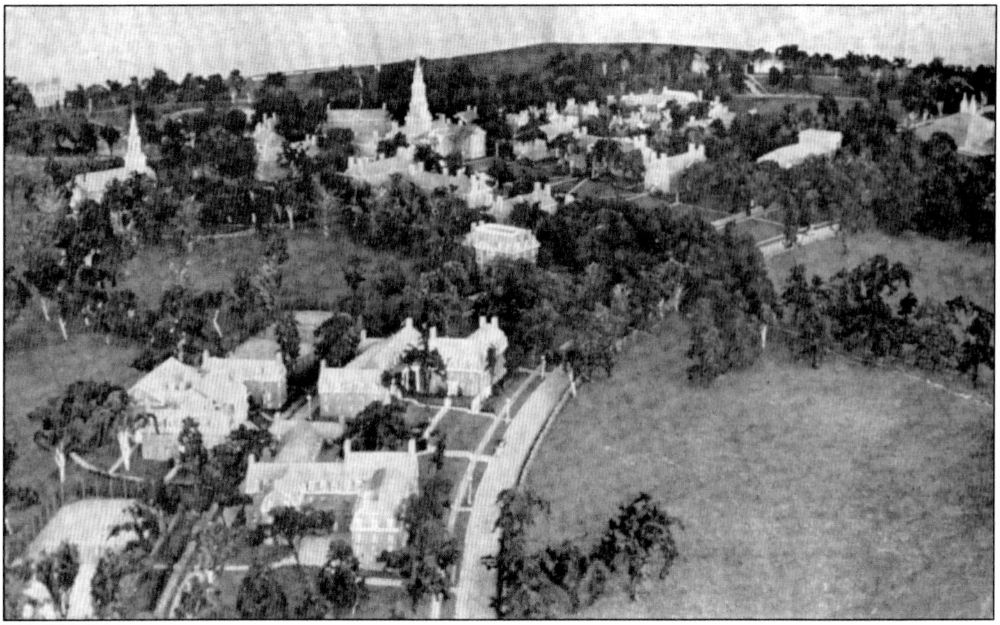

To promote the development of the new campus, the college appropriated $5,000 in 1937 to create a model of the new Colby. This postcard of "the Colby College of Tomorrow" described key features of the model: "The spire on the left marks the Lorimer Memorial Chapel, while the taller spire nearer the middle surmounts the library. In the foreground are the dormitories and social union for women students."

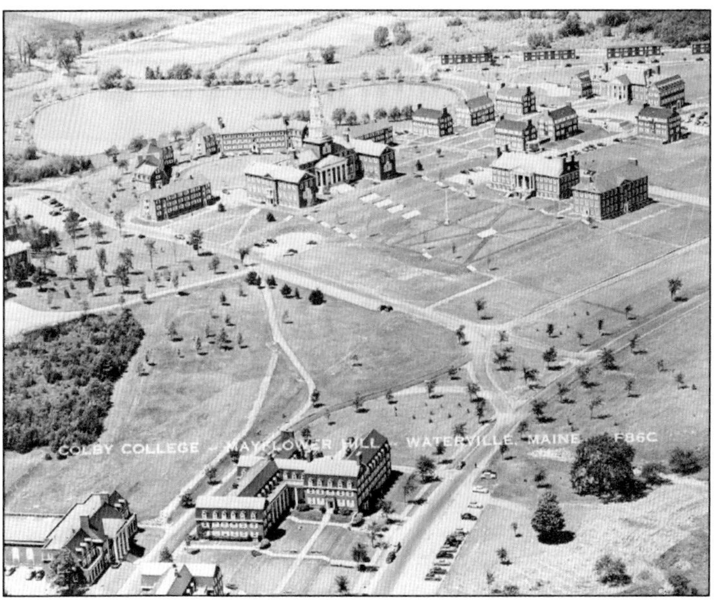

"The Colby College of Tomorrow" was becoming a reality when this aerial view was created in the mid-1950s. Runnels Union and the women's dormitories are in the foreground, while Lorimer Chapel is to the left. Miller Library dominates the upper center, with the men's dormitories behind it. The fraternity houses, Roberts Union, and the two science buildings are at upper right. (Penobscot Marine Museum.)

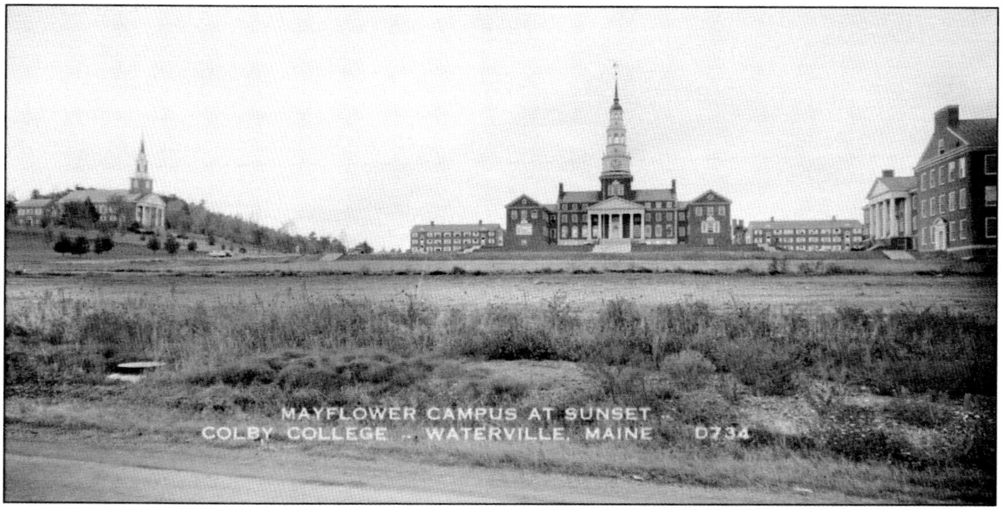

This photograph captures the fresh, unfinished appearance of Colby's Mayflower Hill campus in the 1950s. From left to right are Lorimer Chapel, Averill Hall, Miller Library, Johnson Hall, Keyes Science Building, and the Life Sciences Building. The open site on the left side of the lawn in front of the library awaits the Lovejoy Classroom Building (built in 1959) and the Eustis Administration Building (built in 1960). (Penobscot Marine Museum.)

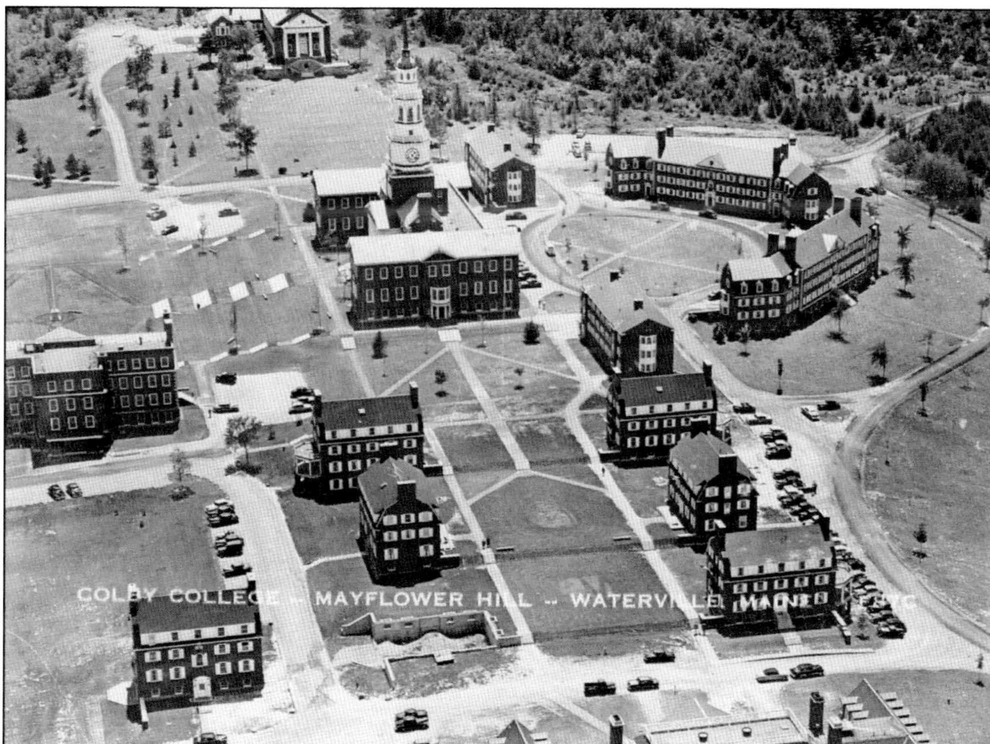

This aerial view of the Colby campus in the mid-1950s shows the roof of Roberts Union in the foreground and six fraternity houses, along with the foundation of a seventh. Keyes Science Building is at left, Miller Library is in the center, and the men's dormitories are at right. Lorimer Chapel is partially visible at the top. (Penobscot Marine Museum.)

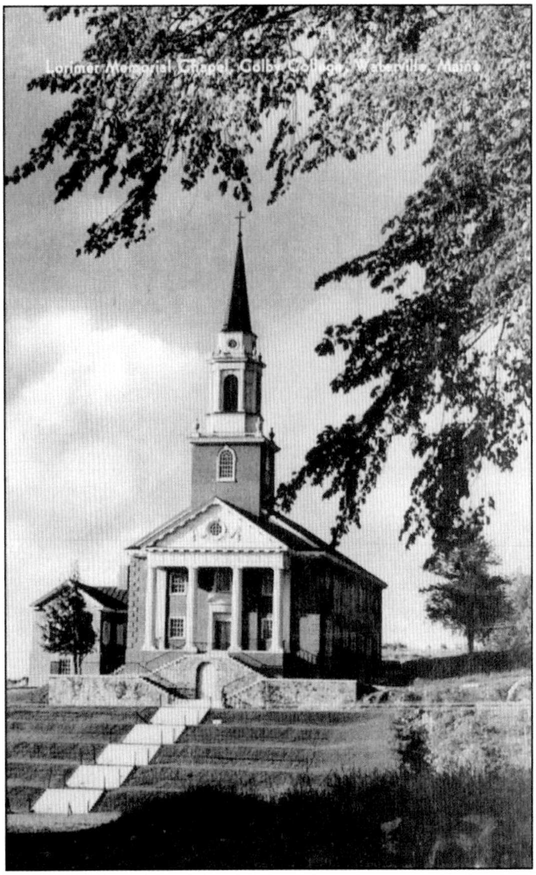

The first building constructed on the new campus was Lorimer Chapel, which was dramatically sited on a high point overlooking the campus. The donor was George H. Lorimer (class of 1898) of Philadelphia, the editor of the *Saturday Evening Post*, who pledged $200,000 to build a chapel in memory of his father, Rev. George C. Lorimer, a noted Baptist minister. Ground was broken in 1937, the cornerstone was laid in 1938, and the building opened in 1947.

This view from Lorimer Chapel looks down upon Miller Library with Averill Hall at left and Keyes Science Building at right. This 1960s postcard shows Averill Hall as it looked when the author lived there in a first-floor room as a freshman.

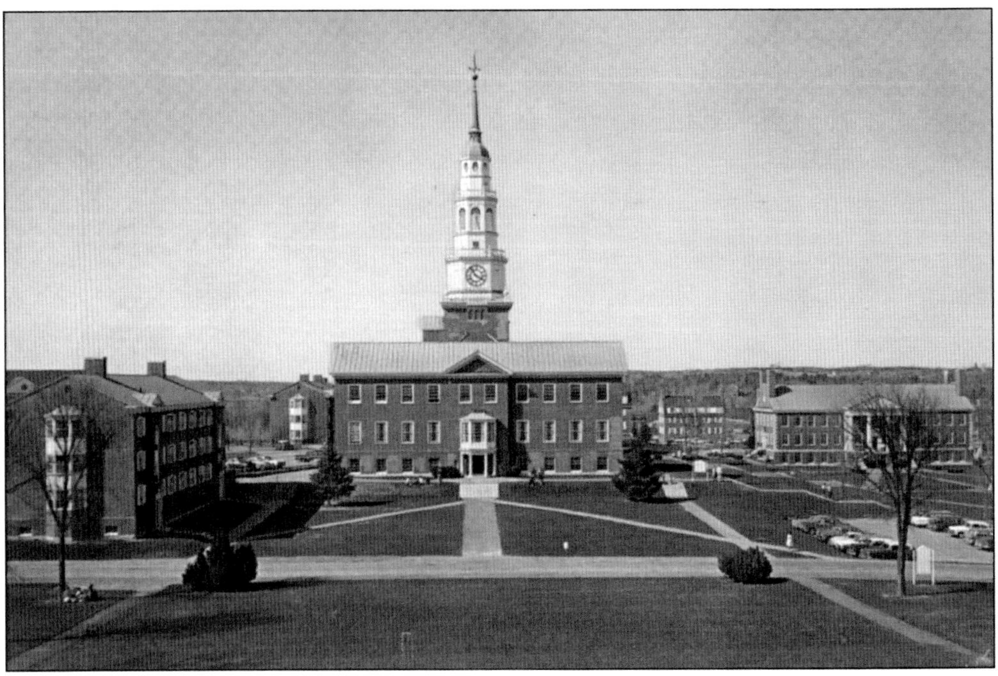

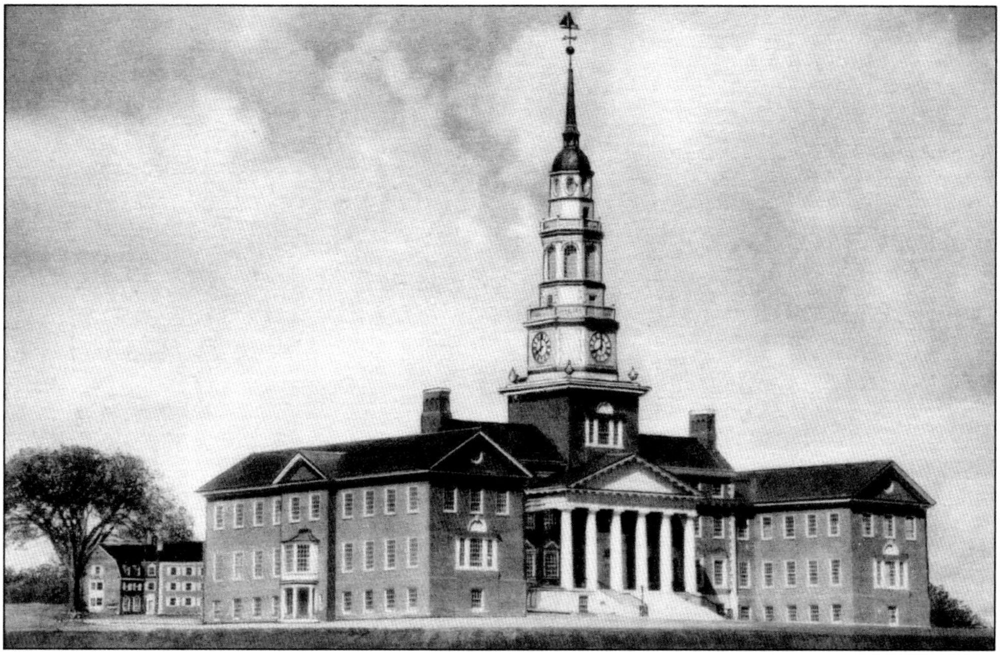

Symbolic of Colby's motto, "Knowledge is the Light of the Mind," Miller Library is the focal point of the campus. It is a stately Georgian Revival building with a classical portico, wings, and a tower. The major donor, Merton L. Miller, laid the cornerstone in 1939, and the building was partially in use by 1947.

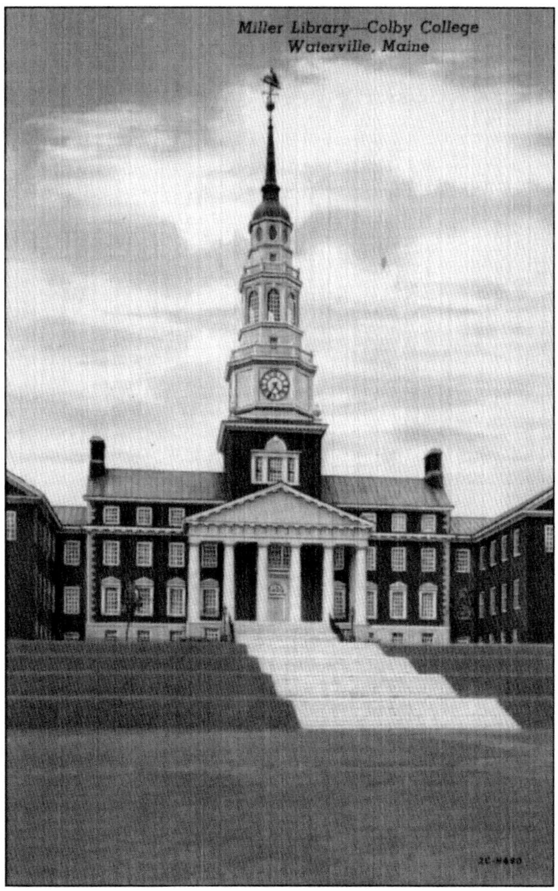

The terraced staircase and lawn in front of the Miller Library have been the site of many college graduations, with noted speakers ranging from Adlai Stevenson to Tony Blair. In 1947, 120,000 books were moved from the old library in Memorial Hall to Miller Library. Since then, the collection has grown to include 900,000 books, plus journals, microfilms, musical scores, sound recordings, videos, and manuscripts.

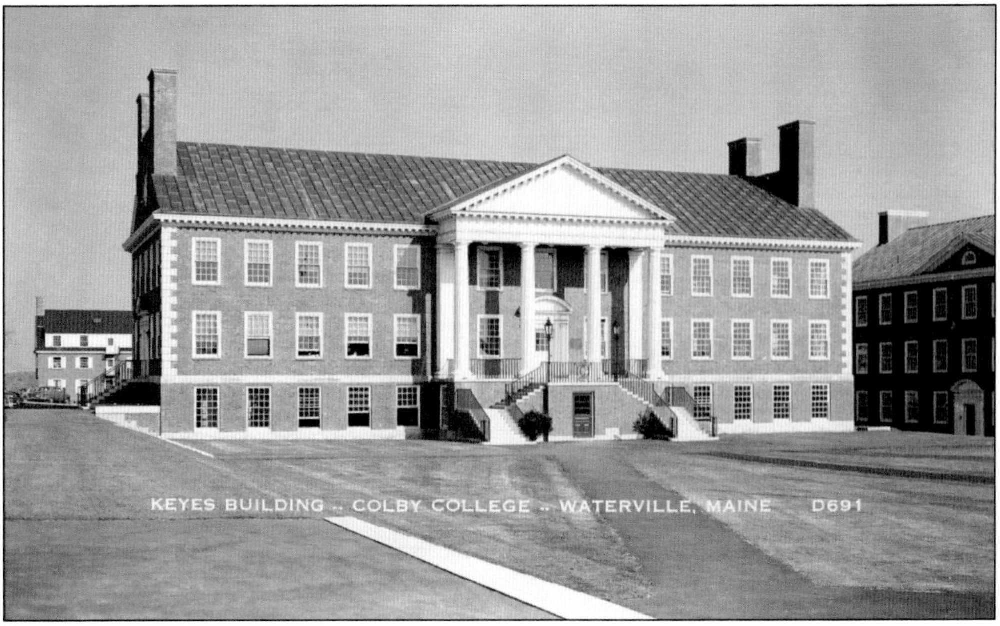

The chemistry and physics departments were located in Keyes Science Building, which opened in 1950. The $600,000 for its construction came from the fortune of Martin Keyes, founder of the Keyes Fibre Company, a highly successful local manufacturer of paper products. Keyes's daughter and son-in-law, Mabel and George Averill, were staunch supporters of Colby and provided the connection that made this support possible. (Penobscot Marine Museum.)

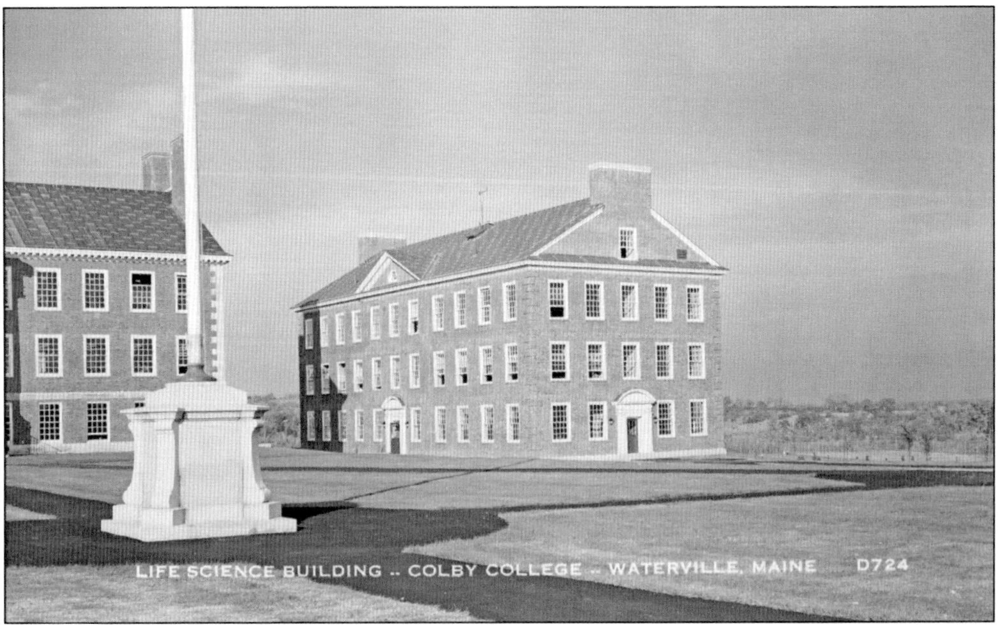

The Life Sciences Building, adjacent to the Keyes Science Building, opened in 1952 to house the geology, biology, and mathematics departments. The Life Sciences Building was renovated in 1978 and renamed the Arey Life Sciences Building; it was connected to the new F.W. Olin Science Center in 1996. A row of four science buildings now stands on one side of the lawn in front of Miller Library: Mudd, Keyes, Arey, and Olin. (Penobscot Marine Museum.)

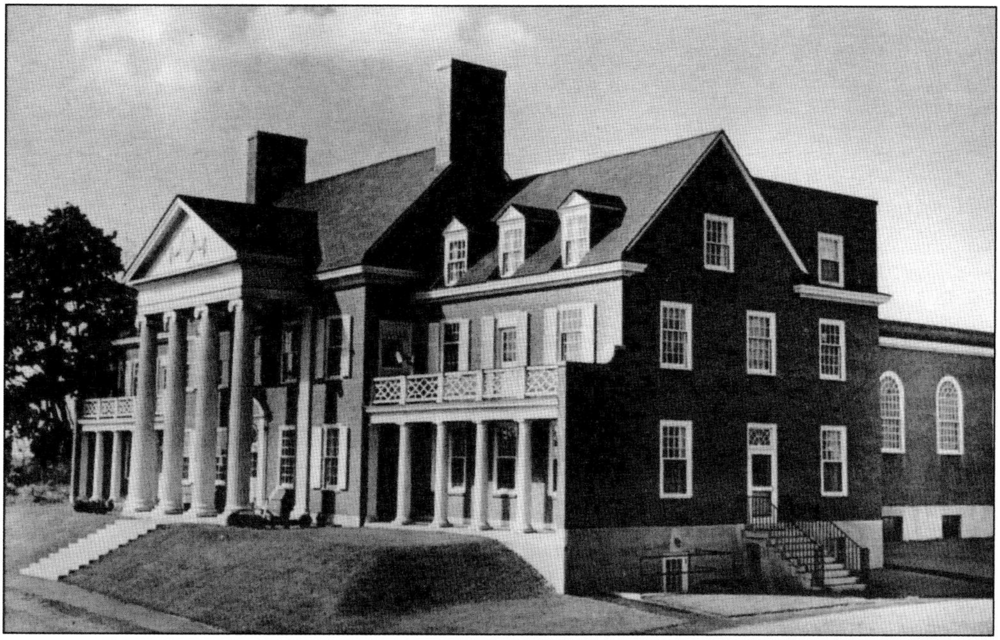

The Women's Union, which opened in 1942, offered several facilities, including lounges, a music room, a dramatics workshop, a dance studio, sorority rooms, and a gymnasium. In 1959, the building was renamed in honor of Ninetta M. Runnals, a 1908 Colby graduate who served as dean of women from 1920 to 1926 and again from 1928 until her retirement in 1949. Runnals helped raise $100,000 from 1,200 alumnae for the union that would one day bear her name.

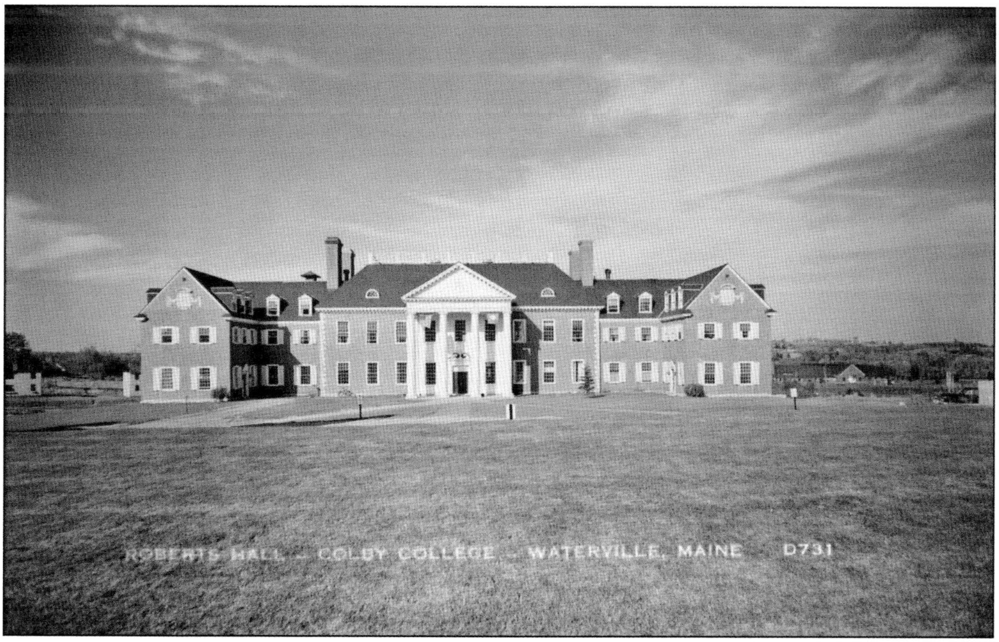

Constructed between 1939 and 1947, Roberts Union served as the dining hall and social center for male students. The cost of the building's construction was covered by gifts from 2,000 Colby alumni in memory of Arthur J. Roberts, president of the college from 1908 to 1927. The east wing of this building housed the college's infirmary. (Penobscot Marine Museum.)

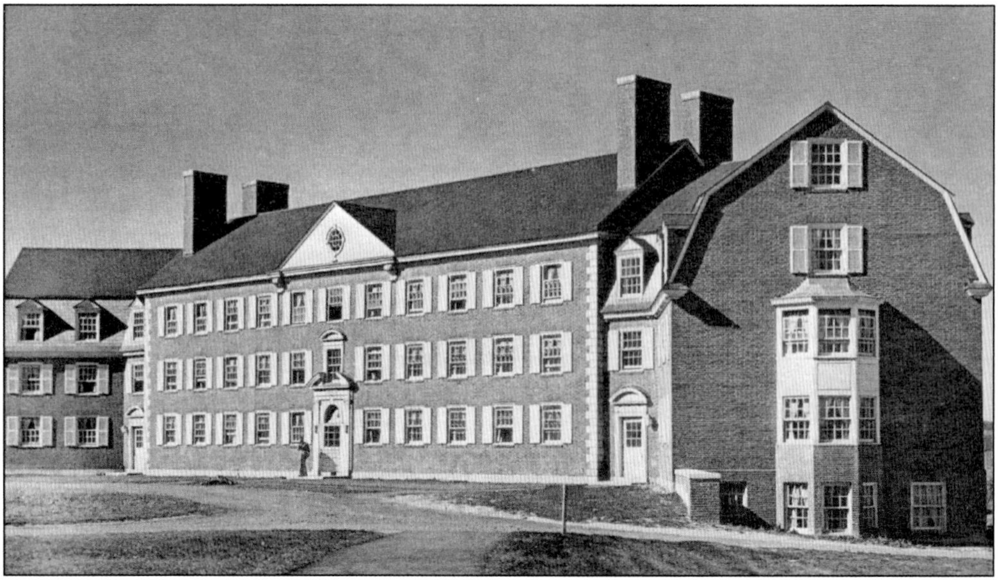

Behind Miller Library are the east and west dormitories for men, designed to accommodate a total of 215 students. Construction of these buildings began in 1938, was halted during World War II, and was completed in 1946. This view shows the east dormitory, which consists of three sections, each named for a Colby president: Butler, Champlin, and Small. The adjacent west dormitory also bears the names of three presidents: Chaplin, Pepper, and Robins.

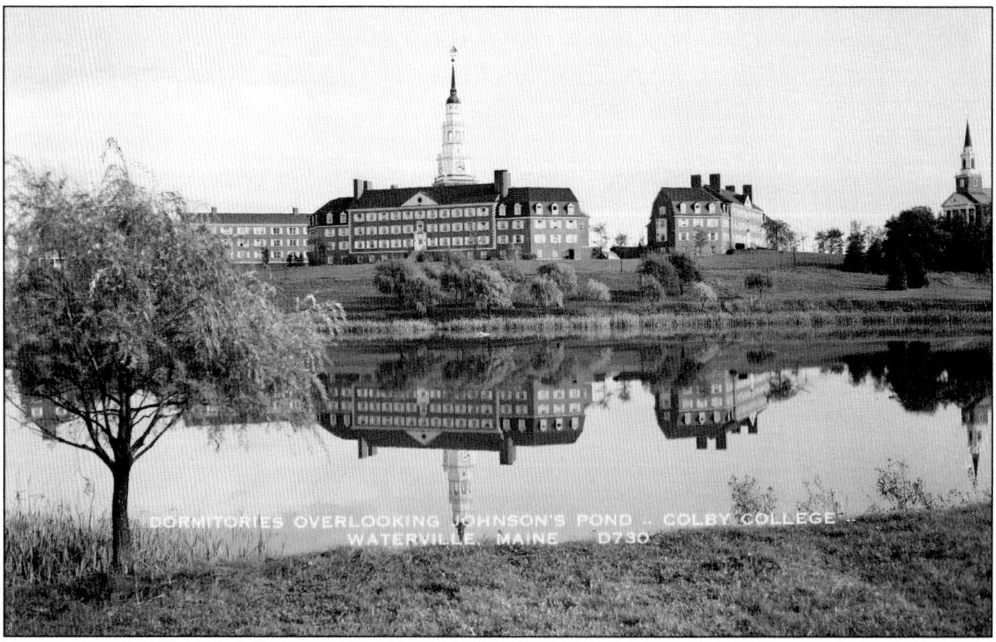

The rear elevations of the east and west men's dormitories are at the center of this view of the campus from across Johnson Pond. Referred to as the "men's resident group," the two dorms were described as follows in a c. 1946 guide to the campus: "Each consists of three sections with separate entrances, lounges and resident faculty members. This arrangement eliminates the conventional long noisy corridors and in this respect resembles the English type of university quarters." (Penobscot Marine Museum.)

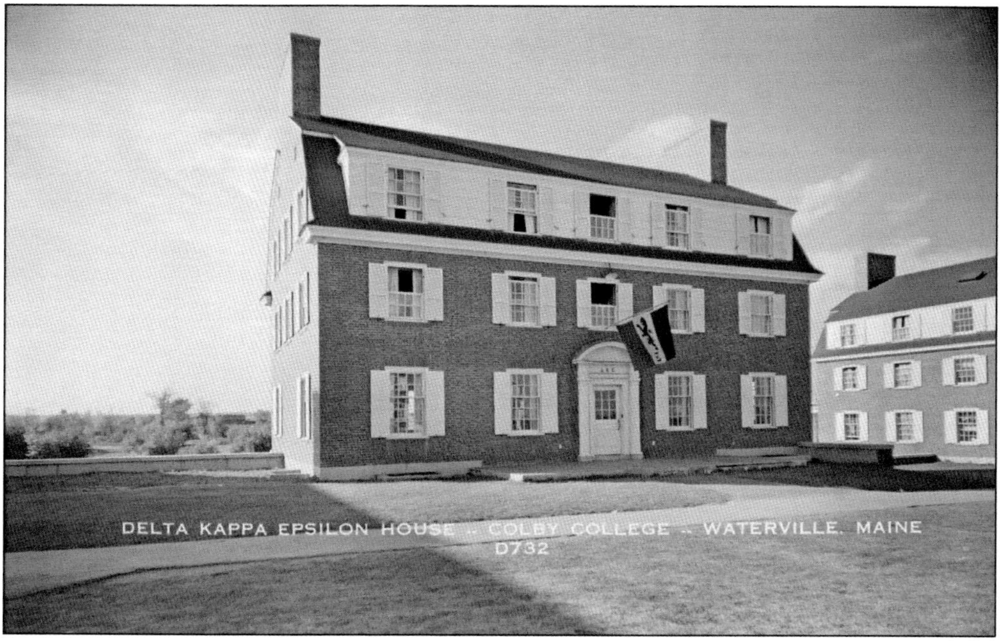

The Jens Frederick Larson plan for the Colby campus envisioned a fraternity row consisting of houses located between Miller Library and Roberts Union. Between 1948 and 1958, seven fraternities built houses at this location in partnership with the college. Delta Kappa Epsilon, shown here, was formed in 1845 and was Colby's first fraternity. (Penobscot Marine Museum.)

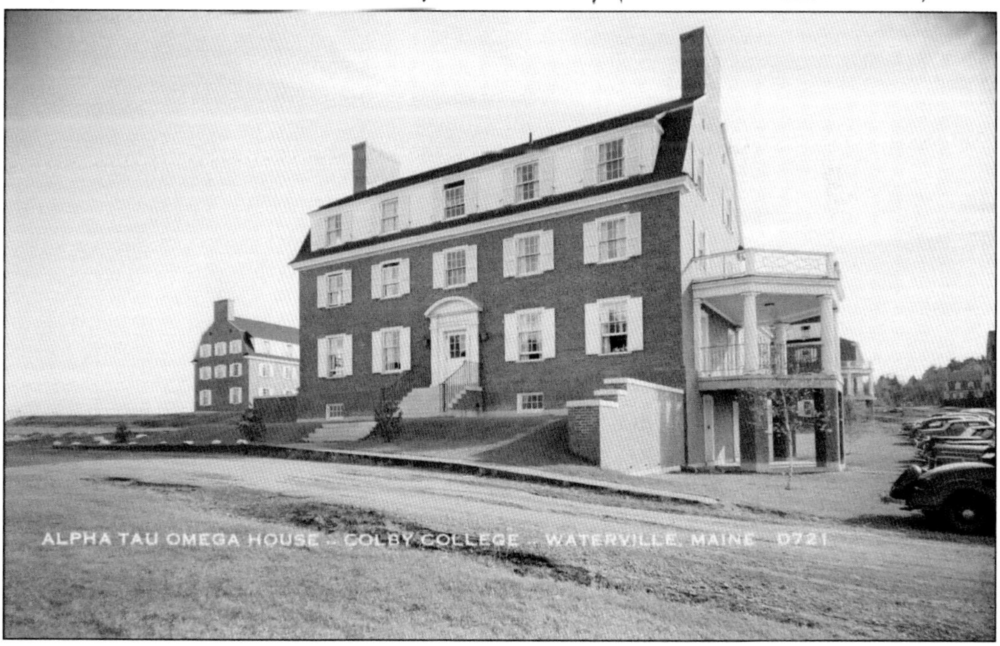

The Gamma Alpha Chapter of Alpha Tau Omega was organized at Colby in 1892 and became one of the college's most popular fraternities. The ATO house, shown here, and the DKE house were the first to be constructed on Fraternity Row. In the 1980s, during the presidency of William R. Cotter, the fraternity system was ended, and the fraternity houses were converted into residences for the general student body. (Penobscot Marine Museum.)

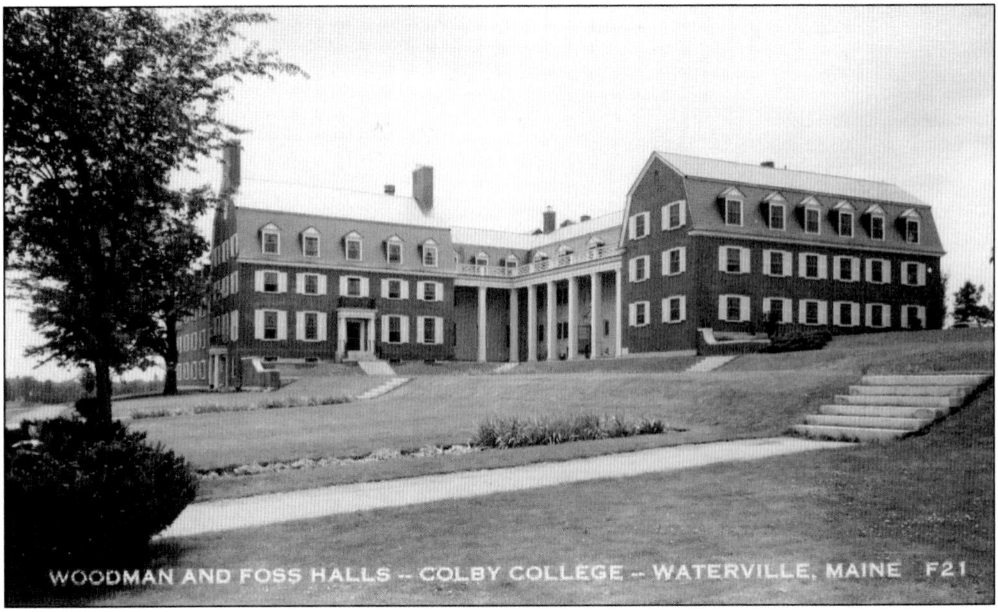

The Jens Frederick Larson plan called for a women's side of the campus consisting of a student union flanked by matching dormitory complexes, each to contain two halls. Construction started on Woodman and Foss Hall in 1951, and both were completed in 1952 for a total cost of $900,000. Woodman was named for Eleanor B. Woodman, a generous supporter of the college, and Foss perpetuated the name of Foss Hall on the old campus.

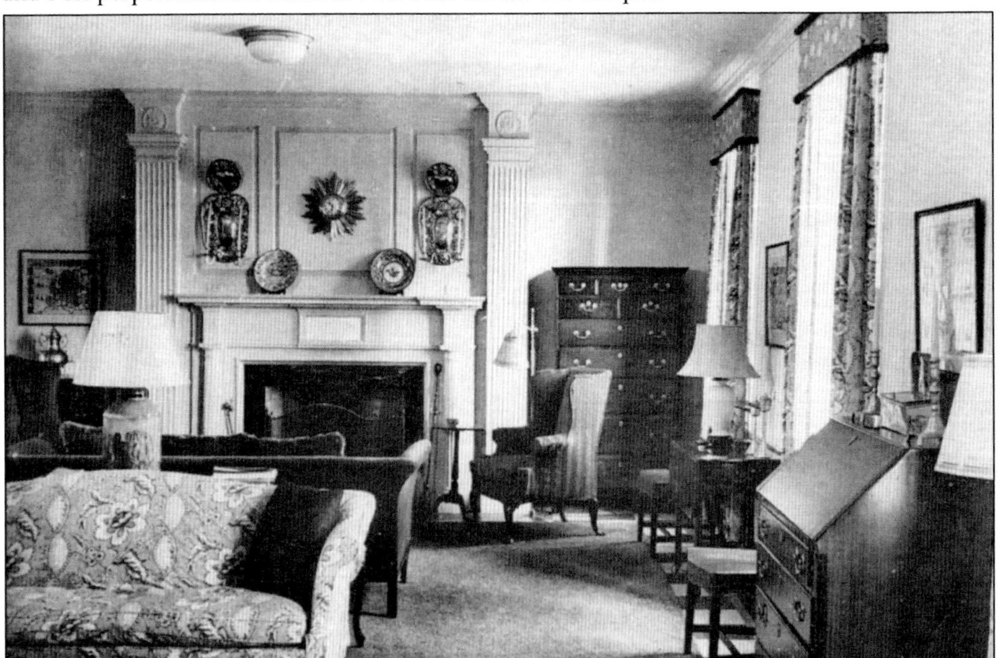

The first floors of the women's dormitories featured beautifully furnished lounges like this, the Lane Room in Mary Low Hall. In 1920, Mary Low Carver (class of 1875), Colby's first female graduate, spoke of the role of women in the college: "A line of Colby Women, coming, ever coming in brave processional, adding touch of color and charm and womanly worth."

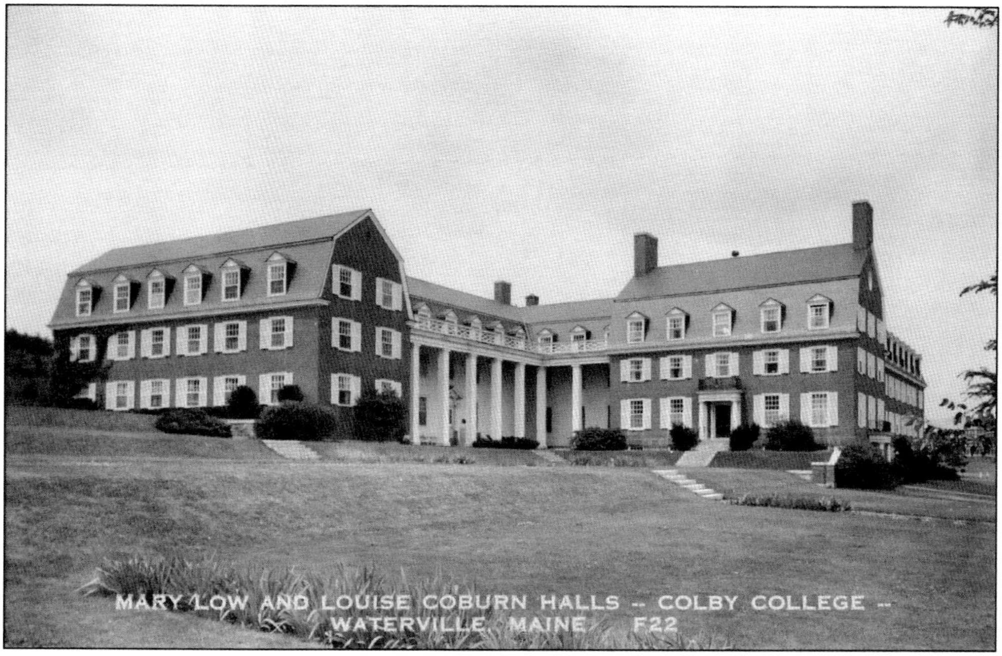

Low and Coburn Halls were completed in 1942 for a total cost of $430,000. Though described in a c. 1946 guide to the campus as under one roof, "the dormitory actually consists of two separate units, each with its own entrance, lounge, and dining room. Each wing accommodates about 80 girls." The wing at left was named for Mary Low (class of 1875), Colby's first female graduate, while the wing at right commemorates Louise Coburn (class of 1877) the school's first female trustee.

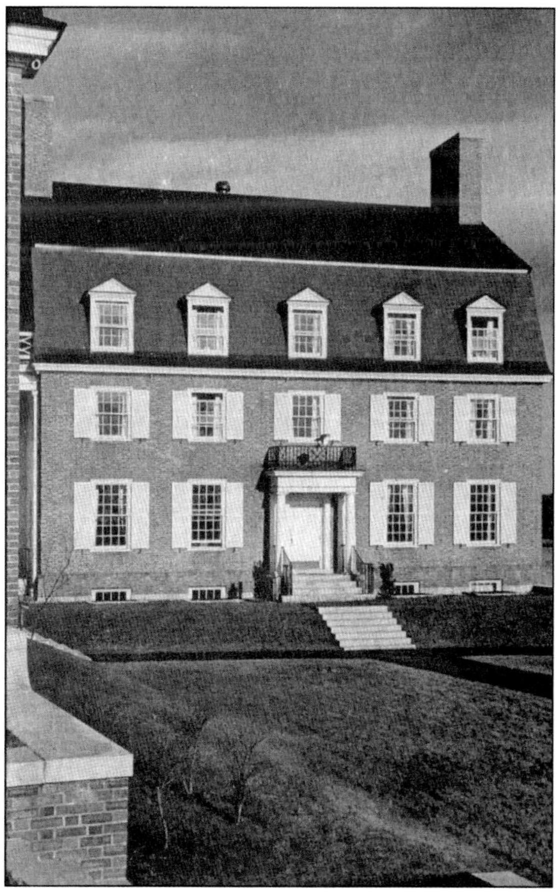

In naming one of its dormitories for Louise Helen Coburn, Colby honored one of its first female graduates. Born in Skowhegan in 1856, Coburn was the daughter of Stephen Coburn (class of 1839), and the niece of Gov. Abner Coburn, one Maine's wealthiest men and a generous supporter of educational institutions. Louise Coburn became an accomplished botanist, poet, and historian who is remembered today for her two-volume book, *Skowhegan on the Kennebec*, a history of the area.

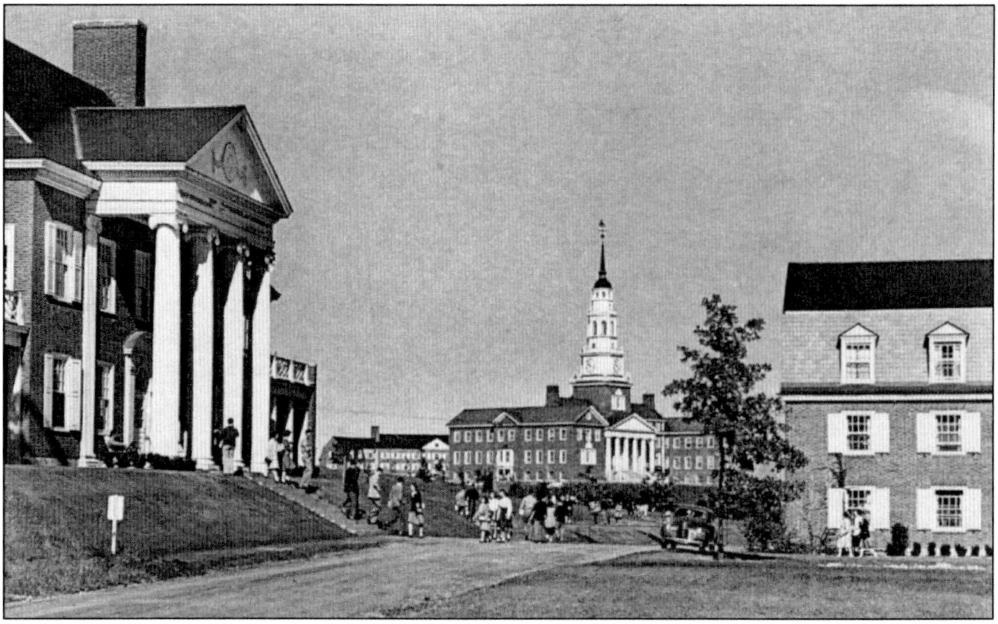

The Women's Union and Mary Low Hall frame this 1940s view looking toward Miller Library. Pres. Julius Seelye Bixler wrote of the new Colby: "I hope that every visitor to our Mayflower Hill campus will perceive that these buildings are not ends in themselves, but rather tools for the attainment of a more effective type of education. The Mayflower Hill campus has been functionally planned to accomplish just that."

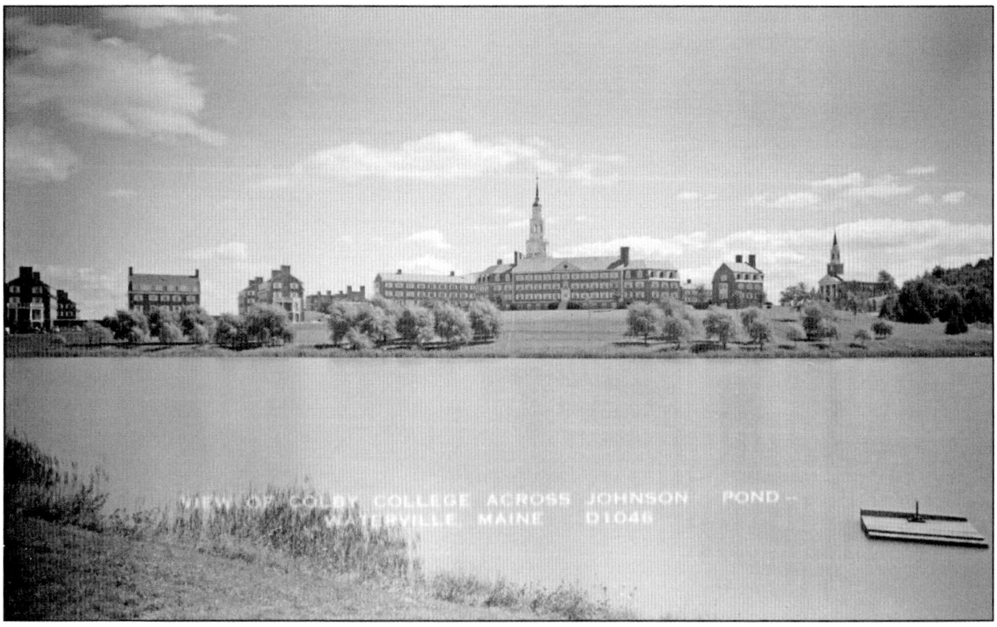

This view of the campus from across Johnson Pond dates from the mid-1950s. From left to right are the fraternities, the men's dormitories (with the tower of Miller Library behind them), and Lorimer Chapel. In 1953, President Bixler called the new Colby "a remarkable achievement when one considers that the work has been done against a background of depression, a world war, inflation, Korea, and the widespread unrest these have brought." (Penobscot Marine Museum.)

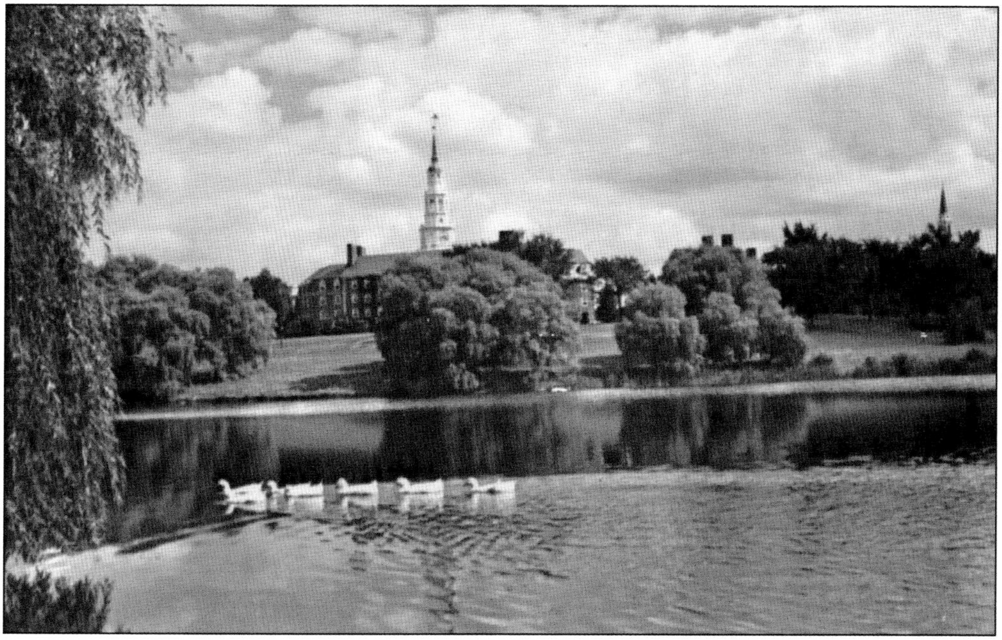

Johnson Pond was created in 1939 with earth taken from a marshy, spring-fed area behind the men's dormitories. In 1948, the pond was dedicated to Franklin W. Johnson, Colby's president from 1929 to 1942 and the man most responsible for the move to Mayflower Hill. Willows were planted on the banks of the pond in an echo of those that grew on the old campus.

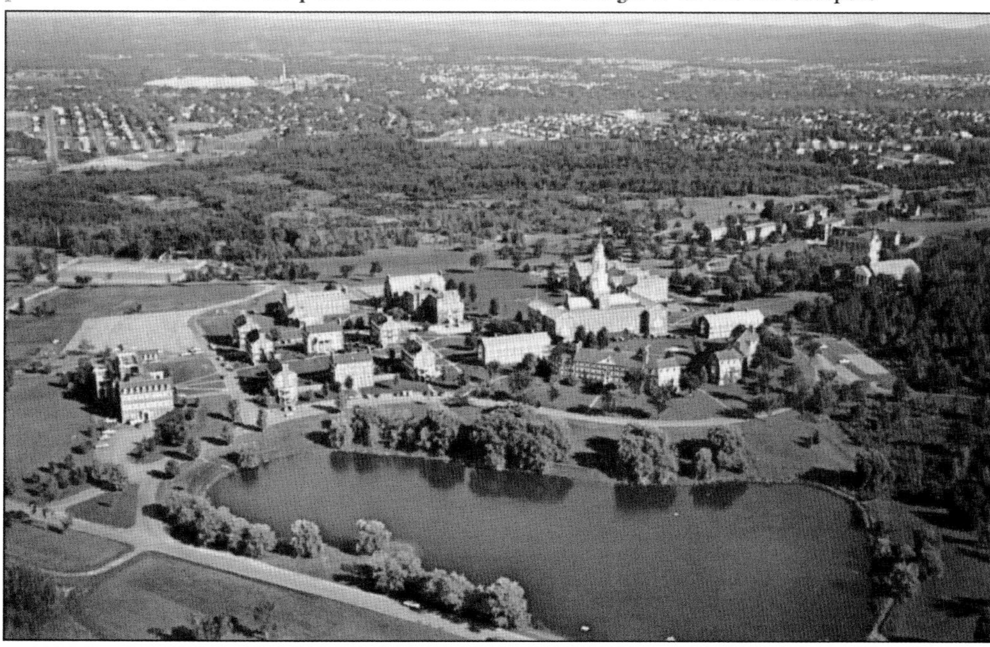

By 1966, when this aerial photograph of Colby was taken, the Jens Frederick Larson plan for the campus was largely completed. That year, construction began on a dormitory complex that would be the college's first departure from the Georgian-style buildings designed in the 1930s. As Pres. Robert Strider said of this decision, "Is it not appropriate for us to expand upon this nucleus with visible symbols of thinking in our own time?"

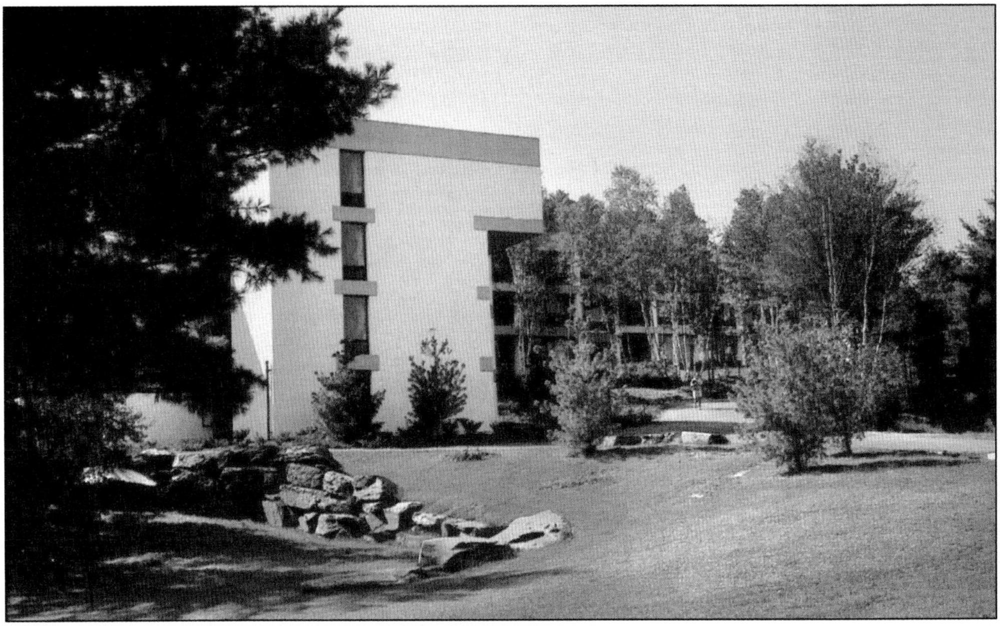

In 1967, the opening of the dormitory complex popularly known as "the new dorms" ushered in Colby's first buildings of modern design. The clean, contemporary lines of these five brick-and-glass structures (Sturtevant Hall, Leonard Hall, Marriner Hall, Taylor Hall, and the KDR fraternity house) fit comfortably next to the birch trees of the hillside adjacent to Lorimer Chapel. Benjamin C. Thompson, a faculty member at the Harvard Graduate School of Design, was the architect.

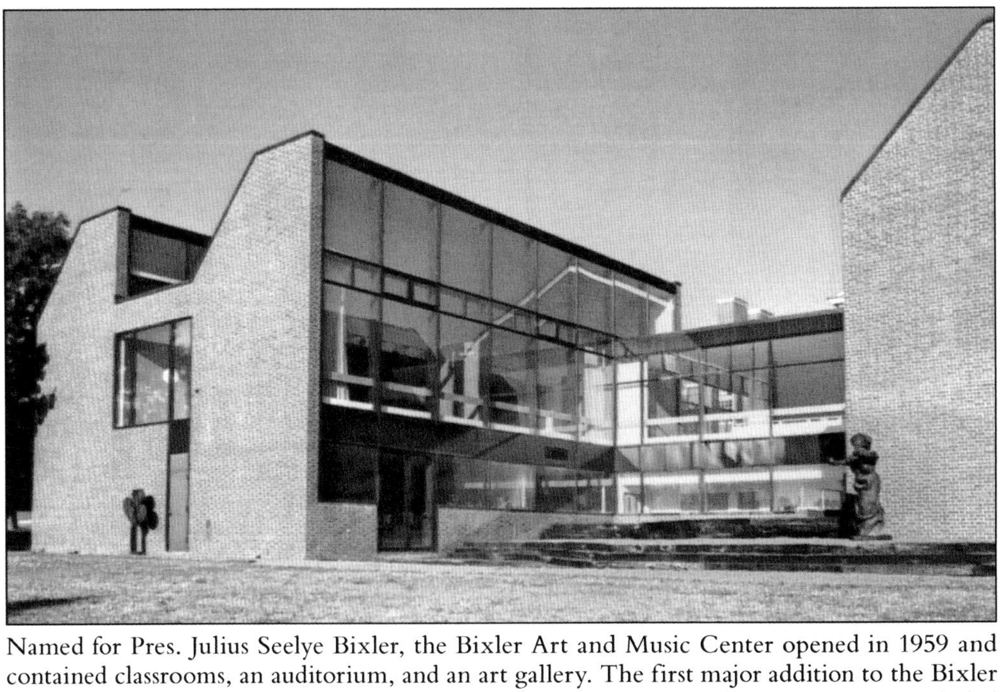

Named for Pres. Julius Seelye Bixler, the Bixler Art and Music Center opened in 1959 and contained classrooms, an auditorium, and an art gallery. The first major addition to the Bixler center, a contemporary brick expansion of the art museum, was completed in 1973 and included studio space for students and faculty; the architects were Verner Johnson and Robert Hotvedt.

Ten

WINSLOW

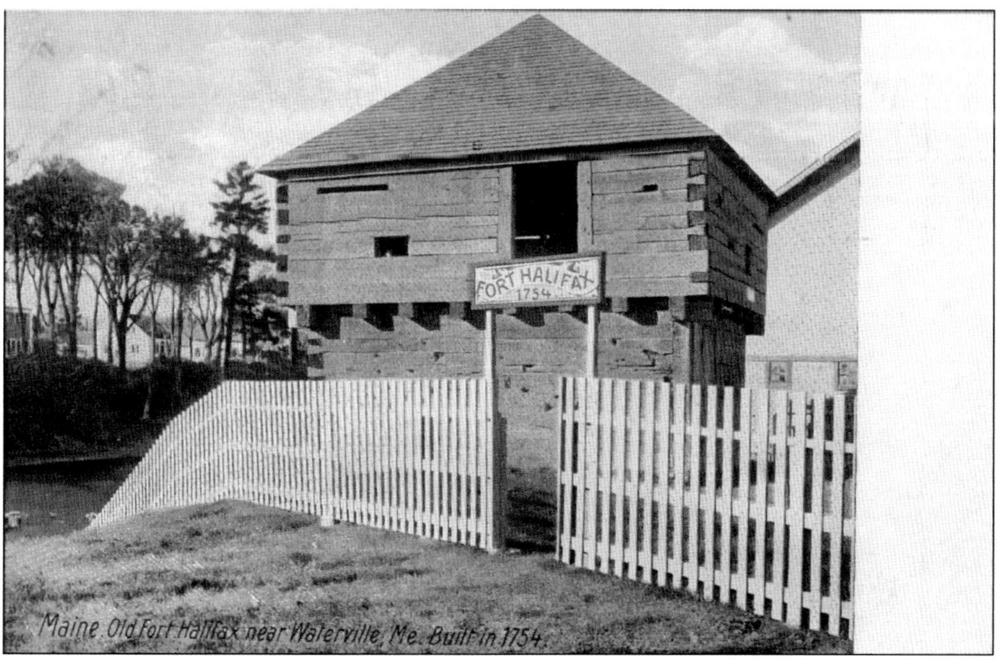

The Fort Halifax blockhouse is a symbol of the Colonial history of the Waterville-Winslow area. Fort Halifax, now a National Historical Landmark, was built in 1754 on the Kennebec River at Winslow to provide defense against the French and Indians. While most of the fort was gone by 1800, one blockhouse survived as a store and later served as a barn. In 1875, this log structure was saved and repaired by the Ticonic Water Power Company.

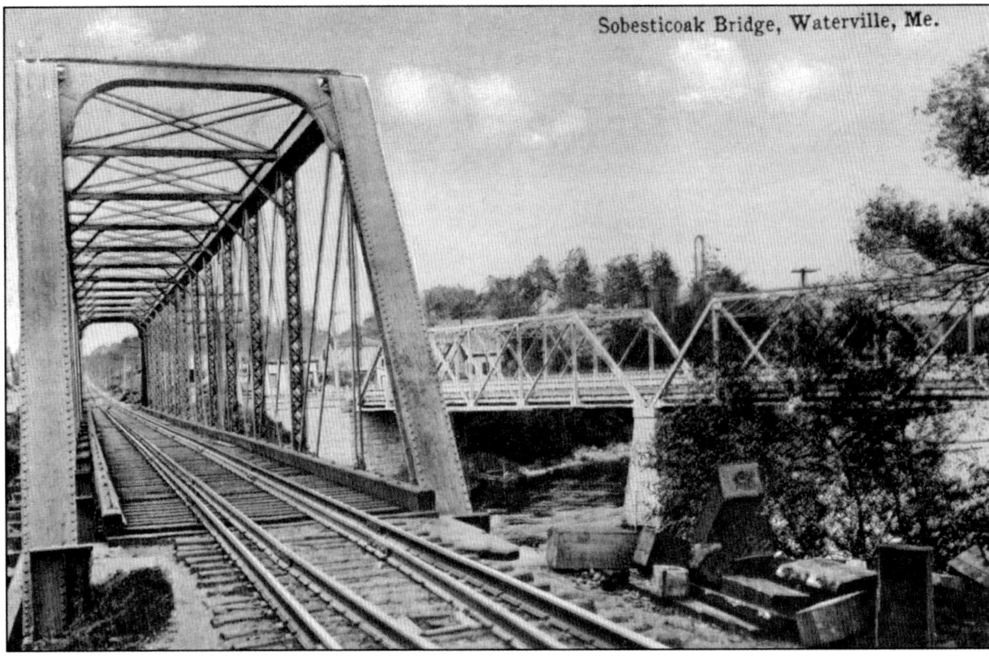

The Sebasticook River joins the Kennebec River at Winslow as its largest tributary. Through Winslow's history, a series of bridges have spanned the Sebasticook. This early-20th-century view shows the Maine Central Railroad's steel bridge (built in 1885) at left and, at right, the steel bridge built in 1902, which replaced a covered bridge destroyed in a 1901 flood.

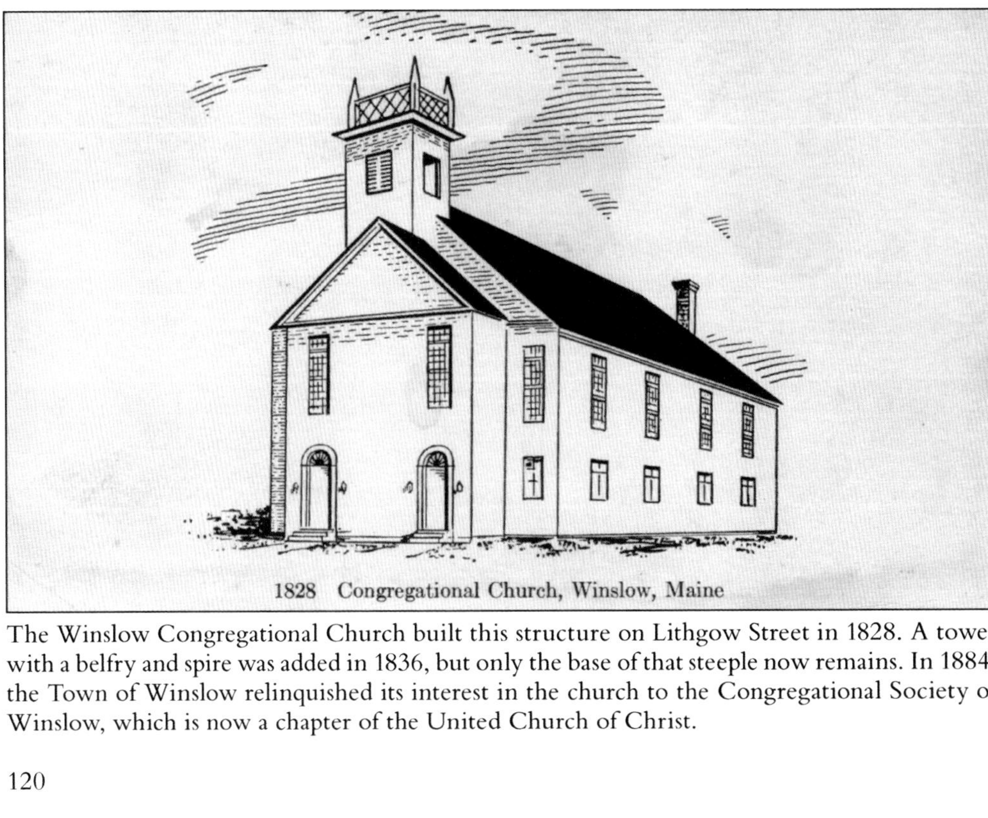

The Winslow Congregational Church built this structure on Lithgow Street in 1828. A tower with a belfry and spire was added in 1836, but only the base of that steeple now remains. In 1884, the Town of Winslow relinquished its interest in the church to the Congregational Society of Winslow, which is now a chapter of the United Church of Christ.

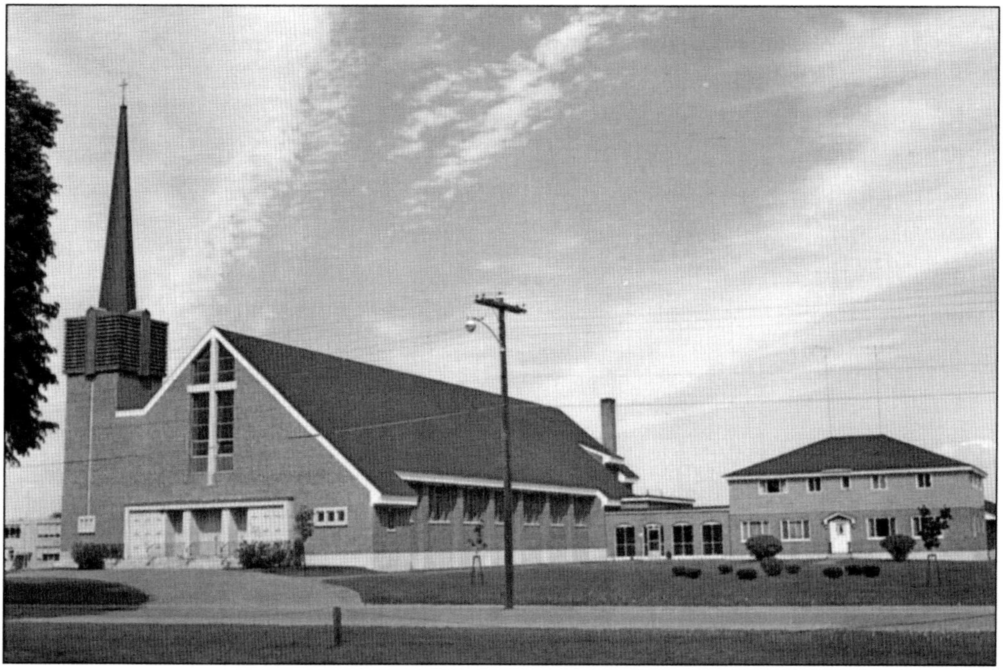

Rev. John W. Frawley founded St. John the Baptist Parish in Winslow in 1926. Within a year, the parish had built its first church, along with an assembly hall and a school. Construction of the current brick church and rectory (pictured) began in 1956 and was completed the following year. St. John the Baptist is now part of the Corpus Christi Parish.

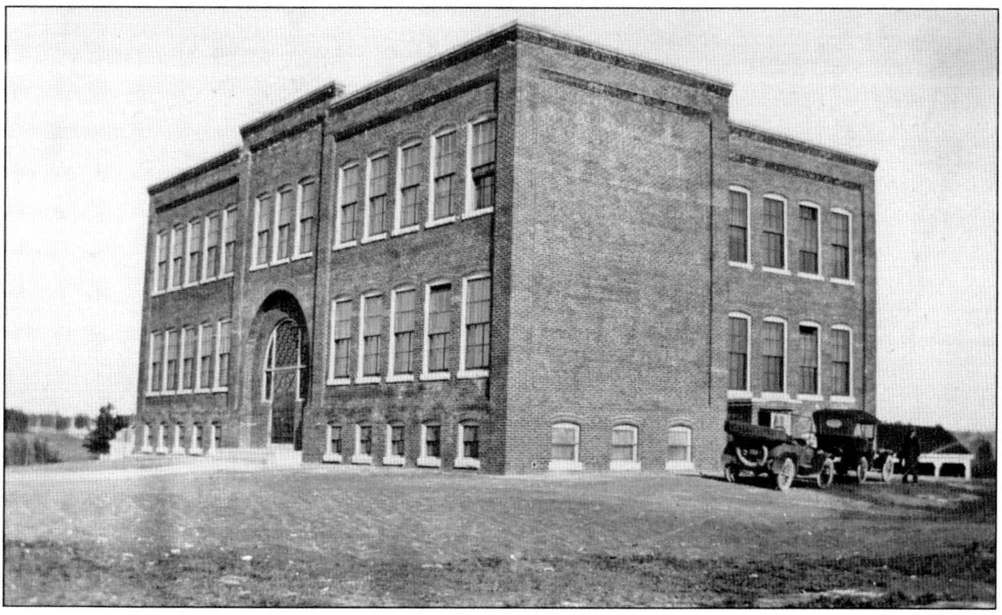

In 1904, Jennie P. Howard, Winslow's superintendent of schools, declared that the town's new brick high school was "all the heart can wish." That year, the town appropriated $9,500 for a lot on Halifax Street and construction of a school designed by local architect O.O. Cross; the project was managed so carefully that $1,043 of the appropriation remained unspent. The Halifax Street School closed in 1993.

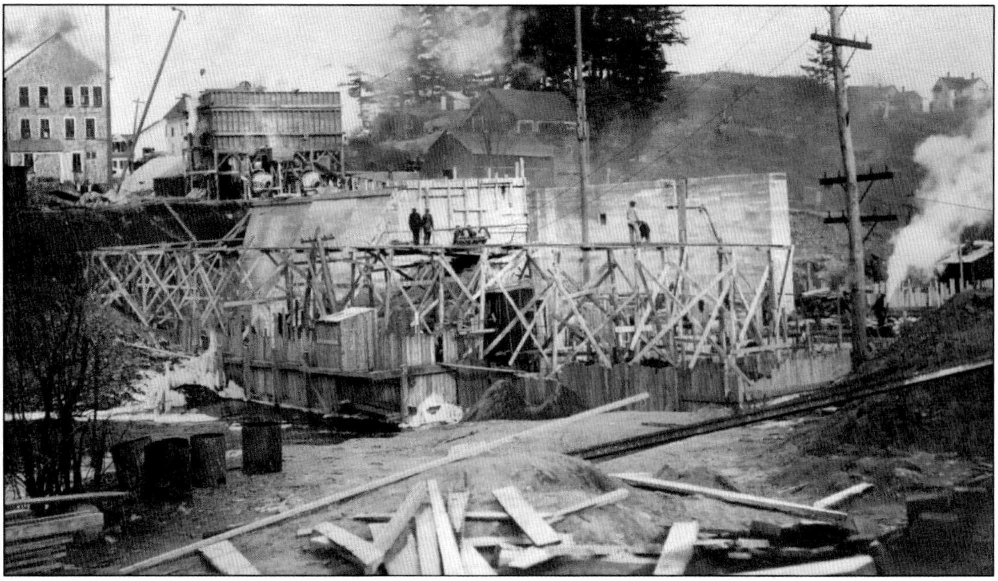

In 1907 and 1908, the Fort Halifax Power Company built this concrete dam and the adjacent brick station to generate electricity for an interurban railroad as well as to provide power for street lighting and industrial power for Waterville and Winslow. The Fort Halifax Power Station was designed by Sellers and Ripley, a noted Philadelphia engineering firm that also planned major hydroelectric stations elsewhere in the country.

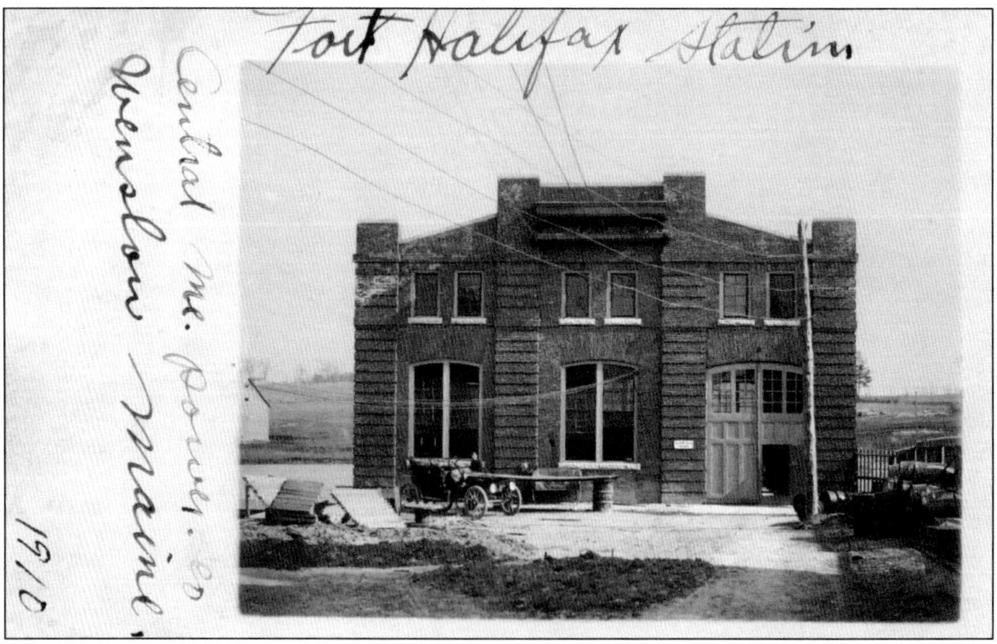

Fostering a corporate image was inherent in the creation of the Fort Halifax Power Station, a powerhouse that successfully combined functional and aesthetic qualities. Brick and concrete construction provided a fireproof enclosure for the machinery, and the building's large windows and white brick interior fostered a well-lighted work environment. Exterior architectural brickwork reflected the importance of the station to the emerging Central Maine Power Company system of power-generating plants.

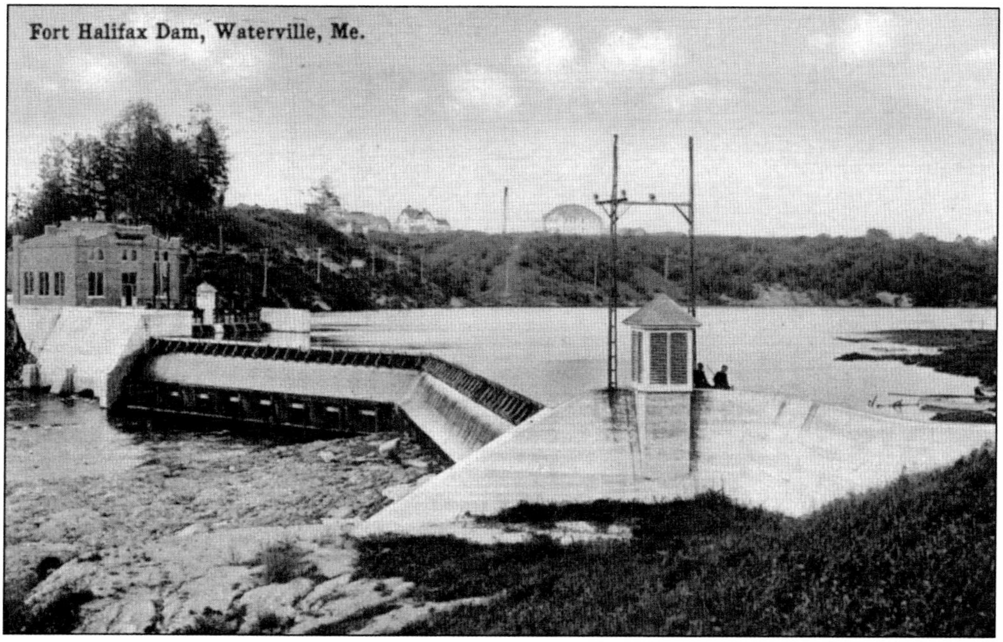

In 1907, Harvey Doane Eaton and Walter S. Wyman established the Fort Halifax Power Company. These two men were the entrepreneurs behind the formation of the Messalonskee Electric Company in 1901. This company became the Central Maine Power Company in 1910, and Eaton and Wyman used that corporation to absorb more than 60 other power companies and dominate the electric industry in Central and Southern Maine.

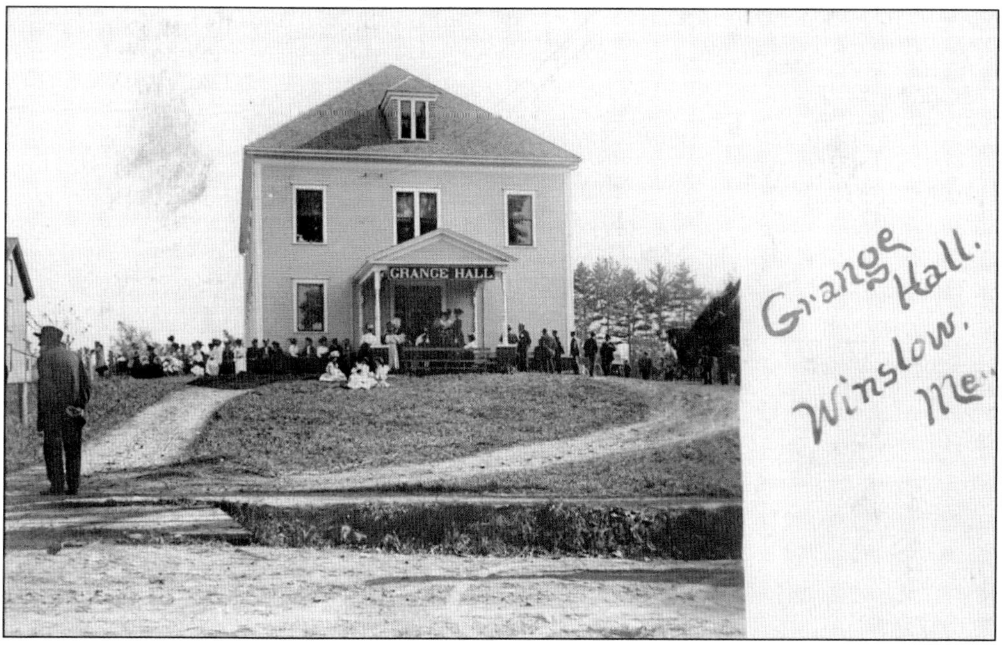

Winslow Grange No. 320 formed on September 17, 1894, with 33 members. By 1900, the organization had grown to the point that it needed its own hall. Work on the grange hall began that year, and members donated materials, time, and money, as well as holding fairs, plays, and suppers to raise funds to complete the building. (Waterville Historical Society.)

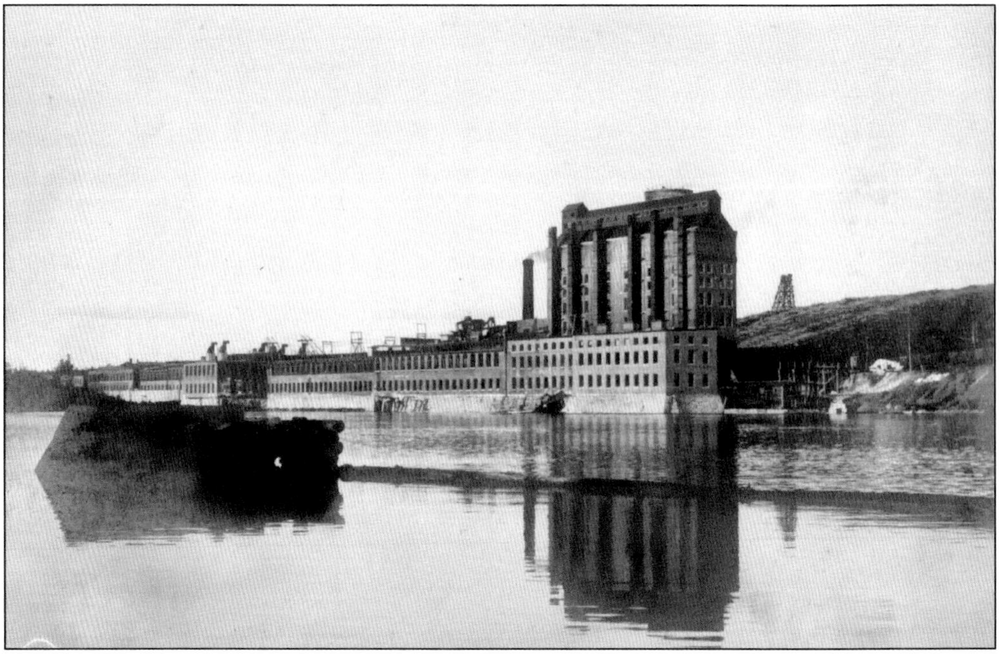

The Hollingsworth & Whitney Company, founded in 1862, manufactured paper at mills in Massachusetts and Maine for more than a century. In 1892, the company built the first section of this massive pulp- and paper-making complex on the east bank of the Kennebec River at Winslow, opposite Colby College's old campus. A major expansion of the plant followed in 1899.

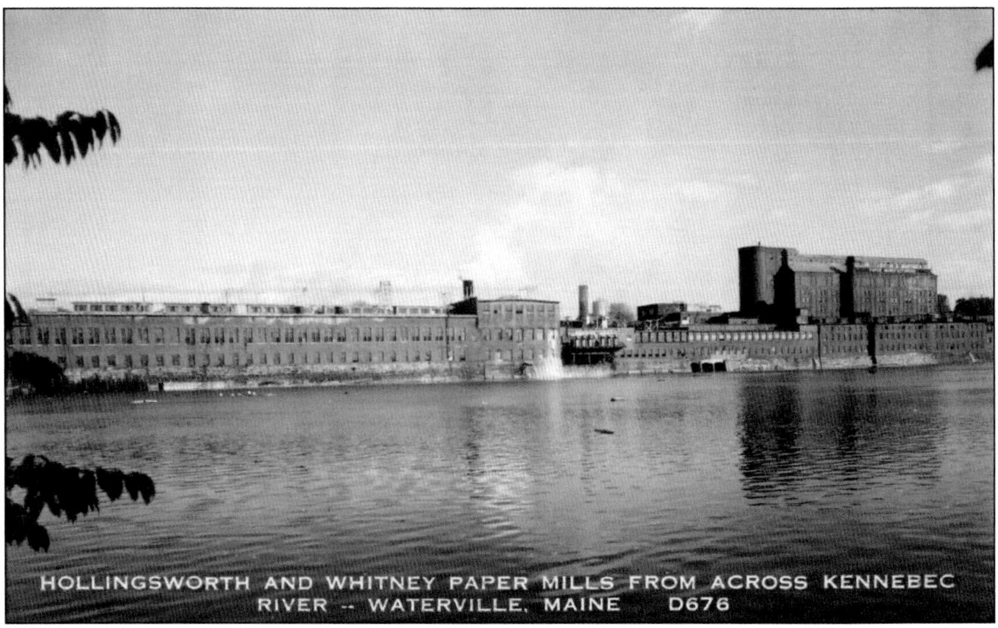
HOLLINGSWORTH AND WHITNEY PAPER MILLS FROM ACROSS KENNEBEC RIVER -- WATERVILLE, MAINE D676

By 1911, the Hollingsworth & Whitney plant was producing 235 tons of paper per day. About 800 men worked for the company, generating a monthly payroll of $40,000. In 1892, employees worked 11- to 13-hour days, earning 15¢ an hour. By 1954, eight-hour shifts were customary, and the hourly wage had risen to $1.61.

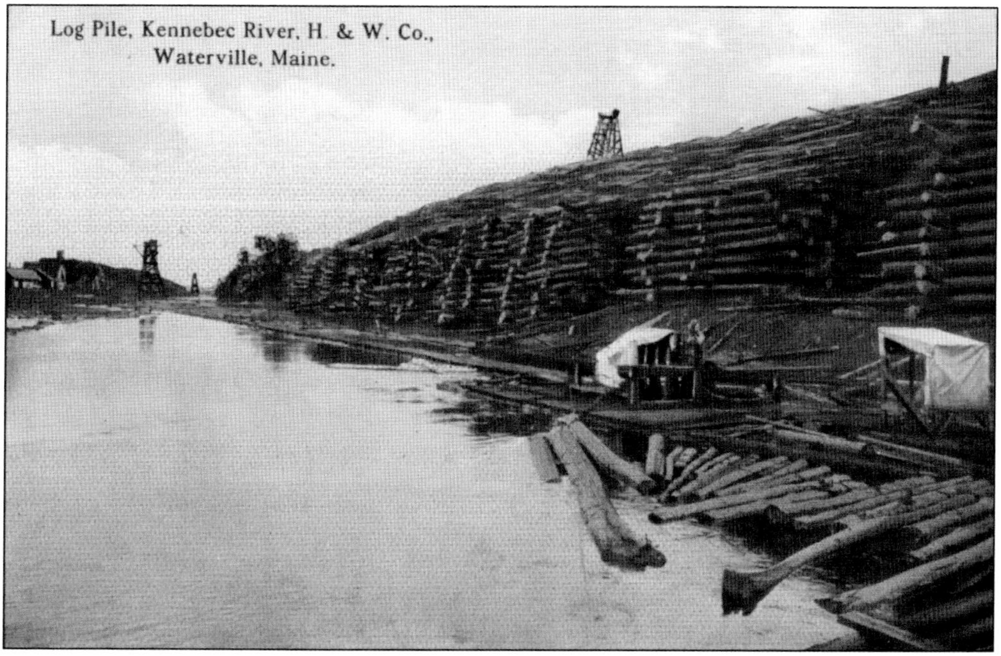

Pulp and paper manufacturing required large quantities of both softwood and hardwood trees, which the forests of Maine supplied. Between 1895 and 1954, Hollingsworth & Whitney amassed 550,000 acres of timberland on the Kennebec watershed. Each year, trees on this land were cut and driven down the river to be collected in this huge log pile adjacent to the plant.

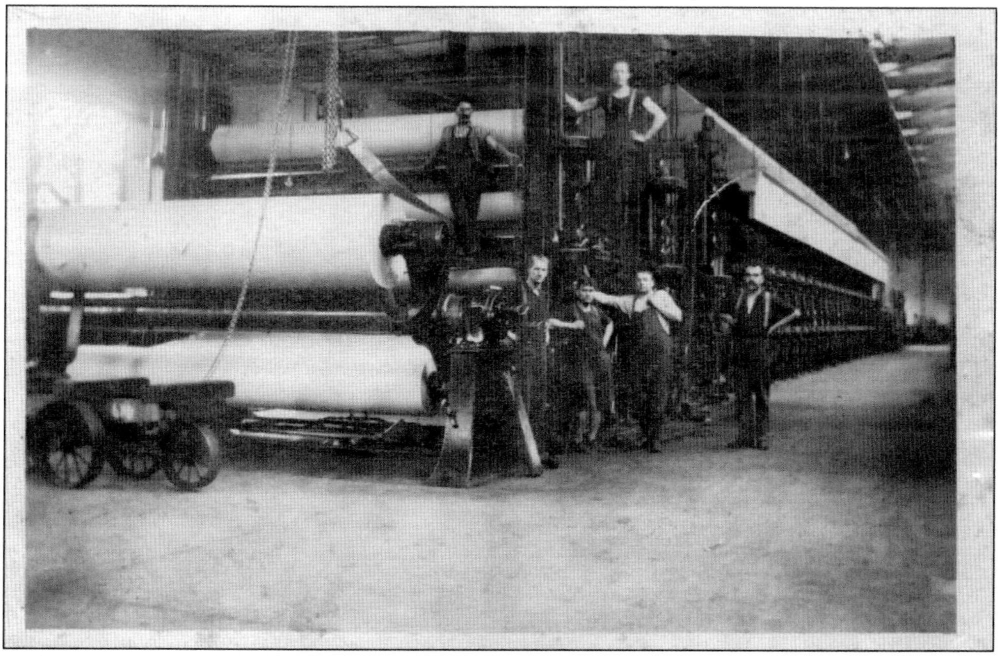

In this c. 1910 real-photo postcard, workmen pose in front of immense papermaking machinery inside the Hollingsworth & Whitney plant. The message on the back—written in French by an employee, Joseph Belanger of Waterville, to his uncle—describes the scene as showing "a machine a papier."

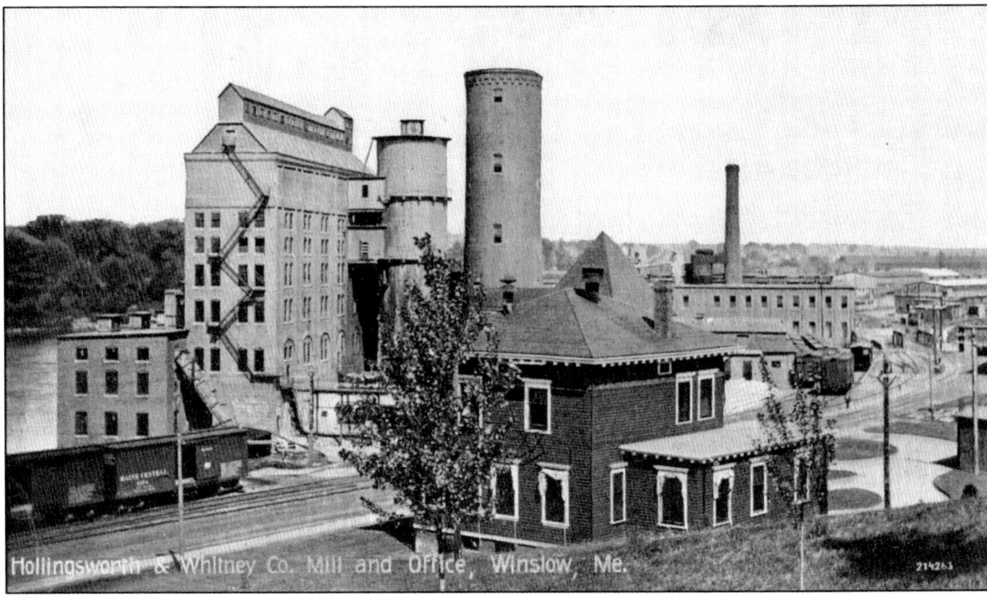

During World War II, Hollingsworth & Whitney's Winslow plant was devoted to defense production. As the nation's only manufacturer of tabulating card stock, production of this item was quadrupled to meet the needs for operating military and defense tabulating machines. Sometime after the war, Hollingsworth & Whitney was purchased by Scott Paper Company, whose 1995 merger with Kimberly-Clark Corporation led to the factory's closure in 1997.

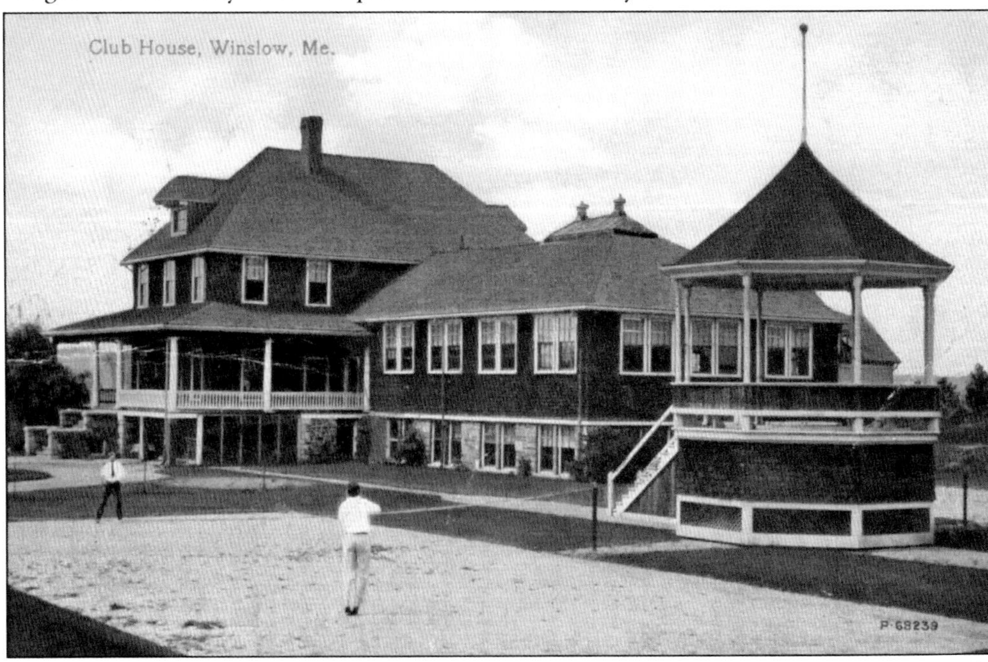

In 1901, the Hollingsworth & Whitney Company built this attractive $20,000 clubhouse for its employees from designs by Waterville architect A.G. Bowie. Edwin Whittemore's *History of Waterville*, published the following year, described the clubhouse as having a 3,000-book library with magazines and newspapers, a billiard room, two bowling alleys, a gymnasium, a smoking room, an entertainment hall, and outdoor tennis courts.

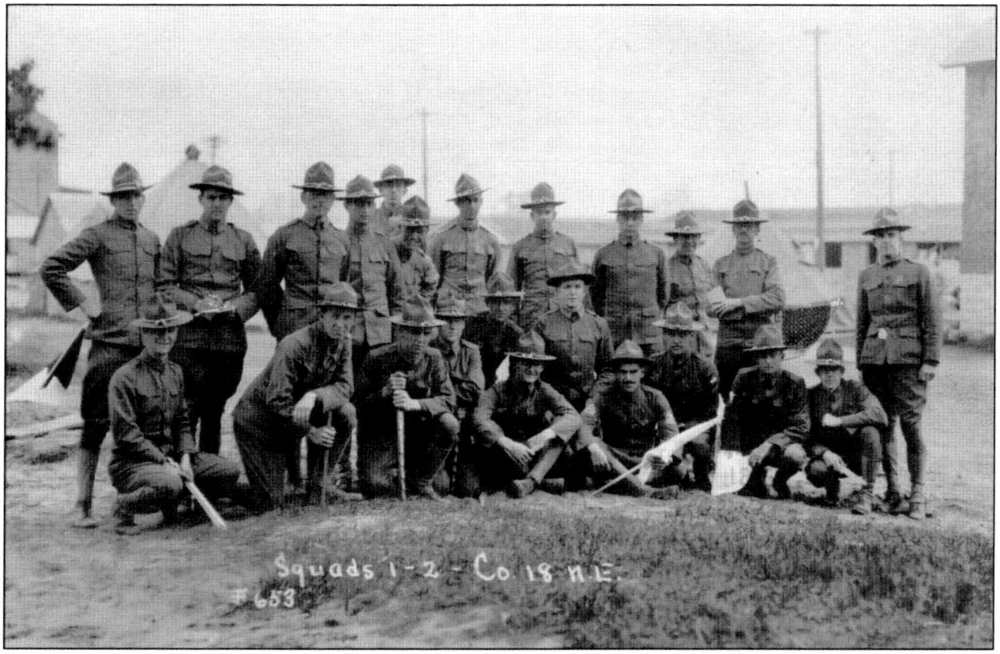

This June 1917 real-photo postcard shows a group of World War I soldiers undergoing training at the National Army Officer Candidate School in Plattsburgh, New York. One of the men pictured here is a French American from Waterville, for he wrote a message on the card in French to Mrs. Joseph Bourque at 4 1/2 Sherwin Street describing his Signal Corps classes.

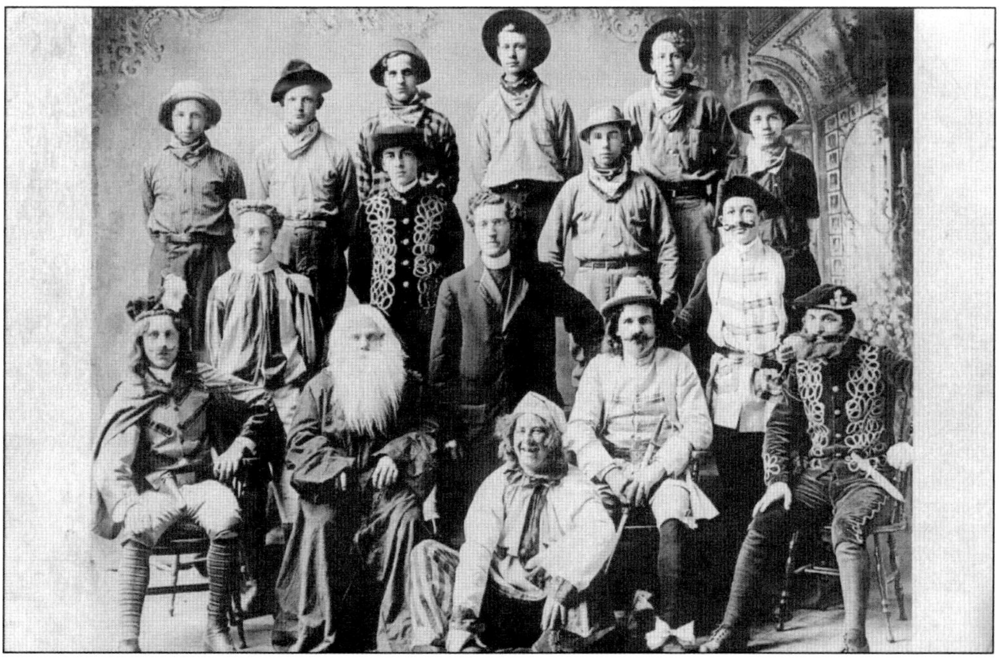

This real-photo postcard mailed from Waterville in 1913 provides no clues as to who these costumed individuals were or why they sat together before the camera in a photographer's studio. Where they attending a costume party, players in a local theatrical performance, or just preparing for Halloween night?